AN AMERICAN EXPERIENCE OF GOD: THE SPIRITUALITY OF ISAAC HECKER

Father Hecker Reading Goethe
Original sketch by John LaFarge, 1866
(Private collection, New York)

An American Experience of God

The Spirituality of Isaac Hecker

By John Farina

Preface by Robert T. Handy
Foreword by Rev. Wilfrid F. Dewan, C.S.P.

PAULIST PRESS
New York/Ramsey

Library of Congress
Catalog Card Number: 81-80875

ISBN: 0-8091-0321-4

Published by Paulist Press
545 Island Road, Ramsey, N.J. 07446

Printed and bound in the
United States of America

CONTENTS

PREFACE ix

FOREWORD xi

INTRODUCTION 1

I A NIGHT IN NEW HAVEN 5

II A SENSE OF DESTINY 9

III THE BUSY SEARCH 21

IV AMONG THE TRANSCENDENTALISTS 46

V THE EFFECTS OF THE ENCOUNTER 61

VI IN SEARCH OF THE SYNTHESIS 72

VII CATHOLIC! 84

VIII A MAN WITH A MISSION 101

IX 1858–1867 118

X THE TRIAL AND THE TRIUMPH 137

CONTENTS

XI A DIFFICULT DECISION 158

XII GOING HOME 164

AFTERWORD 177

NOTES 181

SELECTED BIBLIOGRAPHY 198

ANNOTATED BIBLIOGRAPHY 202

INDEX 205

TO MY PARENTS

PREFACE

The intensity and excitement of the "thaw" in Catholic/Protestant ecumenical relations that occurred during and since the Second Vatican Council (1962–65) has diminished somewhat, but historical and ecumenical scholarship is increasingly making clear the deep significance of that great milestone in modern church history. One of the major outcomes of that remarkable shift is the growing awareness that the history of a given religious tradition, once thought to be of primary concern to those within it (or seeking to interpret it), is now more widely seen as relevant also to the understanding of other traditions and to the interpretation of the larger religious history of a nation. Hence Dr. John Farina's new study of Fr. Isaac Hecker (1819–88), based on a fresh probing of archival and manuscript sources and also informed by pertinent secondary materials, comes at an opportune time. Current trends in American religious historiography have alerted scholars of religion to the importance of spirituality in concept and practice, and the author of this able work has found in Hecker's spirituality a revealing key to the fuller understanding of a convert to Catholicism who became the founder of the Paulist Fathers.

A unique feature of this book is the demonstration of the significance of the earlier, Protestant phases of Hecker's life for the development of his mature spiritual insights and abilities. His encounter with the Transcendentalists has long been familiar (though variously interpreted), but the persisting impact of his original Methodism and perfectionism has not previously been so thoroughly and thoughtfully examined. Small wonder—for Hecker

PREFACE

himself, illustrating "the exclusive power of a new affection," had a new convert's tendency to oversimplify the earlier stages of his life and to minimize the earlier religious influences on him.

This careful study in the voluminous materials relating to Hecker's life, many from his own pen and still unpublished, shows how motifs that guided the young Hecker persisted, usually in reinterpreted form, into his later career as a Roman Catholic priest and leader. Not only the earlier perfectionistic Methodism, which remained of peculiar importance, but his encounters with Orville Dewey and Unitarianism, with Parley Pratt and Mormonism, as well as with Orestes Brownson and Transcendentalism, are analyzed. Hecker's life was marked by various efforts at synthesis: of the ideal and the real, of Catholic and Protestant, of spiritual and ecclesiastical, of Catholic and American, of the individual and the corporate. Thoroughly sympathetic to its subject, this treatment of a fascinating figure in American religious history is not without some critical notes. Informed by a broad knowledge of the religious thought and action of nineteenth-century America, it offers fresh perspectives on the life of a significant and pioneering thinker and leader, a man who anticipated patterns of religious life that have become conspicuous again in the late twentieth century.

Robert T. Handy
Professor of Church History,
    Union Theological Seminary, New York
Adjunct Professor of Religion,
    Columbia University

FOREWORD

Isaac Thomas Hecker was a man thoroughly American and profoundly spiritual. He grew up in mid-nineteenth century New York City eager to imbibe the very best of the cultural values of that exciting society.

Even as a teenager Hecker combined great sensitivity for social justice with a deep interior need for an authentic spirituality that could fill the profound longing within him for the transcendent. His spirituality became rooted in the conviction that God offers himself to each of us, and that the Holy Spirit is the ultimate and best spiritual director.

His search led him on a fascinating spiritual odyssey, until he finally became a Catholic, and even founded his own religious order, the Paulists.

Hecker was bold and clear in his convictions: there is a necessary link between social reform and personal spiritual renewal, Christianity offers the solution for the ills of society, and Catholic Christianity truly lived is the best fulfillment of the whole human person.

John Farina's *An American Experience of God* presents a very appealing picture of Hecker's interesting search for God and the way to bring the Good News to modern people. Especially helpful is the way he traces with great clarity the many influences and people that shaped Father Hecker's inner search. Paulists and the many friends of Father Hecker will particularly appreciate the insightful way Farina handles the mysterious final years of Hecker's life, which to some have been more of an embarrassment than anything else. He shows that Hecker was misunderstood precisely because he never changed his optimistic vision of Paulist missionary efforts to bring the Gospel to the people of America, and in fact began to broaden his vision even more.

The elements of Hecker's search for meaning in life are as modern and challenging now as they were then: being able to read the signs of the times and appreciate the values of one's culture; the conviction that human nature is basically good and free, that community has something to add to the individual search, and that the Holy Spirit will lead those who take the patience and time to really listen.

As one of Father Hecker's successors I am particularly delighted with this fine work of John Farina. May it serve to highlight one of the spiritual giants of nineteenth-century America and spread his influence.

Wilfrid F. Dewan, C.S.P.
President of Paulist Fathers

INTRODUCTION

America during the 1970s witnessed an explosion of interest in spirituality. Out of the action-oriented 1960s had come a countervailing tendency that exalted the values of the contemplative life. Dismayed by the tragedies of Vietnam and Watergate, dissatisfied by the empty promises of materialism, many turned their attention to the spiritual dimension. As astronauts explored the frontiers of space in their lunar stations, myriads of Americans began probing the world within to discover new meaning in their lives.

For some, concern for social action gave way to fascination with spirituality. During the 1970s numerous groups appeared on the scene, each offering an entrée to the spiritual life. Eastern gurus, Korean businessmen, Jesus "freaks," holy rollers turned socially respectable and mainline Church leaders turned holy rollers all offered to appease America's hunger for more meaningful religious experience.

With this new interest in spirituality came a quest for effective guides. The search for spiritual masters sent Americans scurrying to ancient, often obscure, traditions. Without wishing to minimize the value of such an approach, I would suggest that Americans have at their disposal a tradition of American spirituality that can provide rich insights into the spiritual life. This book is a study of the spirituality of one in whom that tradition finds expression—Isaac Thomas Hecker.

Isaac Hecker was both thoroughly American and a man of deep spirituality. Raised as the son of a devout Methodist mother, involved in the world of New York City reform politics, and intimately ac-

1

quainted with New England Transcendentalism, Hecker was immersed in major currents of American religious, social, and intellectual life. Convert to Catholicism, Redemptorist missionary, and founder of the first American Catholic men's congregation, he played an important part in United States Catholic history. He appears as a perfect bridge figure between the nineteenth-century American Catholic and Protestant worlds, one whose spirituality reflected the influences of both.

When one speaks of spirituality, one is immediately confronted with the problem of defining the term. Josef Sudbrack noted in the first part of this century that the word "spirituality" unfortunately conveyed to most hearers an "anaemic unreality."[1] Although one must consent that this is still often correct, the recent rise of interest in spirituality suggests that this once-dead term is taking on fresh meaning. It is, nevertheless, essential to define the term as clearly as possible.

In its most basic sense, spirituality refers to the personal relation of an individual with God. It denotes the fullness of one's experience of God.

In an effort to clarify what aspects of an individual's behavior are dealt with in a study of his spirituality, some have found it useful to make certain distinctions. Louis Bouyer, for example, distinguishes among the inner life, the spiritual life, and the religious life.[2] The inner life, according to Bouyer, is the life of the thoughts, emotions, and affections that exists independent of any transcendent or supernatural dimension. All people experience this life, regardless of their religious convictions.

The spiritual life, Bouyer points out, contains all the dimensions of the inner life, plus a conscious awareness of a spiritual reality, however that is understood. This spiritual reality is something that in the perception of the individual goes beyond himself and is in some way larger than the individual and not contingent upon him for its existence. It may or may not, however, be considered divine.

The religious life, as Bouyer sees it, appears when and only when that spiritual reality experienced by the individual is conceived of as a transcendent deity capable of personal relationship. The spirit perceived in the spiritual life is not only known as a transcendent "something" but also as a "someone."

The study of Hecker's spirituality will deal with what Bouyer terms the inner, spiritual, and religious lives. Although a distinction may be made on paper among these three categories, in the case of an individual like Hecker it is well-nigh impossible to deal with one without dealing with the others. His spirituality, his experience of God, was part and parcel of his experience of life. The broader the picture of Hecker's life experience we have before us, the broader and more accurate will be our picture of his spirituality. To make any strict distinction among his inner, spiritual, and religious lives would be fruitless.

If Hecker's experience of God is best seen in the broad context of his experience of life, then a study of his spirituality will be best carried out in the course of telling the story of his life experiences— or his biography.

Previous studies of Hecker have failed to give an adequate picture of his spirituality. Each of these works has been deficient in at least one of the following ways. The first is a failure to view Hecker's spirituality in its proper nineteenth-century context, assessing the impact of the diverse sources which influenced its development. The result is that the typically American diversity and derivativeness of Hecker's spirituality is not appreciated. In particular, the impact of non-Catholic sources is overlooked. Elliott's *Life of Father Hecker* falls short in this regard.[3]

The second shortcoming results from a failure to properly value the significance that Hecker's experience of God had in shaping his life. The Hecker story is incomplete if the Paulist founder's spirituality is not playing a major role. Holden's fine works, *The Early Years of Isaac Thomas Hecker* and *Yankee Paul,* may be criticized in this manner.[4]

The third deficiency of previous works on Hecker is a failure to deal with the man's whole life. Holden's *Yankee Paul* ends with the founding of the Paulists in 1858, leaving the story of Hecker's last thirty years untold. Elliott deals with the founder's whole life, but chooses to omit many important facts from his account of Hecker's later years. The account Elliott gives us of those final years attempts to portray Hecker's inner life without filling in the details of the rest of that life. The result is an incomplete, mysterious picture of the mature Hecker. One is left with the anxious feeling that something is being purposely left out—that perhaps Father Hecker tottered on the brink of insanity for his final fifteen years.

When, however, Hecker's life is viewed as a whole, such anxieties prove unwarranted. If Hecker's spirituality is understood, the final years of his life present no embarrassment. Hecker in his last years was, as he had been throughout his life, true to his own convictions and understandings. The themes present in his early spirituality were developed consistently and, one can even say, heroically during his later years.

This book had its genesis as a doctoral dissertation written for a degree in religion from Columbia University. I am especially indebted to Professor Robert T. Handy, under whose able and diligent guidance I labored. A word of appreciation is also due James M. Washington of Union Theological Seminary, who during our days together at Yale Divinity School first inspired me to pursue the study of American religious history. Thanks is also due to T. O'Conor Sloane III for his careful reading of the manuscript.

The Paulist Fathers have from the start of my labors been gracious and encouraging. Father Lawrence McDonnell, Archivist of the Congregation, has wholeheartedly supported and assisted my work from the beginning.

The interest shown in my work by the Paulist Press has been much appreciated. Father Kevin Lynch and Richard Payne have shown a sustained concern which has resulted in the publication of this volume.

No list of thank-you's would be complete without mention of two people whose labors of love were responsible for typing and proofreading the original manuscript with unfailing patience and skill. To my aunt, Alice McAloon, and my wife, Paula, I owe my gratitude.

I

A NIGHT IN NEW HAVEN

A brisk autumn wind blew in off Long Island Sound, chilling the throngs of people that waited in line outside the Music Hall on the night of November 16, 1862. Outside the main entrance to the hall the clopping of horse hooves and the distant sound of train whistles blended with the buzzing of a hundred different conversations. There was a sense of excitement in the air, the type of excitement caused by fresh ideas that are capable of inspiring the human spirit.

Such excitement was not unusual in New Haven. For over a century and a half, it had been the home of one of the nation's foremost colleges. Yale had shone as a beacon of the vigorous type of Puritan idealism that had formed and guided New England from colonial times. Yale had a tradition of great minds. Men like Jonathan Edwards, Lyman Beecher, Nathaniel William Taylor, and Timothy Dwight had played prominent roles in the theological life of the nation. It was not uncommon for Protestant clergymen from around Connecticut and educated laymen of a theological bent to gather in New Haven to hear a first-rate lecture on a timely topic of divinity.

What was unusual about the night of November 16 was that these children of the Puritans were queuing up by the hundreds to hear a Roman Catholic priest lecture about Catholicism. The lecture series had been arranged by Father Edward J. O'Brien of New Ha-

5

ven's St. Mary's Church, who had posted a simple notice in the *Daily Palladium*:

> . . . An American Convert to The Catholic Church is desirous of addressing his Protestant Brethren and Countrymen on religious topics. . . . Subject for the First Lecture: 'A Search after Rational Christianity or Why did I become a Catholic?'[1]

Although the lectures were addressed specifically to Protestants, the Catholic faithful turned out in numbers. The Catholics of New Haven had much in common with their Protestant neighbors. Many of them, especially the Irish, the Germans, and the French, were native-born Americans whose parents had long played a productive role in the nation's life. They, like their Protestant countrymen, knew the anguish of the War Between the States that saw Catholics shedding their blood for the cause of the Union as readily as were Protestants. They also shared with the children of the Puritans a vision of America as a land on which God's special favor rested. It was for them as for the Protestants a place of boundless opportunity, a place of new beginnings, new possibilities, new hope.

Though they shared much with their Protestant neighbors, they did not share their religion—a religion that was undeniably part of the warp and woof of American life. They held instead to a faith immersed in the tradition and culture of the old world. Unlike the swelling evangelical churches of the time that presented Christianity in a simplified, folksy manner and won the adherence of countless Americans, Catholicism was, by comparison, a mysterious, detailed system of rites, regulations, and devotions. There were many in New Haven, from the simplest laborer to the learned Yale professor, Samuel F. B. Morse, who said that Catholicism was unsuited for American life, that its values, structure, and practices were out of step with the pulse of the new nation.

The Catholics, however, who approached the Music Hall on November 16 were coming to hear a different idea. They had been instinctively attracted to it on the basis of their own experience, and its boldness intrigued them. Not only did this idea deny that Catholicism was unfit for American life, it forcefully proclaimed that Catholicism was better suited to America than any other religion, including Protestantism.

On the platform of the Music Hall stood the champion of this idea, Isaac Thomas Hecker. He was a man who had been raised in the premier city of the thriving nation, a man who knew the aspirations and hopes of the people. He like them was thrilled by the great potentials of the new world. Like them, he was filled with an enduring optimism persuading him that tomorrow would see the actualization of those wonderful potentials. He knew the political and social climate of the land as well and was himself a member of a family that was fast making its way to a place of prominence in New York's baking and flour business.

He also knew the religious temperament of his homeland. Raised as a Methodist, he had imbibed the spirit of a major force in Protestantism. In his early manhood he had become deeply involved with the New England Transcendentalists, sojourning as a romantic seeker after truth at Brook Farm and Alcott's Fruitlands. His searching had led him at length to the Catholic church. It was within her bosom that this mystically-inclined young man had found the fullness he sought. He was certain that God had providentially guided him, allowing him to experience the rich diversity of American life so as to enable him to understand what Americans longed for. He felt himself called to share with others the blessings he had found.

This young priest from New York had the ability to present these bold ideas to non-Catholics in a manner that many found intriguing. Hecker had been speaking in New Haven for one week. His early lectures were attended primarily by Catholics, but as the handful of Protestant lawyers, merchants, soldiers, students, and divines in the audience heard him speak, they were disarmed of their prejudices and drawn to return with their friends. They heard Hecker appeal to virtues that they as humans and as Americans held dear. They listened as he affirmed many of their most cherished values and were won over by his courteous, even affectionate dealing with their religious beliefs. So successful were Hecker's lectures that by November 16 they had to be moved from Brewster Hall to the more spacious Music Hall. Catholics were bidden to stay away so as to make space for Protestants. On that night over three thousand packed the Hall to capacity. Another several hundred were turned away at the door.

Hecker's ideas about America and Catholicism were grounded, as were the majority of his convictions, on his spirituality. To understand the complexity and richness of his thought and of the man himself one is led back to the study of his spirituality, for Hecker was a man whose life revolved around his experience of God.

II

A SENSE OF DESTINY

The story is told of how in 1822 young Isaac Hecker was victimized by a severe case of smallpox. The child told his fretting mother: "I shall not die now. God has a work for me to do and I shall live to do it." Although it is somewhat hard to believe that this statement came from the mouth of a three-year-old, it does convey the idea, echoed by Isaac's own later recollections, that a sense of God's calling was present from his earliest days. Writing late in his life, Isaac recalled that "from my childhood God influenced me by an interior touch of His Holy Spirit."[1]

This sense of God's special providential calling functioned as the major motivation of Hecker's young life. His psychological and emotional development, his dealing with his own identity, and his efforts to find a suitable life's work all were bound up with his sense of divine calling. Isaac grew up believing that life was imbued with meaning and purpose. The purposefulness of all things was grounded in his confidence that God was the great creator and sustainer. All things were then working together toward a goal—a divinely appointed goal for which they had been created.

That Hecker should have believed in a God who ordered and cared for all things stemmed in part from the fact that his early experiences at home and at school presented him with a world in which God was very much present.

9

A SENSE OF DESTINY

LIFE IN THE HECKER HOUSEHOLD

Isaac Hecker was born on December 18, 1819, on New York's lower East Side. New York City in the first half of the nineteenth century was the premier city of the burgeoning nation. The presence of numerous European immigrants and a lively foreign trade made it a truly cosmopolitan city. To the north, the newly completed Erie Canal ran as a great artery into America's heartland. New York was the focal point, perhaps more than any place in its time, of the confluence of the old and new worlds.

Hecker was, like the city in which he was born, a vital mix of the old and new worlds. His father was John Jonas Hecker, son of a German metal worker who traced his roots to German and Dutch nobility. In 1798 John J. Hecker immigrated to New York City and began working in the shop of James Allaire where Robert Fulton's famous steamboat, the *Clermont,* was built. The senior Hecker was an inventive chap who devised an original boiler design that greatly increased the *Clermont's* efficiency. His knack for originality and creativity was passed down to his sons. The eldest, John Hecker, invented a machine for mixing dough and a patented form of self-rising flour, which helped to bring success to the family baking business. George, the second of the three Hecker boys, was the first in New York to utilize a floating grain elevator system in the loading of grain. His firm, the International Grain Elevator Company, eventually gained exclusive rights on the loading of grain in New York harbor. George became wealthy and throughout his life functioned as his brother Isaac's chief financial backer.[2]

John J. Hecker, Sr. was married to the former Caroline Friend, herself a German immigrant. Their wedding took place in 1811 in the Old Dutch Church of Garden Street in New York City. According to an early chronicler, the Dutch Reformed Church remained the church of Isaac's father. His mother, however, eventually became a Methodist.[3] Caroline Hecker seems to have exercised a dominant influence on the Hecker household. In 1842 a close friend of Caroline Hecker spent a month in the Hecker house and supplied this account of Isaac's mother: "She was fair, tall, erect, a very superior example

10

of the German house-mother. Hers was the controlling spirit in the house, and her wise and generous influence was felt far beyond it."[4] Doubtless, Caroline Hecker exerted a tremendous influence over her youngest son, Isaac. Mrs. George V. Hecker, the wife of Isaac's older brother, recounted that "the influence of his mother was of the most powerful kind."[5]

Reference to Isaac's father in the family correspondence is conspicuously lacking. Although his father lived until Isaac's sixty-first year, the youngest son's letters to his family are, by and large, without mention of his father.

In 1826, Isaac began attending the newly opened Public School No. 7 on Christie Street, between Pump and Hester Streets. The school utilized the Lancastrian method of instruction and stressed the three "r's": reading, 'riting, and 'rithmetic. A fourth "r", religion, was by no means neglected in the New York public schools. The school had been founded by pious men who had no intention of keeping religion out of the classroom. The Public School Society's Annual Report of 1843 gave a brief history of the place of religious instruction in the school's curriculum: "From the beginning it was daily practice to read passages from the Bible in the schools."[6] Early in the Society's history the trustees determined to suspend regular studies on Tuesday afternoons when an association of women came into the classrooms to instruct the children from the catechisms of the various Protestant churches. In addition to weekday catechetical instruction, the children were also required to attend public worship regularly. To facilitate this children were required to assemble at their schools on Sunday morning from where monitors would then lead them to their appropriate places of worship. This practice went on until superseded by the establishment of Sunday schools by various churches. Thereafter, however, the public school continued to support the religious education of its pupils by granting the gratuitous use of their schoolhouses to the church Sunday schools.

The Public School Society's concern for religious education is evident in its 1819 "Address to the parents and guardians." The short document directs parents to see to the religious instruction of their children both by example and by precept:

11

> Seeing, next to your own souls, your children . . . are, or
> ought to be, the immediate objects of your constant atten-
> tion and diligent concern, you ought to limit no opportunity
> to instruct them early in the principles of the Christian re-
> ligion . . . . [7]

Clearly, in the trustees' minds religious training was, in the last analysis, the primary object of the child's formal education. "However de-
sirious they [the trustees] may be to promote the improvement of the
scholars in school learning," the Address continues, they "cannot
view with an eye to indifference the more primary object of an education calculated to form habits of virtue and industry, and to incul-
cate the general principles of Christianity."[8]

In the midst of this faith-filled environment, Isaac was introduced to the fundamentals of Christianity. Isaac's mother, ever
aware of her parental duties, taught her son the Scriptures, reading
to him often from the Bible and encouraging him to study it.[9]

A HEART STRANGELY WARMED

The young Isaac was not only instructed in the Scriptures by
his devoted mother, but was brought into contact with the vital New
York City Methodist community to which she belonged. Through the
New York Methodism of the 1820s and 1830s, Isaac's awareness of
God was formed and nourished. He was presented with a model of
Christian life and action, elements of which found their way into his
own mature thought.

One such element was the Methodist ideal of Christian community. Being a Methodist involved an intense experience of communal
life. The followers of Wesley took seriously the idea of being their
brother's keeper. Methodists viewed themselves as a people specially
called by God to lead America to a higher, more holy Christianity.
The preface to the 1825 edition of *Doctrines and Disciplines* voiced the
following conviction: "We believe that God's design in raising up the
preachers called Methodists, in America, was to reform the continent, and spread scripture holiness over these lands."[10] This refor-

12

mation of holiness could, the Methodists believed, only be brought about by individuals who were themselves going on to perfection. Helping each other along the way of holiness was at the heart of Methodism. The third stanza of Charles Wesley's famous hymn, *Help us to help each other, Lord,* captures the spirit of the Methodist concern for one another.

> Help us to help each other, Lord,
>   Each other's cross to bear,
> Let each his friendly aid afford,
>   And feel his brothers' care.[11]

John Wesley had himself stressed the importance of the communal experience. The way of holiness for him was never to be a solitary journey. Although he admired the Mexican hermit Gregory Lopez, he had an overall distrust of any religious experience which stressed the esoteric or the solitary.

> Not in the tombs we pine to dwell
> Not in the dark monastic cell
>   By vows and grates confined
> Freely to all ourselves we give,
> Constrained by Jesus' love to live
>   The servants of mankind.[12]

Throughout America, those who like Wesley had found their hearts strangely warmed by the Spirit of God joined together. The Methodist communities were places which radiated warmth and affection. Their frequent meetings were animated by the hearty congregational singing of Charles Wesley's hymns. The preaching was simple, biblical, and practical. It took as its frame of reference situations of everyday life with which all could well relate. The pastors and lay leaders who exhorted their brothers and sisters were for the most part ordinary folks with a minimum of theological training. Ministry in the church was by no means the exclusive domain of the professional clergy. Each believer was urged to serve the community according to his gifts. Singers, Sunday school teachers, class leaders, and members of the church governing boards or mission societies all played their part.

When Caroline Hecker joined the Methodists is not known. Her friend, Georgiana Bruce Kirby, described her in the 1840s as a "life-long Methodist," but in fact Caroline could not have converted to Methodism until sometime after her 1811 marriage, which took place in the Dutch Reformed Church.[13] By 1825, however, the year before Isaac was to begin school, Caroline Hecker's name appears on the Methodist rolls. At this time she was a member of the Forsyth Street Church and duly enrolled in one of the small groups known as classes to which all adult members were required to belong.[14] The class was a gathering of not more than twelve adults of the same sex who met together weekly for the purpose of providing the intimate edification and support that was not possible in the larger meetings.

In addition to the class meeting there were three other practices within Methodism that were designed to build community: the Love Feast, the Band Society, and the home visitation. The latter is of particular interest because of the role it played in promoting family religion. Visiting of each church member's home by the pastor or class leader had as its main goal "to banish lukewarmness" and was viewed as essential to "guard against back-sliding."[15] In an urban environment such as New York City where the temptations of the world and the flesh protruded upon the minds of the faithful with unrelenting speed and intensity, it was well-nigh essential that the church provide an influential social milieu that would reinforce the believer's convictions. All too easily could the bright city lights entice a onetime churchgoer to lapse into the unchurched masses of America's great cities.

New York during the first half of the nineteenth century was already a place of numerous entertainments. There was Barnum's famous museum of wonders replete with its fascinating oddities. There were the elegant shops of Fifth Avenue that displayed a seemingly endless array of goods from around the world: the latest Paris fashions, exotic spices from the Far East, and gadgets that purported to do everything from shining shoes to curing rheumatism. Then, for those who sought a more spiritual thrill, there were animal magnetism and faith-healing—practices which, to the consternation of church leaders, fascinated many a nineteenth-century American.

A primary function of the Methodist house visit was to promote family religion in the midst of these distractions. Family prayer was viewed as an "ordinance of God," a means of grace essential to those called to the married state. To encourage family religion, the instruction of children was seen as central. Section XV of *Doctrines and Disciplines* is expressly devoted to the subject of children's instruction. Preachers are urged to meet with groups of approximately ten children one hour weekly or bi-weekly. The preachers should, the directive continues, "procure our instructions or catechisms" for the children and impress their contents upon the children's hearts. Furthermore, the preachers are exhorted to talk with the children "every time you see any at home" and to "pray earnestly for them." These directives are concluded with the following charge:

> As far as practicable, it shall be the duty of every preacher of a circuit or station, to obtain the names of the children belonging to his congregations, to form them into classes . . . [and] to instruct them regularly himself, as much as his other duties will allow.[16]

Classes and home visitations of the type described were a part of Caroline Hecker's church. The Forsyth Street Church was one of the most prominent and active of the five New York Methodist churches of the 1830s. Founded in 1789 as the city's second Methodist society, Forsyth Street had by 1825 become a thriving church. Its members during this time included such prominent figures as the Reverend Daniel Ostrander and Nathan Bangs. Caroline Hecker was in 1825, Isaac's sixth year, an active member of the church, attending a weekly class led by Robert Smart.[17] Her attendance at classes was regular throughout Isaac's childhood and adolescence. In turn, the Hecker house was visited by the enthusiastic preachers and class leaders who, in addition to exhorting their sister Caroline, did not hesitate to follow the directive to instruct the children by talking with them "every time you see one at home," and by organizing classes for regular catechesis.

Concern for the religious education of children during Hecker's childhood led to the establishment of the Sunday School Movement. Interest in the movement among New York City Methodists during the first third of the nineteenth century centered on Caroline Hecker's Forsyth Street Church. The first meeting of the New York Methodist Sunday School was held there in February 1816. In 1827 the most significant event in the development of Methodist religious education, the formation of the Methodist Sunday School Union, took place also in the church. Nathan Bangs was elected general secretary of the Union and chaired the weekly meetings of its board of directors at Forsyth Street. [18]

Under the direction of Bangs, the Methodist Book Concern began publishing a periodical for children entitled *Child's Magazine*. A notice of it in *The Christian Advocate and Journal* outlined its purpose.

> It is intended to embrace in this work short practical essays, anecdotes, narratives, accounts of the conversion and happy deaths of children, facts illustrative of the conduct of Providence, sketches of national history, poetry, etc. The constant aim in conducting this little work, will be to lead the infant mind to the knowledge of God our savior. [19]

In the midst of the keen interest in children's religious education that centered on his mother's church at Forsyth Street, young Isaac was introduced to the fundamentals of Christianity and Methodism in his home through the efforts of his mother, and, on the Sabbath, at Sunday schools. In addition, Isaac attended the Sunday services with his mother and acquired an early familiarity with Methodist liturgy, which he demonstrated years later in an 1842 letter to his parents describing one of Orestes Brownson's services in Boston by comparing it to a Methodist service. [20]

Methodism also presented Hecker with a doctrine of God's special providence. The Methodists believed that they were a people specially called to be agents for spiritual renewal. They were convinced that America could be reformed—that a "scripture holiness" could spread over the land.

This type of thinking had its effect on Isaac's development.

From an early age he believed that he was called by God to do a work. But just as for the Methodists fulfilling one's individual calling was never to be done in isolation, so also was Hecker, as he grew, unwilling to do without the community of believers. Not only was the community of believers to help the individual attain perfection, it was also to be the corporate instrument of God's blessings to the nation and the world. This notion of community was basic to Hecker's later idea of the Paulists.

In addition to the lively experience of community and the highly-developed belief in providence, Hecker also encountered in Methodism the Wesleyan doctrine of perfection. Interest in perfectionism was very much a part of the New York City Methodism of Hecker's day. In 1832, Isaac worked briefly for *The Christian Advocate and Journal and Zion's Herald,* published by Bangs' Methodist Book Concern. During Hecker's employment, *The Christian Advocate and Journal and Zion's Herald,* which had since 1828 been the official weekly voice of the Methodist Episcopal Church, was edited by Timothy Merritt. In the early 1820s, Merritt was gaining notoriety for his preaching on Christian perfection. In 1825 he had published his *Treatise on Christian Perfection, with Directions for Obtaining That State.* The book was enormously successful, taking its place among the standard works of those Methodist clergymen involved in the increased interest in the doctrine of perfection that emerged in the 1820s. The very year in which Hecker worked with the *The Christian Advocate and Journal and Zion's Herald,* the Methodist bishops gathered at the General Conference issued a call for a new concern with holiness. The Book Concern's *Methodist Quarterly Review* carried their statement: "Let us not suppose it is enough to have this doctrine in our standards; let us labor to have the experience and power of it in our hearts."[21]

Interest in perfectionism had been an important part of Methodism from its beginnings. John Wesley himself regarded the doctrine of perfection as a central belief of Methodism.[22] His 1759 *Plain Account of Christian Perfection* became a standard inspirational work among his followers. Wesley had been influenced in his thinking on perfection through reading the Greek Fathers, Clement of Alexandria, Ephraem Syrus, and especially Macarius the Egyptian, a fourth-century Syrian monk whose teaching was drawn from Gregory of Nyssa.[23] Wesley defined Christian perfection in terms of perfect love. Perfect love was love that had been purified from selfishness. Sanctification worked, Wesley believed, a real, not only a relative, change in the believers. The "love of God shed abroad in our hearts by the Holy Spirit" actually cleansed the faithful from inward "evil thoughts" and "evil tempers," as well as from outward acts of deliberate sin.

Wesley held that although perfection was usually the result of a process of sanctification, the believer could receive the experience of perfect love instantaneously.[24] The possibility of full salvation as an experience to be enjoyed in this life functioned as an important part of the Methodist message.

Wesley's doctrine of perfection was embraced by that pillar of the Forsyth Street Church, Nathan Bangs. Bangs himself professed "perfect love" in 1801. An early chronicle of Methodism says of him, "The Wesleyan doctrine of sanctification was to him peculiarly precious, and he delighted to attend services having special reference to this subject."[25] In 1817 Bangs began catechism classes in the Duane Street Church in New York. Among his students were Sara Langford and her ten-year-old sister, Phoebe. Beginning in 1835 Sara and her sister, then Mrs. Phoebe Palmer, started their Tuesday Meeting for the Promotion of Holiness, which was destined to play an influential part in promoting Methodist perfectionism among a broad range of nineteenth-century Protestants.[26]

By emphasizing the doctrine of perfection, the Methodists of Hecker's day showed their love for a religion that was centered in personal experience. Wesley's life was transformed, so he tells us, when he realized that Christ had died not merely for the sin of the world, but for *his* sin. The immediate experience of divine forgiveness served as a foundation of the message that Wesleyan preachers carried throughout America. Salvation was, they proclaimed, for all who would fulfill the biblical conditions of repentance and belief. All who, convinced of their sin, would call upon the Lord could have the assurance of the Lord's forgiveness. Such assurance was based on the first-hand experience of God's saving grace. To be a Christian, the Methodists argued, was not essentially a matter of mental assent to certain truths, or a matter of leading a moral life according to Jesus' teaching. It was essentially an experience of the divine.

This emphasis on experiential religion and on a perfection that was essentially an experience of the sanctifying presence of the Spirit presented Hecker with a God who was near at hand and could be known intimately. His presence could be felt in one's heart; his work could be perceived in one's life. Given this, is it any wonder that Hecker felt from an early age that God had influenced him by "an interior light and the interior touch of His Holy Spirit"?[27] Hecker's radical awareness of God and his efforts to grow in this awareness were shared by every good Methodist who was going on to perfection.

In one further regard, Methodism nourished and formed the young Hecker's awareness of God—in its emphasis on free will and human agency, and its rejection of Calvinism. From the days of its founder, Methodism locked horns with Calvinism. Wesley's belief in free will and Christ's universal atonement flew in the face of the Calvinist schemes of election. The charge of Arminianism was early leveled against the Wesleyans, and by the 1800s the debate was still raging.[28] Once again Nathan Bangs had been in the thick of it. In 1817 Bangs debated the Reverend A. Benedict of the Presbyterian Church of Franklin, New York. Bangs published a series of six letters addressed to Mr. Benedict that were entitled *The Errors of Hopkinsianism Detected and Refuted.* Not to be outdone, the Presbyterians rejoined with a work by Seth Williston entitled *Vindication of Some of the Most Essential Doctrines of the Reformation.* The fiery Bangs, noted for his polemical bent, replied in 1819 with *The Reformer Reformed.* The latter work was a continuation of Bangs' earlier critique. In it he rejected the famous five points of Calvinism.[29] By highlighting the role of prevenient grace he argued against the notion that men are totally depraved until the time of justification. He rejected unconditional election, affirming instead that all are "empowered to repent, believe in Christ and be saved." The worth and abilities of human nature, even prior to regeneration, were affirmed by Bangs. He wrote:

> The doctrine we teach . . . reveals the Holy Spirit, whose divine operations distil as the gentle dew upon the mown

19

grass, or as the showers of rain upon the parched field, to revive the languishing souls of men, and to raise their lapsed powers to divine favor, peace, joy . . . . [30]

Significantly, Bangs declared that the Spirit's influences are poured out upon all and that the Spirit works within men "to raise their lapsed powers." The powers of human nature, Bangs implied, are not totally effaced, but rather "lapsed." The distinction is an important one because it opens the way for affirming the essential dignity and worth of human nature and in effect resembles, in sharp distinction from the Calvinist total depravity doctrine, the Catholic position, which Hecker was later to adopt. Hecker's dissatisfaction with the Calvinist doctrine of total depravity that, as shall be seen, was present in both his early and later writings had a parallel in Bangs' anti-Calvinist polemic.

Nourished by such an optimistic understanding of human nature, Hecker grew up during his first dozen years affirming free will and human agency. He believed that he had a role to play in attaining the divine destiny to which he was appointed. He was confident that his activity could become the channel for divine action. He could be a worker-together-with-God. He could be God's agent.

As a teenager Isaac was soon to become busily involved in other pursuits that took him far from his mother's church. Yet the ideas he had encountered in Methodism remained part of his life.

III

THE BUSY SEARCH

As Hecker moved into the eventful years of adolescence, he continued to be radically aware of the presence of God. This awareness manifested itself in a new social concern. He longed to know how a sense of vocation fitted into the world he saw around him. His perception of God's calling was inextricably bound to the questions of his own identity. In this way it was always present—drawing, leading, beckoning the young Hecker as he strove to find his station in life, to determine what he would *do* in the world. How, he asked, could the inner life he experienced find expression? How could it be practically worked out? Even Hecker's most secular pastimes had at their base the desire to know God's will and to follow his plan.

EARLY POLITICAL INVOLVEMENT

During the summer of 1833 when *The Christian Advocate and Journal and Zion's Herald* was moving into a more spacious residence on Mulberry Street, Isaac took up a new job with a type foundry that did printing for the Methodist Book Concern. His new career as a type founder, however, was destined to be short-lived. In 1834, the family baking business that Isaac's brothers, John and George, had started the year before had prospered to the point where they could use the services of their youngest brother. Isaac began working with his brothers in their busy shop on Rutgers Street. The work was hard

21

and long. Hecker, looking back at those days some fifty-two years later, recalled his labors as a delivery boy.

> How hard I used to work carrying the bread around in my baker's cart! How often I got stuck in the gutters and in the snow! Sometimes some good soul . . . would give me a lift. [1]

The good souls that Hecker encountered were largely members of the working class. Factory workers and small business owners made up the bulk of the population of the Heckers' East Side neighborhood. The working men of the day were accustomed to long hours, irregular wages, and little prospect for improvement. Often laborers were defrauded of their just recompense through the use of bad money that would, when exchanged, yield little or none of its purported value. Inequality between the workers' poverty and the comfortable life of the affluent industrialists and entrepreneurs whose palatial homes lined Fifth Avenue between Washington Square and 20th Street was blatant. While the Astors, the Brevoorts, the Stuyvesants, and the Vanderbilts treated themselves to epicurean fantasies in their mansions, some residents of Hecker's neighborhood—the city's most densely populated—went hungry. During the summer months the overcrowded blocks became breeding grounds for cholera and yellow fever. Large sections of the city still had no decent sanitation system; waste was simply left out in the street or flushed down one of the already polluted streams. It was a long way from the plushness of Fifth Avenue to the decadence of the Five Points neighborhood at the meeting of Baxter, Worth, and Park Streets. Discontent stirred in the bosom of many laborers and calls for reform rang out.

The sensitive Hecker harkened to the popular cry for social amelioration. His heart was moved with the desire for doing good to others, and the political situation of New York in the 1830s made politics an appealing means for accomplishing that end. [2]

In 1825 a law was passed that opened the way for broader popular participation in politics by extending the franchise to those twenty-one and older who had been residents of New York State for at least one year. The move resulted in the widespread formation of workers' political societies.[3] One such group was the Workingman's Party. Founded in Philadelphia in 1827, the group had a New York City chapter by 1829, which in its early days largely was influenced by a group known as the "Free Thinkers" that included Frances Wright, Robert Owen, Robert Jennings, and George Evans. The party put forth an ultra-democratic platform wishing to emerge as the great defender of the rights of the oppressed. The Free Thinkers hoped that by joining with the Workingman's Party they might gain the support of the many lovers of Jacksonian Democracy and thereby implement their radical system of education on a broad scale. The party was from the start splintered by divisions that prevented it from having any large-scale impact. By 1830 the Workingman's Party in New York was defunct.

One of the leading lights of the Workingman's Party, George Evans, remained active in the cause of the workingman and in 1835 co-founded the Equal Rights, or Loco-Foco, Party in New York City, with which the Hecker brothers were soon involved. The new party was composed of what the group's first historian described as "free trade, anti-monopoly, hard-money men."[4] Through the *Evening Post* and *Man* newspapers they took up Andrew Jackson's opposition to the "monster monopoly," put forth an unflinching attack against the banking system and all forms of paper currency advocating the use of gold and silver as the only safe and constitutional currency, and rejected aristocrat-controlled government as a crime against the people's natural rights. Refusing to be silenced by the party bosses, members of the fledgling party succeeded in usurping the chair from monopoly Democrat Isaac Varian during an incredibly raucous meeting of the New York Democratic Republican Electors on October 29, 1835. The demonstration resulted in the Whig papers, the *Enquirer* and the *Courier,* dubbing the new party the "Loco-Focos."[5]

The Loco-Focos continued gaining popular support as economic conditions worsened in New York City. In 1837 a general panic gripped New York's economy when the banks announced the suspension of payment on paper money. The financial market crashed, unemployment soared, and inflation ran wild, plummeting the country into one of the worst depressions in its short history. The price of necessities—flour, meat, fuel, and rents—went sky-high despite suf-

ficient resources, eliciting the wrath of the working class. Flour deal-
ers were the object of much of the popular resentment at this time.
A January 1837 public rally sponsored by the Loco-Focos erupted in
what became known as the "flour riots." One rebellious soul jumped
onto the platform after an address by party leader Moses Jaques and
shouted, "Go to the flour stores and offer a fair price, and if refused,
take the flour!" Before the chairman could restore order an angry mob
was storming off to the nearby Hart's flour store which they left in
shambles.

Soon after the flour riots, in the spring of the same year, John
Hecker's name appears as one of the party leaders.[6] Given the fact
that the Heckers were in the baking business and depended for their
livelihood on flour, it is not at all difficult to understand why they
joined the Equal Rights Party revolt against the political policies that
had resulted in constant inflation in the price of grains. John Hecker
had begun what was to be his long career in politics in 1829 with
the early Workingman's Party and later the 7th Ward Democratic
Association. After the Loco-Focos disappeared in late 1837, John continued to work in the New York political scene. In 1850 he was
named the Free-Soil party candidate for Congress, and in 1865 the
Citizens' Association sponsored him in an unsuccessful bid in the
mayoral contest.[7]

Motivated by the political astuteness of his older brother, the
practical implications that political policies in 1837 had on the
Heckers' livelihood, and his compassion for the plight of the under-
privileged, Isaac joined his brothers in their work for the Loco-Focos.
Having just turned eighteen when John Hecker rose to a leadership
position in the party, Isaac, though not old enough to vote, was old
enough to make his presence felt through political activity. Some fifty
years later he told the story of how he and his brother George had
worked for the purist rump ticket that represented a segment of the
Loco-Focos that refused to compromise with the Tammany Hall
Democrats in the 1837 election.

> I was too young to vote, but I remember my brother George
> and I posting political hand bills at three o'clock in the
> morning. . . . We also worked hard on election day, keep-

ing up and supplying the ticket booths, especially in our own ward, the old Seventh.[8]

What was Isaac's spiritual state at the time of the political involvement with the Equal Rights Party? Writing in 1858, Isaac gave a brief assessment of his development from his childhood. He styled himself as having passed through three distinct states: one of political concern, one of social concern, and one of religious concern. His first stage began, Hecker stated, at age twelve when his "mind began to seek after truth" and his "heart was moved with the desire of doing good to others." Hecker described this political period as lasting "several years." Then he moved into his period of social concern in which he was convinced that "the evils of society were not so much political as social, and that not much was to be hoped for from political action." Hence, he felt that a social reform was called for. "The key to effective social reform was," Hecker thought, "practical application of the moral principles of Christianity to the social relations between men." After this, Isaac realized that all social reform must begin with the individual and ultimately be of a spiritual nature.[9]

The stage theory, however, has its drawbacks since it represents, as might be imagined, an oversimplification. Hecker intended his 1858 letter to be a synopsis of his life and dealt very briefly with the period before his conversion. He was able to describe certain important elements of his past in terms of three states. The tendency to imply that these were totally distinct stages in which the elements found in one stage were not to be found in another is evident in his statement.[10]

But Isaac's life was not as neatly compartmentalized as this three-stage interpretation implies. From his correspondence it is clear that his interest in politics did not end in 1837, but continued until at least 1844.[11] Nor was his concern with social issues limited to the period after 1837. Rather, the notion that essentialized his thinking on social issues, namely that the practical application of Christian principles to social problems was the only proper solution, was fundamental to Hecker's own Loco-Foco party in 1837.

F. Byrdsall's *History of the Loco-Foco or Equal Rights Party* is a first-hand account written by one who was the party's recording secretary for nearly all of its independent existence. Byrdsall provides a clear picture of the importance of the ideas of Christian Democracy to the party's philosophy. The preface to the 1842 edition describes the party's leaders, Moses Jaques, Pascal B. Smith, James L. Stratton, John Hecker, and others, as having encouraged the Equal Rights Party "to have a deeper love for Christian Democratic principles, to seek more knowledge of them, and to find a more abiding faith in them."[12] Byrdsall, together with the man described as the party's "patriarch," Moses Jaques, was one of the two officers of the party, and a Loco-Foco candidate for various offices. His preface is laden with biblical allusions. The book itself, for example, is described as the Bible of the Loco-Focos. Loco-Focoism is cast as a movement with a providential mission to bring back the Democratic Party to the principles on which it had originally been founded. The Loco-Focos are then linked with the religious professors of Hecker's youth, whose mission it was to bring back America to spiritual holiness.

> These Methodists of Democracy [the Loco-Focos] introduced no new doctrines, no new articles into true creed; they only revised those heaven-born principles which had been so long trodden under foot of Monopoly . . . . [13]

The restorationist theme is then blended with its corollary notion: millennialism. In decrying a local newspaper's misrepresentation of Loco-Focoism, Byrdsall interjects: "There could scarcely be a greater proof of the near approach of the Millennium."[14] Byrdsall dedicated his book to one of the party's leaders and often endorsed candidate, Pascal B. Smith. The dedication clearly shows that, for at least two of the most important Loco-Focos, politics was in no way divorced from their view of Christianity as the key to social amelioration: "To a believer who has rejoiced in the light of Loco-Focoism as an outward sign of the inward light of Christianity;—To a Disciple of those principles which would effect peace on Earth and good amongst men . . . ."[15]

The practical application of Christian principles to political and social problems known as Christian Democracy was championed by the party's chief theoretician, Moses Jaques. The February 1838

County Convention issued a declaration of principles that remained the standard for the Loco-Foco platform. The accompanying resolutions written by Jaques end with this summary:

> In short we ask nothing but what is consistent with Christian Democracy, for in the declaration that 'God is no respector of persons . . .' we behold the universal equality of man:—In the denunciation of, 'Woe unto you lawyers, for ye bind heavy burdens and grievous to be borne upon men's shoulders,' we see the strongest form of command against unequal laws on monopolies . . . and in the injunction of 'Be ye perfect, even as your father in heaven is perfect,' we behold the great law of progress. [16]

It is obvious, then, that as Isaac became involved with politics in the Loco-Focoism of the late 1830s he also came into contact with the idea of applying Christian principles to social problems, for this idea was basic to Loco-Focoism.

The three-stage interpretation of Isaac's early life is inadequate, not only in its implication that his social concern was limited to a certain period, but also in its implication that a concern for spiritual things was absent from his adolescence. Even as a youth he remained aware of God's calling. The Loco-Focos provided an example of how the purposes of God could be practically worked out in the world. This was exactly what Isaac was himself trying to do at this time. He wanted to know how the sense of divine calling could take on substance in the world around him. In a statement made later in life, he affirmed, in contradiction of the stage theory, that a sense of divine calling was very much present during his youth. He wrote:

> While I was a youth, and in early manhood, I was preserved from certain sins . . . in a way that was peculiar. . . . I was also at the same time, and indeed, all the time, conscious that God was preserving me innocent with a view to some future providence. Mind, all this was long before I came into the Church. [17]

Yet even though Isaac throughout his adolescence remained keenly aware of God's presence, he did not join the church of his devout Methodist mother.

The Hecker household was one in which religious pluralism was, from the start, tolerated. Caroline Hecker herself had set the pattern in leaving, soon after her marriage, the Dutch Reformed Church of which her husband was a member. Her husband seems likewise to have been tolerant of religious differences, but more out of indifference than generosity. The genuineness of Caroline Hecker's tolerant frame of mind was witnessed by the family's close friend, Georgiana Bruce Kirby, who recorded Caroline's response to the queries of another woman who could not be reconciled to the change of faith of her own offspring. "No," Caroline said, "I would not change the faith of my sons. They have found peace and joy in the Catholic Church, and I would not by a word change their faith, if I could."[18] The tolerant spirit of the Hecker household prompted all three of the Hecker brothers to choose churches other than the Methodist. George eventually joined Isaac in the Catholic church. John, also not uninterested in the high church tradition, became an Episcopalian. As an active member of All Saints Church in New York, John gained a reputation for works of charity. During the torturous winter of 1857, he gave free bread to the city's poor. In that same year, John preceded his brother Isaac into the field of religious publishing by purchasing the *Churchman* magazine, which, under the editorship of Samuel Seabury, Jr., was at the time the official organ of the Protestant Episcopal Church.[19] Of the four Hecker children, only Elizabeth became an actual member of her mother's Forsyth Street Church.[20]

During his adolescence Isaac was distracted from active involvement in his mother's church by the new occupations of his teenage years—his work in the family bakery and his involvement with politics. Although the Hecker baking business was soon to grow into one of New York's most prosperous, in 1834 it was only a struggling new enterprise requiring long hours of toil. The long hours did not leave much time for other activity. The economic situation in the 1830s, as has been noted, made political action an expedient move for the Heckers, whose livelihood depended on being able to turn a profit from their labors. Isaac had the example of his older brothers to follow in entering the Loco-Foco ranks. There was hardly time left for the demanding task of being an active Methodist, constantly bidden by one's brothers to attend to the many ordinances ordained by God for salvation.

In addition to these things there was, however, another factor which kept Isaac from joining a church. Even as a young man, he had certain intellectual problems with the denominations and particularly with Methodism. Writing in 1887, Hecker gave this picture of his attitude toward Methodism in the 1830s and early 1840s: " . . . in our time it had no stated intellectual basis. It was founded totally on emotional 'conversion,' with the notorious exclusion of the intellect."[21] What did Isaac mean by "intellectual basis"? Did not men like the learned Nathan Bangs defend with intellectual acumen Methodist doctrine? By "intellectual basis" Isaac meant not the questions by "insiders" about the propriety of one doctrine over against another, but the more fundamental questions on the nature of belief. The problem over the nature of belief which the young Hecker experienced centered on the issue that was to remain crucial to his whole subsequent search for religious truth. Stated simply it is this: How can one know that one's inner religious thoughts, beliefs, and sentiments conform to objects in the external world? The problem stemmed, obviously, not from a lack of inner religious experience, but from perplexity over how such internal experience of God related to the external world. Hecker was uncertain about how his sense of divine calling could be worked out in the world. It was not that his religious sentiments ran completely cold during his teenage years, keeping him from joining a church, but that he could not see how his own inner religious convictions, beliefs, and sentiments corresponded with those of any given religious group. As a child he had not the reflective ability to doubt the validity of his own experience, but by the time he was a teenager, such doubts began to loom larger and larger, making the question of church membership one that he could, given his family's tolerance and his busy schedule, put off.

Lacking the assurance that he needed to trust and understand his own subjective religious experience, Isaac was attracted to a form of politics that emphasized the social and political implications of

Christianity while largely ignoring the subjective spiritual dimension. Thus he could describe himself and his fellow Loco-Focos as interpreting Christianity "as altogether a social institution, its social side entirely overlapping and hiding the religious."[22]

Hecker's opting for the social side of Christianity was caused not only by what he did not understand about his own religious experience, but also by what he did understand. Often as a teenager, Isaac would run out to the East River during the middle of the night to ask as he gazed across the moonlit water, "What does God want of me? What has He sent me into the world *to do?*"[23] [*Italics mine*] Since he saw God as calling him to action, and since political and social action was, given his situation, both understandable and practicable, Isaac opted for the practical side of Christianity in the Christian Democracy of the Loco-Focos and ignored the uncertain religious side of Christianity and along with it the Methodists.

ORVILLE DEWEY AND UNITARIANISM

In the 1837 elections, the Loco-Foco party suffered a devastating defeat that marked its disappearance from the New York political scene. Although his party was defeated, Hecker's interest in questions of social reform and the ideal of Christian Democracy did not disappear. Compelled to seek new channels for pursuing his concerns, the young man, not surprisingly, turned to the teaching of Orville Dewey. Dewey was a Unitarian minister with an impressive background. A graduate of Andover Seminary, Dewey, before coming to New York in 1835, had worked under the prince of New England Unitarianism, William Ellery Channing. In 1839 Dewey dedicated a new church on Broadway, not far from Hecker's home on Rutgers Street. The Church of the Messiah, as the new assembly was called, attracted others besides Isaac who were interested in Dewey's preaching on a practical Christianity, such as George Curtis, a future resident of Brook Farm and good friend of Isaac's. On Sunday mornings, Isaac made his way up Broadway and settled into the comfortable pews of the new church to hear the eloquent, stimulating sermons of one of the day's princes of the pulpit.

Isaac, though he denied ever having believed in Unitarianism,

30

gave this description of Dewey: "Dewey was a smart fellow and I enjoyed listening to him."[24] What he heard and enjoyed from Dewey was an attempt, not unlike that made by the Loco-Focos, to draw out the implications of Christianity for the relations between men. Whereas Moses Jaques and the Loco-Focos had emphasized the political implications of such an approach, Dewey emphasized the moral and ethical dimensions. Both were concerned with the pragmatic implications of the Gospel. Their focus was on earth more than on heaven.

Dewey's practical religion suited Isaac's inclinations. Practical religion, as Dewey defined it, is "a religion that has the most intimate connection with our daily life and welfare."[25] The intent of his practical religion was not to remove God from the world but rather to show his presence in it, in every aspect of it, even the most ordinary and everyday. Dewey's theology can be seen as part of the movement within Unitarianism that rejected both the distant God of the Deists and the Calvinists' God who was separated from man by man's sinful nature. God, for Dewey, was very much involved in his creation, not only as the grand architect or sovereign Lord, but as the very life of his creatures. Affirming the doctrine of his former mentor, William E. Channing, that there is an essential sameness between human and divine nature, Dewey endeavored to attune men to the marvelous potential of their own nature. In a series of sermons entitled "Discourses on Human Life" delivered at the Church of the Messiah in 1839, Dewey attempted to show that "the history of the humblest human life is a tale of marvels. There is no dull or unmeaning thing in existence, did we but understand it."[26]

The Calvinist doctrine of total depravity received the unrelenting criticism of the New York Unitarian preacher who rejected categorically the implication that sin is in any way natural to human nature. To Dewey this notion was one of "such comprehensive and radical mischief as to infect the religious state of mankind, and to overshadow, almost with despair, the moral prospect of the world." Human nature must rather be seen as having a very real constitutional worth. It contained "a treasure . . . of which most men are not conscious, and with which none are yet fully aware."[27] Calvinism's doctrine of total depravity, as Dewey saw it, removed God from the

31

world by destroying the constitutional bond between human nature and God. By denying man's natural inclination to goodness, the doctrine of total depravity also eliminated the basis for good works, ethical living, and social reform. Religion, Dewey held, did not essentially consist of "something to the mass of men unknown and unintelligible," but rather of "certain intelligible affections" such as goodness, rectitude, and love of truth, which men know by nature.[28]

To say that religion has its basis in human nature did not rule out the transcendent side of faith. Religion is, Dewey held, the "great sentiment of life."[29] Spirituality flowed from an ever-increasing awareness of the treasure within human nature. "Spiritual meditation," Dewey declared in his sermon "The Moral Significance of Life," "interpreting experience, and above all the life of Jesus, will lead us farther into the heart and soul and the innermost life of all things."[30] Spirituality, thriving as it does on the experience of life, finds its proper locus in the whole range of human existence. Everything in creation, everything we do, every situation we encounter is, then, spiritual.

> There is no conviction which is more rare, and more needful for our improvement, than this. . . . To very many life appears at least mechanical and dull. . . . Could the toiling world but see that the scene of their daily life is all spiritual, that the very implements of their toil, or the fabrics they weave, or the merchandise they barter were all designed for spiritual ends . . . what revolution might this single truth produce in the condition of the whole world![31]

Dewey's spirituality was clearly one which rejected the idea that any extraordinary conditions must accompany the religious life. No need existed to go to the cloister. Everyday situations were the *via perfectionis*.[32]

Given his view of the essential goodness of human life and the spiritual nature of all creation, Dewey viewed the Church "not as an empire by itself" but as an institution in service to the world, "the handmaid of general freedom, virtue and happiness." Yet the Church was not a worldly institution, but one which had the pledge of its continuance in its own "eternal principles, and in the power of Almighty God." With respect, then, with love, and with sympathy the Church could address the world, affirming its goodness and directing it more perfectly to its creator and sustainer.[33]

Through Dewey's preaching the young Hecker was exposed to certain notions that he found attractive. In it he heard declared a Christianity that, though it highlighted the social side, did not ignore the religious side. Unlike Loco-Focoism, which did not deal with the questions of spirituality and personal religious experience, Dewey's thought made provision for the transcendent, even mystical element. Unlike the Methodism of his childhood, Dewey's preaching in its emphasis on the spiritual character of all existence presented Isaac with a religion of enlightenment more than a religion of conversion. Here he found a basis for confirming his own aspirations, hopes, plans, and dreams and establishing a connection between these inward experiences and objective reality. Here he saw an opportunity to relate God to a full range of human endeavors, to do all things to the glory of God and to find a practical outworking for his own inner sense of calling. This resonated with his own experience. Dewey encouraged Isaac to do what he was always willing to do: he encouraged him to be radically aware of the presence of God.

PARLEY P. PRATT AND THE MORMONS

About the same time that the young man Isaac was attending Dewey's Church of the Messiah, his quest for social reform led him to investigate the newly-founded Mormon sect. Isaac met two enthusiastic Mormon apostles under whose guidance he undertook a long, careful examination of the doctrines of Joseph Smith. One of Isaac's Mormon teachers was Parley P. Pratt[34] whom he met during the late 1830s while the Mormon preacher was in New York conducting missionary work and pursuing plans to publish a defense of Joseph Smith's doctrines.[35]

The young Hecker, heavily involved in the questions of political and social reform, was attracted by Mormonism's plan for radical social reorganization. A few years after meeting Pratt, Isaac was still impressed and he wrote in a diary entry:

This idea of universal reform has been in the minds of all reformers and founders of sects in Christendom, from Fox to Joseph Smith, and the last gives a greater evidence of success than any of his worthy progenitors.[36]

The Mormons advocated a plan for social and religious reform that centered around an institution known as the United Order. In Joseph Smith's own words, the United Order was "a religio-social system communal in its character, designed to abolish poverty, monopoly, and kindred evils, and to bring about unity and equality in temporal and spiritual things."[37] Concern for equality in temporal things was one of the chief planks of the Equal Rights Party of which Hecker and his brothers had been a part. The Mormons in the late 1830s were offering a more radical, thorough plan for the reorganization of society in such a fashion as to assure an equitable distribution of goods. With these intentions Isaac, who daily rubbed elbows with many of New York's downtrodden, could quickly sympathize. Smith's United Order required its members to turn over to the church all their property, which was then redistributed to each according to need. The success with which Smith's plan met impressed the young Hecker.

The United Order, as had the Equal Rights Party, aimed at the restoration of what it saw as a more pristine social order. In the case of Smith's group, that order was the United Order, or Order of Enoch, which, Smith held, was the socio-economic order that governed the ancient city of Enoch. Practice of this ancient rule, Smith thought, would enable the Mormons to build the new Zion, wherein would dwell righteousness.

The attempts of the Mormons to rejuvenate society by resorting to a long-forgotten truth appealed to Isaac who was concerned with the practical application of the ideal. He greatly appreciated the value of a truth and yet was not content to leave the idea purely in the theoretical realm. Action must flow from the idea; the ideal must in some way become the real. The Mormons were masters of the practical, and although their ideas were in certain cases highly unorthodox, they were able to construct effective, enduring communities that withstood persecution and the ravages of time.

Isaac was attracted to Mormonism for another reason as well. He was disposed, as he himself described it, to "take the side of the under-dog."[38] Both the Loco-Focos, especially the purest rump ticket that the Heckers supported, and the Mormons, who in 1839 sang a song of unfair treatment and oppression at the hands of the Missouri government, were true underdogs whose cause could appeal to the tender youth.

There was one more thing that drew Isaac to the zealous disciples of Joseph Smith: like him, the Mormons were interested in personal spirituality. Although Hecker had been ignoring the spiritual, or, as he called it, the religious side of Christianity, during his days of activity with the Loco-Focos prior to late 1837, he was beginning to open up more to it, as his attendance at Dewey's church attests. In so doing, Hecker had presented to him again certain elements that he had seen in Methodism, namely, the emphasis on religious experience, the importance of the community of believers for the individual's spiritual well-being, the idea that social reform must be preceded by personal spiritual reform, and the belief that God, through a select band of true believers, providentially was restoring his Church.

Had Hecker not been open to matters concerning spirituality, he could never have countenanced for a moment Parley Pratt and the Mormons. Doubtless, for the Mormons there was to be no social reform that did not have personal spiritual renewal at its heart. The United Order, which put forth a scheme for socio-economic organization, also existed to promote the personal piety of its members. In the words of one Mormon historian:

That the United Order, or Order of Enoch was a real order, in the accepted sense of the term, involving a consecration of life and effort, as well as of property, and that also, a religious consecration in the best and highest sense, is amply shown by the rule of the order.[39]

Members of the United Order took up the responsibility to help one another to build the Kingdom of God, as they understood it. The Rules For Members of the United Order lays out thirteen ordinances to which all had to commit themselves, which include pledges to abstain from profanity, uncleanliness, foolish and extravagant fashions of dress, and adultery. Hecker's practice of "abstinence from all luxuries, from all flesh meats, and from all drinks but water," begun around the time of his examination of Mormonism, had a parallel in the United Order's pledge to "be simple in our dress and manner of living."[40]

As the Methodists were out to restore the Church to what they deemed was a forgotten level of holiness, the followers of Joseph Smith in their own right strove to restore the Church's oneness. A number of students have seen in Mormonism an attempt to reestablish, in the midst of the rampant sectarianism of American Christianity, a theology of one, true, authoritative Church. The theology and polity of the Latter-Day Saints, writes David B. Davis, "was a crude attempt on the part of untrained but sincere men to establish a simple authoritative church, the church they had lost and now yearned for."[41]

Smith and his early followers constructed a church system based on the authority of the special continuing revelations that God had allegedly given Smith. The Book of Mormon was regarded as the Word of God, and the belief in continuing revelation through the gifts of prophecy, revelations, and interpretation of tongues was affirmed. According to Smith, each believer could receive the gift of the Holy Spirit through the laying on of hands in a fashion reminiscent of the Book of Acts. Axiomatic to Smith and his followers was the notion that an increased action of the Holy Spirit was to follow the ministry of the Mormons. A time of God's special dealing was upon the earth—a time in which the action of the Holy Spirit would predominate as it did in the early ages of the Church.[42]

This faith in the special action of the Holy Spirit was accompanied by a belief in America's special destiny. God in his special providence had, they believed, determined to gather together Zion and build the new Jerusalem in America. The restoration of the people of God—Israel, and those Gentiles who repent and embrace the

Gospel covenant—is the basic motif of Joseph Smith's revelation. The Book of Mormon purports to give a history of the ancient inhabitants of North America as well as a prophetic picture of the future.

Pratt, in his 1837 *Voice of Warning,* laid out a standard Mormon exegesis of their sacred texts on the subject of restoration.

> From this prophecy we learn—First, that America is a chosen land of the Lord, above every other land. Second, that it is the place of the New Jerusalem. . . . Third, that a New Jerusalem is to be built in America, by the remnant of Joseph.[43]

This American New Jerusalem, Pratt continued, already was being prepared for by the gathering of the remnant of Joseph. During the late 1830s Joseph Smith had indicated that Independence, Missouri, then the headquarters of the Church of the Latter-Day Saints, would be the place where Zion would be built. The writing, which Pratt addressed to the Gentiles in America, declared that unless they repent and respond to this special revelation declared by Smith, they would soon know God's fiery wrath.[44] Such a vivid picture of America's special destiny in the salvation of the world is as clear a statement of the familiar theme of America's manifest destiny as one could find in the 1830s.

As much as Isaac admired the Mormons' attempts at social reform, he never gave his assent to Joseph Smith's peculiar doctrines. Mormonism provided an example of how an ideal could be practically worked out, but the Mormon ideal was one which Hecker found unacceptable. The basic tenets of orthodox Christianity had already been too firmly established in his childhood experience to be supplanted by Smith's strange new revelations.

Yet Hecker continued to be convinced of the need for social amelioration. Motivated by the belief that America could be purged of its blemishes and emerge as a model of righteousness, he sought for the most effective means of reform. The examples of the Methodists, Mormons, and Orville Dewey were convincing him that social reform included personal spiritual renewal and that Christianity was the solution for the ills of society. The claim that Christianity held the key to social renewal was encountered by Isaac in yet another fashion—in the theories of Orestes Brownson.

HECKER'S EARLY RELATIONSHIP WITH BROWNSON

Doubtless one of the greatest influences on the development of Hecker's spirituality was Orestes A. Brownson. In the final article of a series that Hecker wrote in 1887 in *The Catholic World* eulogizing his deceased friend, Isaac described the effect that Brownson had had on him.

> He was the master, I the disciple. God alone knows how much I am indebted to him.[45]

In February 1841, Isaac had just turned twenty-two. His fascination with social reform movements was shared by his brothers John and George who were excited about an event scheduled for later that month. Brownson was coming to town! Controversial, bold, and original, Brownson was one of the most provocative reformers of the day. He was the author of a bombshell, *New Views of Christianity, Society, and the Church,* a book that forcefully argued for a radical application of Christian principles to social affairs. This man had recently taken the Boston intellectual scene by storm, establishing himself as a leading interpreter of the French philosophy of Benjamin Constant, Victor Cousin, and the Saint-Simonian school. His journal, the *Boston Quarterly Review,* was a vital part of New England intellectual life. In terms of philosophical and critical powers he had few equals. Stubbornly he followed his convictions wherever they led, at whatever cost.

Brownson in 1841 and early 1842 was deeply involved in questions of social reform. His activity as a social reformer had begun in the late 1820s when he worked briefly with the Workingman's Party in New York State. After swiftly becoming disenchanted with the machinations of party politics, he decided to launch out on his own as an independent reformer.

In July 1835 Brownson founded the Society for Christian Union and Progress. Along with Constant's work, *De la Religion Considérée dans sa Source, ses Formes, et ses Développements,* the works of French social theorists Chateaubriand, de Lamennais, Lacordaire, and de Montalembert convinced Brownson that the reconciliation of modern society and religion could be accomplished. Both Protestantism and Catholicism were, he believed, unfit to meet the challenges of the present age. Protestantism had placed too much stress on the materialistic, Catholicism on the spiritual. What was needed, he reasoned, aided by Victor Cousin's theory of eclecticism, was a synthesis of the positive elements of both.

After unity, the second great aim of Brownson's Society was progress. With an optimism characteristic of his age, Brownson declared as the Society's motto a statement of faith in the perfectibility of man and the inevitability of progress: "Paradise on earth is before us."[46] When assuming editorship of the *Boston Reformer* in 1836, Brownson declared his belief in the importance of religion as a means of promoting progress.

> When I connected myself with the cause the workingmen profess to have at heart, I had no confidence in religion. . . . Now I embrace it as the lever of reform, as the very soul of progress.[47]

Religion, as Brownson saw it, was to go hand-in-hand with politics in advancing the new society. No contradictions existed between Democracy and Christianity. They were in fact perfectly complementary. In mid-1837 when Brownson founded his own *Boston Quarterly Review,* he declared one of its purposes to be "to christianize democracy and democratize the church."[48]

Brownson's first lecture in New York was held at the Stuyvesant Institute. As Isaac entered the lecture hall that night he was filled with expectation. There on the platform, flooded by the glare of gas lamps, stood Brownson. His large, manly frame appeared to dwarf the podium on which he leaned. His face was framed by a leonine head of hair and a huge black-gray beard. Everything about him gave the air of confidence and strength of conviction.

His lecture was entitled, "The Democracy of Christ." As Isaac listened, he heard a clear articulation of the ideas that had been fascinating him. Years later, he gave the following synopsis of Brownson's talks: "The upshot of the lectures' thesis was that Christ was the big Democrat and the Gospel was the true Democratic platform."[49] A contemporary account of Brownson's lecture appeared in the *Evening Post* for March 1841, which summarized Brownson's attempt to demonstrate that "the Christian Religion as taught by its founder and democracy as it should exist in every rational mind were the same great and eternal principles regarded only in different relations."[50]

A second lecture was given at Clinton Hall, entitled "The Reform Spirit of the Age." The lectures were successful enough to merit plans for future Brownson discourses in the city. The Hecker brothers took the initiative in arranging Brownson lectures in July 1841 and January 1842. Isaac himself wrote to Brownson in November 1841 on behalf of his brothers, inviting the well-known journalist to feel at full liberty in his choice of lecture topics.

> Whatever you make up your mind to do we are always ready
> to cooperate with hearty cheer as long as it makes a stir,
> a shaking amongst the People. In fact if we could think of
> any other than the ordinary course to pursue so as to excite
> enthusiasm, we would do it with all our might. We hate
> the beaten track.[51]

Brownson, to the delight of the youngest Hecker brother, accepted the invitation. What was even more thrilling, he would lodge with the Hecker family during the course of his lectures. Isaac would have the chance to interact with this fertile and innovative mind which he so admired. It was a mind that, as he readily perceived, had long been traveling the paths he had only recently discovered. From Brownson he could receive direction and be guided in a study of the ideas he longed to pursue.

Brownson, an apt teacher for those who could bear with his domineering ways, obliged his eager admirer, introducing him to the study of German philosophy. Stealing moments during his busy schedule in the bakery, Isaac plunged into the works of Fichte and Kant. As he read, his mind was lifted from the monotonous routine of preparing countless loaves of bread to a new realm, a realm of boundless possibilities. In that realm he was free to explore, free to search where his curiosities led, free to soar to new heights on the wings of fresh ideas.

Brownson delivered a series of four lectures on Civilization and Human Progress in January 1842. An outline of the discourses appeared in the January 17, 1842 New York *Tribune*. The first lecture was a general survey of civilization and "the law by which it is advanced." The second took as its subject "Modern Civilization, its Elements: Influence of Religion and Philosophy in advancing it." The third, the "Influence of Property on Legislation and Political Institutions," and the fourth, "The Part this Country has played, and is destined to play in advancing the Civilization of the Race."[52]

When Brownson delivered his 1841 and 1842 lectures in New York City, he was putting forth the essential idea of Christian Democracy that he had been developing for over a decade. The lectures on "The Democracy of Christ," "The Reform Spirit of the Age," and "Civilization and Human Progress" all reflect themes that were basic to Brownson's thought of the 1830s. That he was chosen by the Heckers and their political comrades to lecture in New York is understandable given the popularity of the ideas of Christian Democracy as put forth by the Loco-Focos' own Moses Jaques. When Isaac heard Brownson develop his notions of the role of religion in social reform, he heard something that was by no means new to him. Brownson did, doubtless, develop the notions of Christian Democracy far more completely than had the Loco-Focos. For Brownson politics was only part of a much larger picture. The keenness of his philosophical abilities enabled him to put forth a scheme not only for political reform, but for far-reaching societal and religious renewal as well.

The effect of Brownson's lectures on the young Hecker was not, as some have suggested, to "turn him to religion as a means of social reform and to Jesus as a teacher of social theories."[53] This had clearly already been done not only by the Loco-Focos but also by Orville Dewey who, like Brownson, attempted to draw out, though again in a less broad-ranging fashion, the social implications of the Gospel. Even the Mormon United Order was in its own way an attempt to

41

do this very thing. It is true though that Brownson presented Hecker with a more forceful, more impressive exposé and that Hecker was now older and had personal access to Brownson, all of which accounted for the added impact that Brownson's ideas had on him.

A second effect of Hecker's 1841 and 1842 meetings with Brownson was that Isaac was initiated into the study of philosophy that resulted in his plunge into subjectivism.[54] It is clear that Hecker struggled with subjectivism in the course of his philosophical studies between 1842 and 1844. Later in life he told of how he and Brownson fought the battle against radical idealism shoulder-to-shoulder. Hecker testified that he fell into a belief in subjectivism from which "it took much to lift me."[55] But the problems with which Hecker struggled were not new. His awareness of God and of his internal dealings with him was present long before he ever became aware of the more precise vocabulary of the philosopher. The meeting with Brownson marked the beginning of his serious dealing with this problem as it emerged in its philosophical dress. It was, however, no stranger that Hecker met, but rather an old acquaintance in new clothing. As he himself said when describing his first interview with Brownson, "I had begun my mental life in politics, and in a certain sense in religion, but to my philosophical life I was yet unborn."[56] His mental life was begun in religion, in the sense that it was in reference to the inner workings of God that Isaac first began to question the reality of his own subjective experience and to attempt to see the correlation between his own inner experience and objective reality. This question, the one with which every individual who dares to think of God must eventually struggle, became increasingly urgent to him as he matured.

The urgency with which this question began to assault him during 1842 can hardly be overstated. The desire to see it resolved grew as the intensity of Isaac's own internal operations of the soul increased. During this year the young searcher was drawn, often seemingly against his own will, to deal with his subjective experience. The things of the external world became more and more of a distraction. As he sought the time and energy to sort out the elements of his own inner life, he found himself unable to cope with the demands made on him by the baking business. Try as he might, he could not ignore the voice within that kept calling out for meaning, substance, and significance in his life. The emotional stress soon began to take its toll on his physical health, resulting in severe fatigue. His family, perplexed by his condition, called in doctors, but their medical remedies brought little improvement. Soon his loved ones realized that Isaac was suffering a malady of the soul, not the body.

During this time Isaac had opened to him, to a degree unparalleled in the past, the world of the internal, the mysterious, the supernatural. A series of dreams so affected him that six months later he was still under their influence.

> How can I doubt these things? Say what may be said, still for all, they have to me a reality, a practical good bearing on my life. They are impressive instructors, whose teachings are given me in such a real manner that they influence one, would I or not . . . . [57]

The most impressive of these dreams occurred in July 1842. Hecker gave this account ten months later:

> I saw (I cannot say I dreamt for it was quite different from dreaming as I thought since I was seated on the side of my bed) a beautiful angelic, pure being and myself standing along-side of her, feeling a most heavenly pure joy. And it was as if . . . our bodies were luminous and they gave forth a moonlike light, which I felt sprung from the joy that we experienced. We were unclothed, pure and unconscious of anything but pure love and joy, and I felt as if we had always lived together and that our motions, actions, feelings and thoughts came from one center. . . . Now this vision continually hovers over me. . . . I am charmed by its influence, and I am conscious that if I should accept anything else, I should lose the life which would be the only existence wherein I could say I live. [58]

Isaac felt that he had to give his undivided attention to the questions troubling his soul, and that this could not be done in the midst of the many responsibilities and distractions of his home environment. He planned to go to a place that would allow him the time and energy to read, study, and ponder.

His family, although sympathetic, could not understand the details of Isaac's struggle. His mother perceived rightly that Isaac was undergoing a profound religious change, which she described as a striving to give over his "whole mind to Christ." Isaac's eldest brother, John, thought his condition had been brought on by too much study. Both Isaac and his family looked to Brownson for counsel in the matter.[59] Perhaps, they thought, he would be able to understand Isaac's condition and offer timely advice. Brownson suggested to the family that they allow Isaac liberty to pursue his interests. Despite John's own disinclination, the family decided to support Isaac's decision to spend time away from home in study.

To the satisfaction of all, especially Isaac, Brownson suggested that the young inquirer visit him at his home in Boston. Late in December of 1842, Isaac arrived at the Boston reformer's Mt. Bellingham home in Chelsea. There Isaac found the time to open his eager soul to one who could sympathize with him.

Isaac was aware that a rather dramatic change had taken place in his life. He was bewildered and not a little frightened by it. With increasing intensity he had found himself alienated from his former life and seemingly from those who meant so much to him. At the moment, all he saw were the differences between his former way of life and the path he felt compelled to take. It seemed that he must leave all behind, and that was painful. Yet although he did not know specifically what it was that he desired to replace the old, he knew he had to seek it with vigor.[60]

As dramatic as this change was, it was not without certain antecedents in Isaac's own experience.[61] From his earliest introduction to Christianity as the son of a Methodist mother, Isaac was shown a faith that had both a social and a personal dimension. Personal religious experience was constantly before his eyes, whether in the form of the Methodist quest for holiness, the Mormon experience of the gifts of the Spirit, or even Dewey's practical religion that encouraged a greater awareness of God as present in his creatures. Hecker had chosen to ignore this religious dimension in favor of the social, but his attempt to do so was ultimately unsatisfying. When the change occurred in 1842, he was still not yet willing to identify himself with any church. His experience of God remained an inner, private one that he could not yet share with others. But now this inner experience demanded his attention as it had not done before, and fidelity to it appeared as the only way to "the something more" he wanted. The notion that the inner life was the key to the higher, richer existence had been presented to him through Methodism and Mormonism. In addition, through his contact with Dewey and especially Orestes Brownson, he was being introduced to a movement in New England intellectual life that stressed the very notions that were becoming so important to him. That movement expressed in a uniquely American style the Romantic mood of the Continent with its stress on the value of the mystical element. That movement was New England Transcendentalism.

IV

AMONG THE
TRANSCENDENTALISTS

During his visit at Brownson's home, Isaac became increasingly aware of his inner life. Exploring it was like opening a great magical box. As he opened the box, there flew out bright, dazzling phantoms all full of promise. Some pledged to tell the secret of his individuality. They claimed to be able to show him who he was and what he was to do in life. Others promised to give him the key to the marvelous powers that he felt stirring within. They told the young man that the development he had experienced was only the beginning—that within his nature dwelt the capacity for greatness. These brilliant creatures also testified to a spiritual world—a world of the supernatural, the transcendent, the divine. They told Hecker that his aspirations for a richer life could be fulfilled by entering into this world and communing with its inhabitants. Moreover, they told him that the great reality behind all things was a God who was both immanent and transcendent, both the sovereign Lord of all creation and the dove-like Spirit who could be personally known and experienced.

But out of the box also flew dark, ugly creatures. They often tried to frighten the dazzling ones away. These benighted creatures shouted that the good things the brilliant ones had told him were lies and that the promises of a higher, richer life were only the products of his imagination. They discouraged him by saying that he had no great untapped potentials. There was no supernatural realm which gave substance to his aspirations. Only those things which could be seen with the eyes were real. His destiny was to go the way of the world, to labor and toil for perishable things, to be ever unfulfilled in his quest for something more.

The story of Isaac's development between 1842 and 1844 is the story of how he learned to attend more fully to the brilliant ones. During these years he became increasingly confident that he had indeed been called by God to participate in a higher, richer, more meaningful life. He became certain that there existed a transcendent, supernatural dimension into which he could enter. In the face of doubts he grew in his ability to affirm that the God whom he experienced within was indeed the God who had created all things and was fully able to bring all things to their appointed end.

As Hecker's spirituality developed during these years it demonstrated the following characteristics: fascination with the inner life, perplexity over the nature and validity of his internal subjective experience, a desire for synthesis, harmony, and communion, and a radical awareness of the presence of God in all things that was expressed by an emphasis on the spirithood of God. These elements continued to be important parts of his mature spirituality.

BROOK FARM AND FRUITLANDS

As 1842 drew to an end, Isaac and his family were faced with a dilemma. More than ever, Isaac felt the need to be in an environment that would nourish introspection and study. Though Brownson's home had provided such an environment, both Isaac and his family realized that they could not impose on Brownson's good graces much longer.

Aware of this situation, Brownson suggested that the newly-formed community at Brook Farm in nearby West Roxbury might be the ideal place for him. Isaac was pleased by the idea, and so, with his family's blessings and a letter of introduction from Brownson in hand, the young seeker journeyed to the Farm on January 4.

Brook Farm had been founded in 1841 with the intention of establishing an "agricultural, literary, and scientific school or college." As a cooperative subsitute for "selfish competition," the community sought to "dignify bodily labor by uniting it with the intellectual and spiritual life."[1] Among the early members were its founder, George Ripley, his wife Sarah, Nathaniel Hawthorne, Mrs. Minot Pratt and her children, George Bradford, and Warren Burton. By the time of Hecker's arrival the group had grown to some ninety people.

The sense of equality that pervaded the community appealed to the former associate of the Equal Rights Party. Isaac was impressed by how the New England "brahmins" worked side by side in the most menial tasks with those of more humble backgrounds. George Ripley's calm, humble demeanor set the pace for the community. With the greatest ease, the one-time pastor of the prestigious Purchase Street Unitarian Church in Boston could go from cleaning stables, milking cows, and hoeing gardens in the morning to teaching German philosophy and discussing the latest trends in theology with Theodore Parker in the afternoon. Charles Dana, who because of his scholarly bent and Harvard degrees was called "Professor," blended his love for studying German and Greek with a humble willingness to work the two hundred acres that belonged to the Farm.

Life in the community was marked by a genuine sense of merriment. After the evening meal, the chores were quickly dispatched and the dining hall cleared for the evening's entertainment. Singing, dramatic readings, concerts, plays, and the ever-favorite group dancing filled the main building called, rather appropriately, the Hive. In between events there was lively conversation, which ranged from discussions of Kantian philosophy to whimsical punning.

On his arrival Hecker was treated well by the Brook Farm folk. They studied their new guest with a penetration typical of those who love ideas. George Curtis was impressed with Isaac's gentle, affectionate manner and his air of self-reliance. Ora Sedgwick was attracted by his earnestness and truthfulness. Georgianna Bruce Kirby spoke of him as a mystic by inclination who had been "nearly crazed by the direct rays of the moon."[2]

Isaac remarked to his family that his lodgings in the section of the Hive designated for newcomers were most pleasant. Soon he found that his skill as a baker could be profitably employed, and a short time after his arrival he took charge of the community baking. But the main reason Hecker had come to the Farm was for study and reflection. An impressive array of courses were offered to all the residents. George Ripley taught philosophy, while Charles Dana handled German and Latin. Belles Lettres were taught by George Bradford, and modern languages by Sarah Ripley. Hecker availed himself, to a moderate degree, of these educational opportunities. George Curtis recalled that Isaac was not particularly studious but could often be seen popping into the various classes taught at the community as his fancy led him.[3]

Having the time to devote himself fully to study and meditation delighted Isaac. He found the Brook Farmers generally congenial and supportive. Yet despite this, he did not feel as if he were truly part of the community. With some, like the Curtis brothers, George Ripley, and Charles Dana, he developed a warm friendship. Respectful as he was of their convictions, however, he could not abide long in their company. He was seeking something different. The lifestyle at Brook Farm in his opinion was too much like that of the rest of society. It did not call individuals to a radical enough change and was too self-indulgent. Isaac sought something more extreme that would demand a more thorough departure from the status quo.

This desire for a more ascetic lifestyle led him to Bronson Alcott's Fruitlands in July 1843. Alcott, whose pioneer work in progressive education won for him the title the American Pestalozzi, had founded his community one month earlier. He was joined by a group of Englishmen—Charles Lane and his son William, H. C. Wright, and Samuel Bower.[4] The group traced its origin to 1825 when the English reformer, James P. Greaves, had formed a circle of mystically-inclined social reformers in London. After receiving a report of Alcott's Temple School, the Englishmen opened a correspondence with Alcott that resulted in their forming a high estimation of Alcott and his thinking. Greaves, Charles Lane, and their English cohorts established an experimental school near London that they named Alcott House in honor of their newly-found mentor. Alcott himself visited England in May 1843 and began discussing plans for the establishment of a utopian community in America.

Central to Alcott's vision was the belief in the necessity of self-denial. Through practicing an ascetic way of life, Alcott believed that a higher, purer life could be attained. The asceticism included abstinence from all animal foods, frequent cold-water showers, and hard physical labor seldom eased by the use of animal power.

Hecker was invited by Alcott to join the Fruitlands community prior to its actual inception. Alcott wrote personally to him in February 1843 while the latter was at Brook Farm.[5] Hecker's status as a partner in a lucrative New York baking business made him attractive to the economically impoverished Alcott. Despite Brownson's objections, Isaac responded to Alcott's invitation a few months later. He remained at Fruitlands for only two weeks, but, as shall become apparent, the two weeks in July 1843 were an important time in his spiritual development.

The Fruitlands experiment was destined to be short-lived. Lacking money, foresight, proper planning, and even ample fruit trees, the little community disbanded not long after Isaac's visit. Lane left for the Shaker community in Harvard and Alcott continued effusing his Orphic sayings which earned him the reputation for being the most transcendental of the Transcendentalists.

After a short stopover at Brook Farm to pick up his belongings, Hecker returned home to New York. His diary and letters written between 1843 and 1844 reflect his experiences at Brook Farm, at Fruitlands, and at home. On their pages young Isaac poured out his heart. He struggled with his fears, wrestled with his uncertainties, delighted in his hopes, and grew in his resolve to find life's meaning.

A FASCINATION WITH THE INNER LIFE

Evident in his diary entries and letters from this time is the continued commitment to attend to the inner workings of his soul. Often he found that the study he undertook was a hindrance to the spiritual growth he sought. He became increasingly convinced that attending to the inward spirit was the all-sufficient method of attaining enlightenment. His statement of November 1843 is typical of his attitude during this time. "There is no virtue which the Spirit does not teach," he wrote, "if we would hear its whispering voice in our hearts."[6]

Hecker believed that studying the thought of others was not the primary way to knowledge of ultimate truths, since each individual possesses within his nature potentials which, if unfolded, would enable him to partake of divine life. "Man is not aware of his godlike capacities," he wrote. "May not man transcend humanity?" He continued his July 1843 entry:

> Every man is an unconscious prophecy to me. I would awaken him to the wonder of his being. . . . Every human being strikes me as a wonderful becoming, as if a god were struggling for birth in him. He is an imprisoned god . . . .[7]

Isaac desired to affirm the worth of human nature and the importance of self-knowledge. By attending to one's own essential nature, or true self, one comes, he believed, into a deeper knowledge not only of the human but also of the divine.

Hecker's concept of the self was, then, even from his earliest writings, a transcendent self. Constantly he attempted to know a reality that went beyond the subjectivistic world of the individual. An implicit belief in a transcendent force, in something bigger, more powerful, more eternal than the isolated individual, was basic to him.

Related closely to the notion of human nature as containing a true, transcendent self was Hecker's individualism. Each person had, as he saw it, a responsibility to participate actively in the development of his true self. All of us must strive to become more fully the godlike creatures we were created to be. As Isaac put it: "Each of us has an individual character to act out, to realize under the inspiration of God, and this is the highest, the noblest thing we can do."[8]

CONTEMPLATION AND ACTION

Hecker's belief in the individual's responsibility to pursue his destiny reveals how important action was to him between 1842 and 1844. The youngest son of what was quickly becoming one of New York's more successful families was by nature a man of action given to wholeheartedness and singlemindedness who pursued his goals with an uncommon seriousness and intensity. His sense of divine calling, which reached back to his earliest days, was more intense than ever. He had felt it as a child, and it had been reinforced through his contact with Methodism, the Christian Democracy of the Loco-Focos, Mormonism, and Orville Dewey's preaching. Methodism had stressed an active spirituality, a social holiness that worked out the practical implications of perfection. Loco-Focoism had had as its guiding light the application of Christian principles in politics. Mormonism had blended a scheme of spiritual restoration with socio-economic reform. Dewey had made much of practical religion that drew out the significance of the spiritual life for everyday affairs. But now, when Hecker attempted to follow the Spirit's leadings, he was disturbed, for the Spirit seemed to be leading him to do nothing but to cease from his own activity and to passively submit to its biddings. Isaac felt himself drawn to contemplation, yet the contemplative life had not yet been born in this action-oriented young man, and its birth was to bring with it not a few pangs. He had had presented to him forms of religion that stressed religious experience, but none of these previous influences had introduced him to passivity in the radical form that now confronted him. To experience the workings of the Spirit on the soul was one thing; to embrace the contemplative life was another, which did not necessarily follow from the first.

Hecker's struggle to accept the contemplative dimension and to balance it with a continuing commitment to action consumed his energy. His diary for the years 1843–44 reflects this struggle. During his last month at Brook Farm uncertainty about a future course of action festered to the point where it was driving him to the limits of his psychological strength. "Living is madness," he blurted out in a June 13 entry. "I am, I am not, are correlative. . . . Christianity and atheism are correlatives."[9] Not being able to see any goal or direction for his immediate action devastated him. The thought that his brothers were hard at work in New York while he sat, as it were, paralyzed in West Roxbury frustrated him deeply. He longed to be active: ". . . the meanest of all would be heaven to me if this inward impulse had action . . . ."[10] But the work he saw others doing he could not bring himself to do, for it did not conform to his inner sentiments. "Your work is to me the devil's work. . . . I want God's living work to do. . . . My labor must be a sermon. I deny Christ in every act that I do which is not done with and from His spirit."[11] Yet he could not bring himself to wait patiently until the way was opened to him.

> You say, good adviser, you must accept things as they are—
> be content to be—have faith in God—work that which thy
> hands find to do. Good: but it is taken for granted we know
> what things are, which is the question. And what to be?
> 'Be content to be.' Be what? That is the question.[12]

Earlier in the month of June, when Isaac was at Fruitlands, he participated in a conversation on the highest aim of life and the greatest obstacles preventing its attainment. Isaac named "Harmonic Being" as the highest aim and doubt over the validity of his inner leadings as the greatest hindrance.[13] Significantly he did not name action as the highest aim, but being. During the next week at Fruitlands, he seems to have come to the point where he could begin to accept the uncertainty of his present situation and rest content until he received further light. His July 17 diary entry shows a growing acceptance of the mysterious and incomprehensible. "I cannot understand what it is that leads me, or what I am after. Being is incomprehensible."[14] Being is incomprehensible! Not just his own particular situation, but Being in general. Isaac was beginning to see that part of his problem rested in the attempt to know the unknowable. He realized something of the ineffable nature of the transcendent life he sought. As a result he became more willing not only to accept mystery but, with humble trust, to delight and wonder in it.

> It is useless for me to speculate on my future. Put depen-
> dence on the spirit which leads me. Be faithful to it and
> work. Leave results to God . . . . [15]

Isaac's willingness to embrace this passivity developed steadily. As he grew in his desire to submit to the Spirit, he grew in the practice of denying everything that was contrary to the Spirit's will. Although asceticism had been a part of his life even before Brook Farm, he now continued with more zeal the practice of abstaining from meat and limiting himself to small amounts of simple foods. He was resolved to attend more fully to the inward life and not let the outward tempt him.[16] He wrote in July: "Lord, what Thou wouldest have me to do is no question with me. What I want is to be governed by Thy Spirit."[17] Man must, Hecker declared the same month, experience the "birth of the feminine in him."[18] A passive obedience to the will of the Spirit must be cultivated.

Isaac's new willingness made Quietism appealing. He wrote in August 1843:

> I feel that daily I am tending more and more to Quietism; being less wilful and more peaceful. What is not spoken from the Spirit is profane . . . . [19]

The selfish, willful nature must be annihilated. The extent to which the destruction of the willful self was to be taken was not carefully qualified by Hecker, who in his diary gave vent to his sentiments with little concern for balance and moderation. Even the Hindu doctrine of the annihilation of the self and the absorption of the individual into the Absolute held its appeal for him. He saw this Eastern doctrine as a mere logical extension of Quietism. In a moment of sympathy with such a notion of radical passivity, he declared: "This incessant activity of men is most devilish. I would that all men should be made to stand motionless and still be men . . . ."[20] Even his journal writing, he blurted, was a foolish, fruitless activity that sprang from "a diseased irritation."[21]

As Isaac attempted to submit to the Spirit's will and deny all that opposed it, he became more willing to accept the situation in which he found himself. Central to his new willingness was a growing faith in God's providence. Providence was for Hecker, in effect, the Spirit's action in and through the events and situations of life. The Spirit which led the individual by immediate inspiration also led him by arranging the circumstances of his life in a purposeful way. Through providence, as well as through direct leadings, the divine Spirit brought the individual to the end for which he was created. In his characteristically aphoristic style, Hecker summed up this truth in July 1843: "Destiny is Providence."[22] This new understanding of providence was reflected in his decision to return home to New York. His trepidation about the distractions to his spiritual life that his home environment would provide was overcome by his trust that with his family's cooperation and the "help of Divine Providence" the situation could be worked out.[23] On August 15, 1843, Isaac arrived home peaceful and content.[24]

At home he continued seeking to grow in his ability to obey the Spirit's leadings. During the year following his return his commitment to learning the contemplative way increased. In his final entry of the first volume of his diary, Isaac compared his present inner state with that of the time when he began his writing. He knew well the difference between his earlier impatience and the more peaceful submission of the present. "I am more quiet and will-less," he wrote. "I ask no more where it shall lead me, but submit to be led."[25] In June 1844 he gave evidence that this newly-worked submission had drawn him at last to the summit of contemplation.

> The Spirit draws me ever inward and will not permit me
> to read, think or do anything else but attend to it.[26]

At the same time, however, Hecker remained committed to action. As he became more willing to wait for the Spirit's leading, as he grew in an awareness that his ways were not always God's ways, his desire to act was qualified by his concern that his action be according to the divine will, that it be, in effect, God's action working through him. He continued to believe that the individual must act out the unique role for which one is destined and labor to reform society. What became clearer during 1843 and 1844, however, was the necessity of God's grace to enable the individual to do this. Thus by August 1843 Isaac prayed this prayer that illustrates both his high estimate of human action and his dependence on God's uncreated grace, the Holy Spirit:

> O Lord, awaken me more to the divine capacities Thou hast
> endowed man with, and wilt Thou make my sight clearer
> and my hearing delicater, that I may see and hear more of
> Thy divine voice of love. O may I become more obedient,

humble, like Jesus Christ, my Master, Lord and saving Redeemer, to whom and to Thee and to the Holy Spirit my
soul is indebted wholly. . . . O Father, why should my
heart be so pained after Thy loving spirit? Thou hast said,
Ask and it shall be given. Now, O, Lord, I ask in Jesus'
name, give unto me more and more of Thy loving spirit. Fill
my whole being.[27]

Grace was not only necessary, Hecker felt, for the realization
of the divine nature in the individual, but also for the transmission
of grace through him to others. Again, it was the Spirit to whom he
appealed for aid. "O dear Christ," he wrote in a letter to Almira Barlow of Brook Farm, "baptize me with Thy Spirit and loosen my
tongue that I may speak of Thy love to man."[28]

A NAGGING PERPLEXITY

Hecker's commitment to pursuing the inner life was accompanied by a good deal of perplexity over the nature and validity of his
own subjective experience. He could not doubt that he had been
strongly impressed through certain abiding feelings and dreams to follow the course of attending to his own inner life. In April 1843, he
still held to the importance of the dreams he had had in the autumn
of 1842. "They have to me a reality, a practical good bearing on my
life," he wrote; "if I should not follow them I am altogether to blame.
I can have no such adviser upon earth . . . ."[29] Yet though he had
remained committed to following these inspirations, he could not
suppress the notion that the greatest problem confronting him as a
seeker of truth was doubt "whether the light is light."[30]

Hecker could not, even during the time of his sojourn among the
Transcendentalists, rest with anything that smacked of solipsism.
The fact that the ideas that captivated him were to him clear and distinct did not guarantee their validity. He could not agree with the
radical notions of Emerson who could declare himself a "transparent
eyeball" through whom the currents of the Universal Being circulat-
ed. Issac had to know, as he said writing some fifty years later,
whether "the yearnings, aspirations, unappeased desires or religious

feelings" were "genuine, real, corresponding to and arising from the reality of certain objects external to the soul."[31] To imply that the objects of religious affections must remain a purely subjective reality was to undermine any reconciliation between religion and reason. He viewed the philosophies of Kant and Fichte as opposed, in their skeptical tendency, to the establishment of the reality of subjective religious experience.

What was leading Isaac was often as much a question as where he was being led. "What drives me, and where I shall be driven, is unknown to me," he wrote in February 1843.[32] A few weeks later he tried, with no more success, to describe to his brother George what had led him to Brook Farm.

> What was the reason of my going? . . . The reason I am not able to tell. But what I felt was a dark, irresistible influence upon me that led me away from home. What it was I know not.[33]

These references to the mysterious, powerful forces are found in Hecker's papers alongside mention of the Spirit. Even in July 1843, when he reconciled himself more fully to following the leading of the Spirit, his language revealed an uncertainty about what that Spirit was.

> What the spirit may be, is a question I cannot answer; what it leads me to do will be the only evidence of its character. I feel as impersonal as a stranger to it. I ask: Who are you? Where are you going to take me?[34]

These somewhat perplexing references to a mysterious influence or spirit are intermixed with entries which identify this spirit with the Spirit of God. The earliest diary entry, for example, contains a prayer which states, "Thy spirit has led me in all present judgements."[35] During the next month, Isaac inscribed a prayer for the continued guidance of God's Spirit. "Grant, O Lord," he wrote in February 1843, "Thy Spirit to me that I may be willing to do Thy will."[36]

From early in 1843 Isaac's writing showed an awareness of tra-

ditional Christian concepts of God. In particular, the redemption of
Christ and the need for the regeneration of the individual were notions with which he was familiar. He stated that although he would
not take it upon himself to say that he had been "born again," he
knew that he "had passed from death to life." He then extolled the
greatness of Christ's redemptive sacrifice, and prayed, "O Lord, may
I daily come into closer communication with Thy Son, Jesus
Christ."[37] Isaac's Methodist roots were showing! He was at home
with a spirituality that stressed the value of the inner life, the importance of human capacities, and the place of emotions and feelings.
These romantic themes in his spirituality during this time represented developments of ideas he had encountered as the son of a devout
Methodist mother. Methodism as the common man's version of romantic religion had prepared Hecker for the more sophisticated notions of the Transcendentalists. But as much as the young Isaac
delighted in the airy speculations of men like Alcott and Lane, he
could not abandon Christ for the nebulous gods of the New England
Romantics.

Christ was seen as more than a model for leading a spiritual life.
He was seen, rather, as a living person whose life could be shared
by those who believed in him. This sharing was a communing, a partaking of Christ's Spirit. Christ's Spirit was not merely conceived of
as the sense or significance of Christ. It was instead the very principle of life that animated him. In this manner Hecker again reflected
the influence of the Methodists who placed a considerable emphasis
on the person of the Holy Ghost as the Spirit of Jesus—God in us
and with us. The concept of real participation in the divine, or divinization, was one of the things that most attracted Wesley to the
Church Fathers, especially Gregory of Nyssa.

Isaac's July 1843 act of greater resignation that resulted in an
increased willingness to accept the uncertainties of his present situation was also the beginning of a growing confidence that the Spirit
which led him was in fact the Spirit of Christ. After July 1843, the
vague references to a stranger-like spirit disappeared. Mention of the
"Holy Spirit" increased, and the Spirit was placed with the Father
and Son in traditional Trinitarian formulas. He prayed in August
1843, "O Lord, I ask in Jesus' name, give unto me more and more

of Thy loving spirit."[38] His increased willingness to submit to the Spirit's leadings was matched by a growing conviction that, as he said in March 1844, "He that follows the Holy Spirit is never led astray." His only aim became more and more "to fulfill the Spirit," to humbly receive the Spirit's inspirations.[39]

A DESIRE FOR SYNTHESIS AND COMMUNION

A desire for synthesis and communion also characterized Hecker's spirituality during his stay with the Transcendentalists. From the start of his odyssey in 1842, Isaac desired to share with others the new life he had begun to experience. He searched, somewhat in vain, for another to sympathize with his struggles. He felt, in his own words, "the want of a person to commune with." Thus motivated, he turned to God. In Christ he hoped he would find the comfort he sought, but, interestingly enough, Isaac appears in his diary dissatisfied with the thought of divine comfort alone. He is pressed with a desire to utter his inmost sentiments, to bring forth his thoughts and aspirations.

> Who will be unto me now a friend, a comforter? Will it be said Christ? Alas! in this I drink too deeply, and how shall it get utterance?[40]

Gradually, however, as his willingness to submit to the Spirit grew, so did the ability for fellowship with the divine. "Increase Thy Spirit in us," he prayed in August 1843, "until between Thee and us there is no more we or thee, but only thou, O Father."[41] Earlier that same month he prayed that he might be "wholly lost in the sea of the spirit, wholly lost in God."[42] Such union with God, Isaac uttered in a characteristically exaggerated manner, was to be total:

> When the Spirit begets us, we are no more. The Spirit is all, and there is nothing else.[43]

A mystical union between the individual and God was the essence of the perfect Christian life, as Isaac understood it.

Hecker's concern with the categories of unity and harmony manifested itself in a desire to see the synthesis of opposing elements. Worked out in matters of religion, this meant that the true components of various religions could be synthesized into a more perfect whole. The influence of Brownson's thought in *New Views* and his efforts at establishing the Church of the Future which would reconcile Catholicism with Protestantism, modernity with Christian tradition, is obvious here. In April 1843, Hecker recorded his response to Schelling's statement that the Church was in substance first Petrine, then Pauline, and must become love-embracing, Johannine—Peter corresponding to Catholicism, Paul to Protestantism, John to the future Church:

> The statement struck me and responded to my dim intuitions. Catholicism is solidarity; Protestantism is individuality. What we want, and are tending to, is what shall unite them both as John's spirit does—and that in each individual. We want neither the authority of History nor of the individual; neither the infallibility nor Reason but both combined in Life.[44]

The synthesis Hecker looked for was to be an organic, living thing that reflected the real, unified nature of all being.

Hecker's desire for synthesis is also evident in his ideas about the relation between religious and scientific knowledge. He believed that both could be grounded in fact, one as surely as the other. The age in which he lived was, he maintained, one during which humanity would come into a greater understanding of the nature of religious knowledge. "Man will reduce the facts of the inward world to the same certainty as he has done in the outward world," he wrote in August 1843.[45]

V

THE EFFECTS OF THE
ENCOUNTER

Isaac's time among the Transcendentalists was one of undeniable importance in his growth. Were the themes which emerged at this time as the focuses of his spirituality parallel to ones which were popular among his New England Transcendentalist contemporaries? In particular, what were the effects of his encounter with Transcendentalism on the development of his spirituality?

THE INNER LIFE

In his emphasis on attending to the inner life as a means for apprehending primary truths, Hecker was in line with his New England contemporaries. The assertion that human nature contained the ability to in some way intuit transcendent moral and spiritual truths was the central idea of the Transcendental movement.[1] The movement had arisen in the 1830s out of a growing dissatisfaction with the then predominant philosophical theories of Locke that, it was felt, erred in underestimating the subjective intuitional element. As a reaction to the sensism of the Enlightenment, the Transcendentalists embraced an idealism that emphasized man's intuitive apprehension of the truth. The rationalistic tendencies within the New England Unitarianism of the time were errors attributable to the dominance of the Lockean system. Drawing on varied sources, the Transcendentalists stressed the importance of intuition and sentiment, the place of self-understanding and reflection, the value of the individual as over against the society, and the categories of the non-rational and mysterious.[2]

George Ripley, founder of Brook Farm and one of Hecker's best friends among the Transcendentalists, wrote the following 1836 reply to Andrews Norton, in which he contrasted the transcendental philosophy with Norton's Lockeanism.

> For the philosophy [Locke's] I have no respect. I believe it to be superficial, irreligious and false in its primary elements. The evils it has brought upon humanity, by denying to the mind the power of perceiving spiritual truth, are great and lamentable . . . . [3]

The great mission of the age was, as Ripley saw it, to cure the evils brought about by Lockeanism. This was to be done by returning to an idealism that made room for the spiritual dimension. Ripley continued:

> I wish to go back to the philosophy of the most enlightened Fathers, to that of the giants of English theology . . . to the lofty spiritual faith which is now held by the most eminent philosophers of the continent.[4]

The result would be a true reform of theology in which "the living and practical faith of the heart" would displace the "bondage to a dead letter."[5]

When Hecker met Brownson in 1841 he had met not only a political and social reformer, but one who was involved in the Transcendentalist movement, especially in its early phase. His book, *New Views,* and his important articles in the *Christian Examiner* on French philosophy were among the most significant documents of the movement. Although Brownson was never to accept the thoroughgoing idealism that marked the Emersonian brand of Transcendentalism, he clearly was in agreement with the whole move to establish a philosophy that found within human nature the means to perceive transcendental truths. This emphasis on the inward turn can be seen even in Brownson's political writings of 1836. In his initial statement as editor of the *Boston Reformer,* he announced that he would from then on "look mainly to the inward" to find the truly effective means for social reform.[6] In his 1836 work, *New Views,* Brownson put forth the notion that the Church of the Future must establish human nature as the basis for true religion. Asserting the doctrine common among Transcendentalists that only like can know like, he declared that "truth itself is nothing else to us than that which our nature compels us to believe."[7]

HECKER AS AN AMERICAN SCHOLAR

In pouring out the questions and perplexities of his heart, Hecker employed a literary style that he had learned from his reading of works in vogue among the Transcendentalists. From these works he learned how to express his emotions as well as his reasonings.

Raised with a knowledge of German, Hecker by his late teens was ready and able to plunge into Goethe, Schiller, Novalis, and Jean Paul Richter. After the War of 1812, interest in German literature was running high among New Englanders. Men like Edward Everett, George Ticknor, and George Bancroft returned from Germany praising the merits of German culture. Ticknor and Everett instituted changes in the Harvard curriculum that gave many of the budding Transcendentalists an exposure to German literature while they were still in college. When the Transcendentalists first turned in the 1830s to German literature, they did so often through the commentaries of Madame de Staël, Coleridge, and Carlyle, whose works provided an enthusiastic introduction. Soon, after learning German with the aid of texts prepared by Harvard Professors Charles Follen and Carl Beck, they went to the primary sources. Goethe, Schiller, Richter, and Novalis, the very names that occur most often in Hecker's diary, were the favorites. The pages of major Transcendentalist journals, the *Dial,* the *Harbinger,* the *Christian Examiner,* and the *North American Review* soon were filled with comment on these authors.[8]

One of those most responsible for the spread of German literature in New England was George Ripley. Ripley edited a series of volumes containing English translations of German classics entitled *Specimens of Foreign Standard Literature*. Ripley was also deeply interested in German philosophy, the study of which he advocated in his Brook Farm journal, the *Harbinger*. Fortuitously, it was he who taught a course in German philosophy at Brook Farm during Hecker's stay.[9]

When Isaac journeyed from Brook Farm to Fruitlands, he was going to a place were German literature was no less esteemed. In 1834, Alcott had begun to discover German philosophy with great excitement after becoming disenchanted with the popular English works of his day. Although relying totally on the English versions, Alcott became enthusiastic about Goethe, Richter, the Schlegels, and, most especially, Jacob Boehme. The Fruitlands library contained copies of works by these and other German authors.

Richter was among Hecker's special favorites. In August 1843 he wrote that Richter had provided "more nourishment for my heart, such as no other author has given me." Richter's massive novel *The Titan* seems to have fascinated him during late 1842 and early 1843. His diary opens with a reference to his just having read *Siebenkas*, *Hesperus, Titan,* and *Life* by Richter. Hecker went on to say that he felt especially close to three characters in *The Titan*—Carl Roquairol, Schoppe, and Albano of Titan. Isaac said of Schoppe's apostrophe, "It was like tearing out my spirit, because I have not yet attained the power to speak it; it rests in me yet undeveloped." The section of *The Titan* that Hecker referred to finds Schoppe uttering: "I am surrounded by humanity turned into stone. . . . I am totally alone. . . . I am only conscious of my higher non-consciousness within me mute, blind . . . working in disguise and I am he himself."[10] This sounds a great deal like Hecker, who wrote in a January 1843 entry: "I feel as if life is too much for me, it is inconceivably painful for me to live. . . . There is none that I can commune with . . . ."[11]

The idea of the true self as a transcendent self is also quite evident in the Richter passage cited. Indeed Hecker's concept of the true self as both unique and yet intimately connected with a transcendent reality whose dimensions stretched far beyond the individual was fertilized by his reading of German literature. Goethe and Schiller, as well as Richter, were each deeply influenced by German classicism which, like the *Sturm und Drang* (Storm and Stress) movement that preceded it and the Romantic movement that followed, stressed the importance of the individual's developing his own powers. Yet this self-actualization could not be carried out without some regard for society. Even Richter, who was more of a Romantic than Goethe, did not allow individualism to run rampant. The very concern for harmony with society was what in part caused the struggle of the individual who, like Schoppe, was pained by his loneliness and separation from the "humanity turned into stone" that surrounded him.

Hecker's struggle over the legitimacy of his subjective experience runs along these same lines. He feels drawn by a mysterious force to leave family and friends and to attend fully to the inner mentor. Yet all along he complains of the loneliness, cries out for communion, and struggles to find his true self and to see how his inner sentiments are related to the external world. His constant desire to do something, to carry out an active role in society, shows how important it was that he as an individual ultimately be properly related to something bigger than himself.

German literature provided for Hecker a rich symbolic framework that allowed him to probe in search of an acceptable understanding of individuality. Thus even Hecker's famous dream-vision of the angelic being—a symbol, as it were, that summed up for Hecker his quest for the higher life—is curiously parallel to Albano's description of his idealized love for Liane which Richter gave in *The Titan*.[12]

Hecker also looked to Goethe with great interest. He noted reading Goethe's *Dichtung und Wahrheit* and during his first month at Brook Farm asked his family to send a copy of his *Götz von Berlichenger*. In a particularly interesting note written at the end of the turbulent year of 1843, he tells of having read Goethe's *Die Leiden des jungen Werthers*. He related to his family that it had appealed to him, since "just at that period there was much in it with which I deeply sympathized . . . it was written in a period like what I was passing through."[13] What exactly did Isaac mean by this? Did he wish to imply that he, like the young Werther in Goethe's tragedy, had been devastated by his powerful feelings of love for a fair lady? Or did he merely wish to suggest that he, like Werther, had passed through a time when his own sentiments and emotions so affected him as to consume his every energy? Whatever may have been the case, his comment offers another insight into the passionately introspective mood that dominated a good part of his journal.

Goethe's and Richter's works provided the searching youth with something with which he could build a relationship. They provided the chance to act out his own feelings and hopes and assured him that his sentiments were not wholly peculiar. His was a deeply personal involvement with the text. He wanted to know what the work set before him could say to the questions of vital concern with which he was presently dealing. Richter and Goethe appealed to him because they were "food for the heart," and in fact this is what Hecker sought from most things that he took the time to peruse. In no way could he be described as a careful, scholarly reader who studied and analyzed the texts before him with a detached air. Certainly Hecker never could be compared in this regard to the master critic, Brownson, who, in his role as a literary journalist, had few peers.

Hecker's manner of reading was more like that of the radical Transcendentalists of his time than like Brownson's. If we dare speak of him as a scholar, we can only do so in terms of his being an "American scholar" along the lines defined by Emerson in his famous address of that name. Hecker would certainly agree with Emerson that "books are for the scholar's idle times." They were essentially "to inspire."[14]

Isaac demonstrated a familiarity with what may rightly be labeled the classics of Transcendentalism.[15] Yet his familiarity was with only those elements of these works that, as it were, fitted his own person. His diary is filled with quotations used either to inspire his own speculations or to buttress his own conclusions. Few of the ideas he expressed, however, can be perfectly traced to some other mind. Hecker was in this regard the Emersonian "scholar" who combined in himself "all the ability of the time, all the contributions of the past," and yet who never merely parroted the ideas of others, but shaped and fashioned them according to the fresh inspiration he directly received from the great Source.[16]

SYNTHESIS AND COMMUNION

The characterization of the Transcendentalist movement as primarily a reassertion of the mystical basis of all religion finds support in the utterances of a number of Hecker's contemporaries.[17] Bronson Alcott stressed the importance of the Spirit as a way to knowledge. Spirit is reflected, Alcott held, in nature. "The various kingdoms of matter," he wrote in a September 1835 journal entry, "are emblems and significant types of the Divine Spirit in whom alone is absolute Being and Life, Growth and Vitality."[18] Alcott, who read books in much the same way Hecker did but with greater fervor, was bolstered in this conviction by his study of Plato. After Plato he was more convinced than ever that "Spirit [is] all in all—matter its form and shadow."[19] From this basis, he went on to reason that the contemplation of Spirit in its manifold emblems and in the human self is the chief means of coming to truth.

Behind this assertion is the belief that one becomes what he beholds, that as one contemplates Spirit he becomes more fully united with Spirit. The channel through which this notion found its way into New England Transcendentalism can, in all likelihood, never be exclusively defined. The fact is that this thought rests behind the brand of idealism to which the New Englanders had become attracted through a variety of ways. Coleridge's *Biographia Literaria* ranks as one of the standard works of the Transcendentalist school. Alcott, like all the major lights of the movement, was well acquainted with the work and with Coleridge's teacher, Schelling. Schelling's view of the artist as one who penetrates by his vision to the Absolute represented a revival of Neo-Platonism. But it was Thomas Taylor's 1833 English translations of Plato and Plotinus that made the most ancient advocates of the contemplative ideal available to New England audiences. Plotinus especially offered a succinct statement of this ideal, maintaining that all things are "striving after contemplation, looking to this as their one end." For Plotinus, the object contemplated "becomes progressively a more and more intimate possession of the contemplating beings, more and more one with them."[20]

Alcott's theory of contemplation and union differed from Plotinus' in regard to the place of asceticism.[21] For Alcott, the soul must be purified if it is to grow in its ability to contemplate Spirit. Thus he advocated, as is obvious from the life-style of Fruitlands, a strict regimen of self-denial. In this tendency he was more in line with certain Christian mystics who made place for self-denial. Among his favorites was Jacob Boehme, whose works, he told Emerson, should be in the hands of everyone interested in the spiritual life.[22] The Fruitlands library, in addition to eight different titles by or about Boehme, contained works by Julian of Norwich, St. Bridget, Hermes Trismegistus, Molinos, De Sales, Madame Guyon, Fénelon, Thomas à Kempis, William Law, Henry More, and Emanuel Swedenborg.[23] It was a veritable goldmine of mysticism—certainly one of the best collections on the subject to be found in New England during the first half of the nineteenth century.

Alcott was taken with the notion that the one ideal substance, the one Spirit, lies behind all the phenomenal objects of the world. If individuals could see beyond the forms of matter to the Spirit, the basic unity of all things could be realized. This emphasis on unity was by no means unique to Alcott, but was essential to Transcendentalism. It followed from the premises of the idealistic philosophy behind the Transcendental movement.

The belief in the unity of Spirit led those influenced by it to seek with unfettered optimism the reconciliation of opposing ideas and systems of thought. Faith and reason, Protestantism and Catholicism, the individual and society, science and religion—all were seen as capable of being reconciled. Victor Cousin's eclectic philosophy, which attempted to synthesize opposing systems by realizing the truth contained in each, enjoyed popularity in New England after being introduced to American audiences by Brownson's articles in the *Christian Examiner*.[24]

Thus it is not surprising, given the fact that men's minds were, as one reviewer put it, "dimly groping after the point of union between the supernatural and the rational," that there was among the

Transcendentalists an interest in mysticism, which holds that the union of God and man can be experienced to a significant degree in this life.[25] The *Christian Examiner* ran an article on St. Teresa of Avila and one on Fénelon by William Ellery Channing. The March 1841 issue carried an article on the life of Bernard of Clairvaux. The author drew a highly favorable picture of Bernard as a "mystic living in an age tending to rationalism." He praised Bernard's life as one in which "contemplation [was] preferred before action," and added sarcastically, "This ideal would be wretchedness to an American . . . ." The chief characteristic of Bernard's spirituality that the author pointed out was, however, one that was more congenial to the American mind. Bernard's was a spirituality in which mystical experience was blended with a "practical tendency." Although contemplation preceded action, it did not preclude it. Like Emerson's "American Scholar" or like Hecker himself, Bernard was pictured as one who blended the active and passive dimensions of spirituality.[26] The interest in mystical religion resulted in a new openness to Catholicism on the part of certain segments of the intensely anti-Catholic New England. The *Christian Examiner* ran a series of three articles dealing quite favorably with Roman Catholicism in the September 1837 issue.[27]

Seen in the light of trends within the New England Transcendentalism of his day, Hecker's interest in unity, synthesis, and mystical religious experience was, then, not at all unusual. Hecker read the mystical writers whose works were enjoying a certain vogue within Transcendentalist circles. Two weeks after leaving Fruitlands, Hecker joined Alcott in his praise of Jacob Boehme, whom he described as "the most inspired man of modern times."[28]

In addition to the mystical writers already discussed, Hecker indicated in an April 1844 letter to Brownson that he had been eagerly reading the works of "Dionysius, Johannes Scotus Erigena, Bernard, Hugo and Richard of St. Victor, and Meister Eckhart."[29] In June he mentioned his affection for certain of the ideas of Emanuel Swedenborg, the influential eighteenth-century Swedish theologian.[30]

Hecker's fascination with mystical writings was not limited to Western sources. With the Transcendentalists, he shared a certain interest in the classics of Oriental spirituality which had been made available to the English-speaking world for the first time in the early part of the nineteenth century. Hecker quoted from the "Vishnoo Sarma," *Buddha Commandments* of Pictus, and was intrigued by the concept of Brahman.[31]

What were the effects of Hecker's encounter with Transcendentalism? At a time in his life when he was preoccupied with understanding his own identity and exploring his own capacities, Hecker became involved with the New England Romantics. Transcendentalism gave him the encouragement to do the very thing to which he was inclined—to explore the full range of intellectual and emotional facets of his personality. Within Transcendentalism, he was able to do this in a freer, more broad-ranging way than he could in Methodism. At Brook Farm there was no class leader to reprove him for his imaginative speculations, no one to tell him what he must do to be saved. He was able to search out the myriad aspirations and questions of his soul in his own style, at his own pace. He could test his emerging abilities to know and feel, and still move toward the transcendent, still follow after that sense of divine calling which had long been with him.

Through his encounter with Transcendentalism, he was not only thus encouraged, he was also introduced to new sources from which he could gather wisdom about the spiritual journey. The Transcendentalist culture brought him the German and English Romantics and the wisdom of the Eastern sages. But most importantly, it opened to him the world of Catholicism. Through the eyes of Romantic seekers such as Alcott and Lane, Hecker had presented to him the Catholic faith in the most attractive light. It was introduced not as a moribund system of creeds and doctrines, but as a living testimony to the reality of spiritual values. In Catholic mysticism he caught a glimpse of the radical synthesis of the real and the ideal for which he longed. Transcendentalism showed Isaac not a picture of Rome as the great Harlot, but a picture of Catholicism as the storehouse of precious mysteries and wonders.

As influential as Transcendentalism was on him, it nevertheless did not elicit his full support. Rather, he took from Transcendentalism that which fed his soul. He took from it inspiration to search out his inner life and to seek the transcendent, and he took from it a style of expression that gave full vent to the inner sentiments. But as has been seen, he never accepted the radical Transcendentalist position that man possessed everything necessary for full communion with the Transcendent. At this point he retained the evangelical understanding of the work of Christ and the need for grace that he had learned from Methodism.

In the final analysis, Hecker remained the unique blend of forces and feelings, affections and hopes that made him an individual. His spirituality was as varied and unique as was his own broadranging experience of life. He had assimilated the ideas of Methodists and mystics, politicians and social theorists, bards and utopians in his own style. Through it all he grew in the awareness of the presence of God. Despite his very real doubts and struggles, despite his perplexity and frustration, he was strengthened in his faith that God had destined him for a special task and was guiding him to the fulfillment of it.

In this sense Hecker was the Romantic hero striving to attain the ideal in the midst of an imperfect and often hostile world. The ideal, the divine call, burned within his bosom. When he resisted it or tried to compromise it, he had no peace. Its presence often made his life appear to him like a huge anomaly. He was unable to embrace his mother's Methodism, unable to work at the family business, unable even to find consolation in the Transcendentalist communes.

Hecker was by his twenty-fifth birthday an idealist. Yet he was the type of idealist for whom the ideal is so real that it must have practical here-and-now significance. This desire to realize the ideal that motivated him led him to investigate that ancient tradition which claimed to be the visible embodiment of the Christian ideal: Catholicism.

VI

IN SEARCH OF THE SYNTHESIS

Isaac's desire to realize the ideal motivated him to grapple with the Church question during his 1842–1844 period of searching. If the ideas he had about God were true, he asked, what was their here-and-now significance? If grace were needed to elevate man to communion with God, then was there a church through which Christ's life was to be brought to the world? He wondered if there were a way in which his own private experience of God could be shared with others without compromising it. Could his experience of God be validated by the testimony of a believing community in a way that would lessen doubt, or was that possible only at the cost of his individuality? He mused also if there were a way in which the Church could function to reform not only the individual, but the society as well.

Isaac's struggling with the Church question was shaped and molded by his longing for synthesis and communion, his interest in personal and social reform, and his desire to submit to the Spirit's leadings—themes that in the years 1842–1843 were basic to his spirituality.

LONGING FOR COMMUNION

There were two streams of thought that ran through Isaac's mind as he meditated on the idea of communion. While he dwelt among the Transcendentalists he considered, on the one hand, the value of attending to the inner life. He viewed fidelity to the unique dealings of the divine with the individual as the necessary, sufficient means to communion with God. On the other hand, Isaac thought about the idea of communion with other like-minded humans and saw such communion as beneficial to the individual's relation with God. The two streams ran side-by-side in Hecker's early diary. On February 4, 1843, he boldly asserted: "I commune not with man. . . . It is only in Thee that I find communion." But the next day he prayed, "Lord, lead me into the Holy Church which I am now seeking for, by the aid, I hope, of Thy Holy Spirit."[1]

Isaac even at this early date was well aware of the Catholic church and certain elements of Catholic piety. The above-quoted February 5 entry contained a prayer to the saints for their intercession. On Easter Sunday, 1843, Hecker visited a Catholic church in West Roxbury. He recorded in his diary for April 17 his observation that "a sanctified atmosphere" seemed to fill the church and to penetrate his soul when he entered.[2] During the month of April, while at Brook Farm, he also discussed the Catholic church with Ripley, Dana, and other members of the community, as well as beginning J. A. Moehler's *Symbolik,* a copy of which he borrowed from Theodore Parker. An April 19 letter to his family told of perusing parts of the book and thinking that it would be helpful in determining the Church question.[3] Moehler systematically compared Lutheranism, Calvinism, and Catholicism on key theological issues. The work certainly represented what was, for its time, a fairly even-handed approach to apologetics. The main thrust of Moehler's argument, however, was boldly engrained in every section of the work: Catholic doctrine is clearly superior from both a logical and a theological standpoint to Protestant teaching.[4]

Around the same time Hecker was studying the *Catechism of the Council of Trent.* This work seems to have had a lasting effect on the young seeker. Even in 1887 he recalled how he had been struck with the Catholic doctrine of the communion of saints, which he first read in the *Catechism.*[5]

In addition to *Symbolik* and the Trent *Catechism,* Hecker at this time was also reading some of the Oxford Tracts. He discussed them with Brownson during a February 25, 1843 visit to Chelsea and wrote of his reaction to them in a letter to his family dated March 1, 1843. Hecker told his brothers, who were themselves reading the Tracts, that he was thrilled by the similarities among the doctrines of the Tractarians, the Protestant bishops of Geneva and Prussia, and the Roman Catholics. He looked forward to a growth in unity among the churches.[6]

During April 1843, Isaac struggled with the Church question, oscillating from one opinion to another. On April 18 he wrote: "I feel that either it [the church] has nothing to give, or that what it has is not that for which my soul is aching."[7] Less than a week later he seemed to have changed his mind rather thoroughly. He wrote: "The Catholic Church alone seems to satisfy my wants, my faith, my soul. . . . My soul is Catholic and that faith answers, responds to my soul in its religious aspirations and its longings . . . ."[8] But in another four days, he was torn again with uncertainty: "What shall I say . . . ? Shall I submit myself to that which does not engage my whole being? The Church is not for me the great object of life . . . . Is not the best way for me to live my own nature rather than to attempt to mould its life to some object?"[9]

Hecker's struggle continued into May 1843. A sense of isolation and separateness, fueled by a ravenous appetite for asceticism, gripped him. The feeling persisted that the more dedicated he was to his true self, the more cut off he would be from those around him. Confusion over who the Spirit was and where it was leading and perplexity over his own identity and purpose crowded in upon his mind, making concerns about the nature of the Church seem secondary. At one point he began a diary entry with a discussion of the Church, but then found it impossible to continue. "Stop! Why need I try to pierce into the future. All is so dark before me . . . I meet with no one around me . . . I cannot speak from my real being to them. There is no recognition between us."[10]

As Isaac had continued his quest for the higher life, he had grown in his conviction of the need for grace. But the question remained: What are the channels of that grace? He knew that God had led him by means of the interior working of the Spirit upon his soul. Attending to the inner life was the way to the higher life. But was it sufficient? Did it need to be complemented by the grace of God as mediated through the Church? In a May 24 entry Isaac argued with himself: "Possess thyself. How much in two words! Rightly understood they are enough."[11] Yet he could not rest with this anti-Church philosophy. In the same entry he went on to refute it. He based his argument for the Church upon themes which were obviously the same as those developed by Brownson. He proceeded to contrast the anti-Church advocates with the children of the Church and concluded that fruitfulness had more abundantly blessed the labors of the latter. Despite this, he could not yet come to the point of joining himself to the Church. He still felt, as he wrote two weeks later, "inwardly cramped in."[12]

CONCERN FOR REFORM

In the summer of 1843, after returning from the Transcendentalist communes to his family in New York, Isaac became freshly concerned with questions of social reform. Having to some degree experienced a higher, richer life, he was convinced that the social situation could be improved. He took to heart the advice of his friend George Curtis who encouraged him to stand fast in the situation in which he found himself and work for the betterment of those around him.[13] He began by making some improvements in his brother's sleeping quarters. At the bakery, to which he had returned, he also tried making things better. He established an employees' lounge and strove to deal with those under him in a kindly, humane manner.

The reform that Isaac sought was at its core a spiritual one that could be realized by following the Spirit's leadings. On November 1, 1843, he wrote: "Once we are born of the Spirit we shall be led by it in all reforms to the full and complete harmonious life of the Spirit in us . . . ."[14] Again the question arose, however, of the role of the Church. Is the Church as a social institution necessary to bring about societal reform? This question was in fact a corollary of the one that had already exercised Hecker: Is the Church necessary for individual reform? That is, may the individual rely solely on his own inner experience of the Spirit, or must he be aided by the ministry of the Church? Isaac's attempts to individually bring about some measure of reform in his New York environment thrust the Church question at him with renewed vigor. Thus he wrote in a November 11 entry: "My disposition has been of late to look into the Church matters with more interest than it has for six months back."[15]

As he reached out to reform his society, he realized, as he had in attempting to reform himself, that he needed grace. "No man raises himself alone," he wrote early in December. Increasingly he grew in his acceptance of the Church's role as a channel of grace. He drew a triangular figure in his diary that represented the Church as the center of all reform. The three sides of the figure were labeled "personal reform, political reform, and social reform," respectively. In the center was written "religion, Church, Unity."[16] The Church was thus represented as the place where personal and societal reform were united.

Isaac was also being pressed to consider the Church question from another direction. During the closing months of 1843 his friend Brownson was hammering Hecker on the necessity of both the Church's role in social reform and the need for him as an individual to be joined to the Church. In a November 8 letter Brownson declared: "No work of reform can be carried on with any prospects of success till we have recovered the unity and the Catholicity of the Church as an outward, visible institution."[17] He ended his letter suggesting that Isaac might join the Episcopal church. Brownson had for some time been convinced of the need for the institutional church in social reform, but in late 1843 he had not yet become convinced of the idea that the Roman Catholic church was the one that conformed to his model.[18] His efforts to found the perfect Church of the Future had more or less been abandoned, however, and he was less opposed to working with existing institutional churches.

Isaac, likewise, was not yet convinced that Rome was the church he sought. In fact he was still not fully convinced of the need for the Church in theory. Doubtless, one of the things that impeded his progress in this regard was the divided state of Christendom. When he looked to the Christian churches to find the expression of the one body of Christ, the idea of which was becoming increasingly agreeable to him, he saw instead a divided, quarreling house. Sectarian controversy disgusted him and discouraged him from looking to the Church to find the help he needed to live a holy life. The divisiveness within the Christian community repulsed him. It seemed antithetical to the life that he had begun to experience inwardly— a life of harmony and unity. Writing to his family in May 1843, he confessed his lack of sympathy with either the Anglican or the Roman polemics. "The spirit of all the sects," he wrote, "appears to me to have the tendency of narrowing and hampering my sympathies." He felt it his duty "to labor to do away with this sectarian tendency." But how could this be done? By joining a sect and laboring therein? Doing this would not solve the problem. He would only thereby become a sectarian himself. [19]

When Isaac recoiled from the idea of joining himself to an institutional church, he found encouragement from some of his old Brook Farm acquaintances who were not as willing as Brownson to accept the existing institutions. George Ripley, who himself had resigned his post as a Unitarian clergyman before founding the West Roxbury community, was not at all convinced of the necessity of the Church in the process of social reform. In an October, 1843 letter to Hecker, Ripley put forth his theory of reform. Discussing the problem of slavery Ripley stated, "Faithfully serve your nature, and no stain of falling country or shattered Social system need disturb you." He continued with a succinct statement of the self-reliance theme, so common among the Transcendentalists: "The wiser man lends himself to no organization. He is his own Society and does his own reforms." [20] Thus did Ripley urge the young seeker to rely only on himself the very same day that Brownson was writing to him of his conviction that the Church as an outward, visible institution was absolutely necessary for reform. [21]

Isaac, nevertheless, still was captivated by an increasing awareness of the idea of the Church as a channel of grace for both the individual and society. By the end of 1843, Brownson's arguments had convinced him of the necessity of the Church. He wrote to Brownson in December acknowledging that he had come to highly value his ecclesiology.

> The necessity for a medium through which the Spirit can act—that man as man can be no reformer—and that the church is the only institution which has for its object the

bettering of men's souls, by giving to them a diviner love
. . . are clear and important truths to me. [22]

Brownson's ecclesiology had persuaded Isaac with the cogent
type of philosophical argument for which the Boston journalist was
famous. The argument had two crucial steps.

The first step involved a rejection of German idealism, as put
forth by Kant and Fichte, which, according to Brownson, led to the
error of subjectivism. As Hecker expressed it years later when re-
counting the impact of Brownson's thought on him, subjectivism implied that ". . . the aspirations or unappeased desires of the soul
toward the infinite are the renderings of the sentimental imagination
. . . mystical impulses toward no corresponding realities . . . ." [23] Giv-
en the value he placed on the inner life, such a position was unten-
able.

Brownson led the way in finding an alternative to the theories
of Kant and Fichte. He drew heavily on French philosophy, particularly Pierre Leroux's *L'Humanité*. According to Hecker, he and
Brownson carefully studied Leroux's work during Isaac's time among
the Transcendentalists. Leroux established to their satisfaction that
there is a necessary element of objectivity in every act of the subject. [24] Every act of the subject supposes an object and involves objective certitude and real union between the thinker and the thing
thought. On this basis Hecker became convinced that the yearnings,
aspirations, and religious feelings of an individual correspond to and
arise from, in his words, "the reality of certain objects external to
the soul." [25]

Such a "sound realism," as Hecker called it, served as the foundation for demonstrating the necessity of grace. Every act involved
both the subjective and objective element, or, as Leroux reasoned,
communion between the Me and the Not-Me. Life centered in communion. As the subject communed with an object of a lower order
of being it was brought down; as it communed with one of a higher
order, it was elevated. Only, then, by communion with an object of
a higher order could humanity be elevated. Thus had Brownson come
to the conclusion that all efforts at social reform which relied on the
merely human were in vain. Man could not, he reasoned, pull him-

self up by his own bootstraps. He must instead commune with, partake of, divine life itself.

The theory of life by communion pointed not only to the necessity of grace, but also to grace as mediated through a supernatural, revealed, authoritative religion. For Brownson, belief in the necessity of grace was not separated, even in his early life, from this type of religion. Brownson wrote in *The Convert* that, even before his conversion, "I felt, as I had felt from my boyhood, that I had need for an authoritative religion, and that a religion which does not and cannot speak with divine authority is simply no religion at all."[26] The notion of the Church as a people through whom the voice of the living God spoke to the world appealed to him. The idea of an invisible Church that had no concrete human dimension was unsatisfactory to one whose interests in social amelioration always ran high. His study of the social philosophy of the Saint-Simonians had convinced him of the need for the Church as a social institution to take the lead in the process of reform. But it was Leroux's doctrine of Providential men that presented Brownson with the idea that humans could in fact be the channels for the divine life to other humans. In discussing Leroux's doctrine, Brownson aptly described it as "Leroux's attempt to convey his version of the Catholic doctrine of infused grace."[27] The theory simply stated maintains that certain individuals have enjoyed a more direct, more immediate communion with God. By communing with these Providential men, mankind may enjoy a direct communion with the divine life that these Providential men have experienced to an extraordinary degree. This theory, Brownson stated, opened the way for his acceptance of the doctrine of apostolic succession.[28]

The concept of Church as a society of Providential men was nothing new to Hecker whose first picture of the Church was that of the Methodist communities who believed that they had been providentially called to spread throughout the land the holiness of God that they had experienced. What Brownson's theory of the Church presented to him was a more radical understanding of the reality of divine grace than had Methodism. Grace, the divine life in the world, was seen as a real substance. It was the very life of God, not merely the individual's consciousness of that life.

Belief in the reality of the communication of the divine life to man led to an understanding of the Church as an organism uniting divine and human life. The individual was, by reason of the life he shared, part of the Body of Christ, the Church. The Church, united as the one Body of Christ, alone possessed authority in matters of religion. The Church was then, as Brownson argued in *The Convert,* "in some sense the continuation of the Incarnation."[29]

Despite his realization of the need for the Church, Isaac still searched for that ideal church in the real world. Between the alternatives of naked self-reliance and affiliation with the existing institutional church lay the hope in a new church that would better meet the needs of the age. The search for such a new church was widespread among Hecker's contemporaries. It formed the basis for Mormonism, Brownson's Church of the Future, and Swedenborg's New Church. Hecker himself had been thrilled by his reading in early 1843 of Schiller's vision of a new church that would synthesize the Pauline and Petrine, the Protestant and Catholic elements. Charles Dana wrote to Hecker in January 1844, declaring his belief in the dawning of a new church, a "Third Dispensation," which eclipsed the existing institutional church as the Church of the New Covenant did that of the Old.[30] Dana had an idea of the holy, catholic Church that he was convinced Isaac shared. "In this idea," he wrote, "of a society which shall be a church and a church which shall be a society—lives, as far as I can understand, that Holy, Catholic Church which we, both you and I, have at heart." This ideal church was not, however, the present church. The present church would remain, but no longer, he reasoned, "as the medium of God's inspiration." The new church would arise, one which was "more universal than the Old" and hence better able to meet the needs of the times.[31]

Hecker's experience at Brook Farm, Fruitlands, and at home had made him a bit weary of the idea of founding new social institutions to replace the old. He had also seen Brownson's attempt at founding the Church of the Future fail. With Brownson, he was now far more willing to consider reforming the existing institutions as opposed to starting new ones. By March 1844 he decided to join either the Episcopal or Roman Catholic church and to devote his whole energy to "becoming a laborer in the cause of the Church."[32]

IN SEARCH OF SYNTHESIS

SUBMITTING TO THE LEADINGS OF THE SPIRIT

Isaac's devotion to the Spirit during the months preceding his decision to join a church grew in intensity. In April he reported to Brownson that he had been deeply involved in reading mystical writers—Dionysius the Areopagite, Erigena, Bernard of Clairvaux, Hugo and Richard of St. Victor, and Meister Eckhart.[33] In May he wrote to his brother John's wife, "We must be filled with the Spirit of God."[34] June, likewise, saw him keenly aware of the Spirit's presence. He wrote on June 4 to Brownson that his conscious union with the Spirit was "a source of so much more life in every direction" that all other sources, including the books he was trying with limited success to study, seemed "lifeless and dry" by comparison. He went on to state his intention to more fully resign himself in humble submission to the Spirit's leadings. "Man rules his destiny," he wrote, "only by perfect submission to God."[35]

This notion of submission played a key role in Hecker's choice of churches. Ever since the end of 1842 he had desired to submit to the divine Spirit's working within his soul. When he became convinced that the same Spirit, in its fullness, worked within the Church, he then determined that he had to submit to it. Brownson again helped him along at this point, chastising him for what he deemed his excessive tendency to "mere private meditation and prayer."[36] "You are wrong," Brownson chided. "You must put yourself under the direction of the Church. . . . Your cross is to resist this tendency to mysticism which is really enfeebling your soul." He concluded, "You must either be a Catholic or a Mystic."[37]

In responding to Brownson, Isaac agreed that it would be in his own best interests to join the Catholic church and indicated that any hesitation he felt was only the result of an ungodly willfulness, founded on no good reasons. The main questions had been settled. He stated that the Catholic church, unlike the Protestant, "answered the demands of nature," thereby indicating that he now saw that by entering the church, he would find the fullness of divine life that he had to some measure experienced in his own soul and toward which his inner sentiments aspired. He also believed that the Catholic

81

church was "the channel of the Holy Ghost . . . the inspired body illuminated by Christ's Spirit."[38]

The demands of obedience and submission that the Catholic church made helped to convince Isaac that the Roman Catholic and not the Anglican was the one, true Church. Once he admitted that the Church was in a real sense the Body of Christ, animated by the very Spirit of God, the claims to authority made by the Roman church seemed a logical necessity. Anglicanism, with its less strict discipline and emphasis on "comprehension," did not appeal to the zealous youth. He once said of Anglicanism that he could remain as he was and still be an Anglican.[39] In June he spoke of the Catholic church, in contrast, as demanding one's all. "It seems to me the difference between embracing the Roman Catholic church and any other is the same as between remaining as I am and selling all I have and following Christ."[40] The Catholic church, like the Spirit that had been leading him, called him to a higher life. He came to believe that there could be no contradiction between the Spirit's work in his soul and that Spirit's work in the church. His own personal experience would not be contradicted but confirmed and aided. As he said some years later, "The work of the Holy Ghost is one whether in the Church or in the soul."[41]

In June 1844, Isaac visited Bishop John McCloskey, assistant to Bishop John Hughes of New York. McCloskey, who had made the acquaintance of William Ellery Channing's brother Edward, was familiar with the tenets of progressive Unitarianism and was able to perceive Isaac's sincerity and understand some of the ideas that drew him to the church. For six weeks he instructed Hecker in the Faith mainly through a series of recommended readings. By the end of July Isaac was able to demonstrate a solid understanding of the Catholic Faith in his discussions with the bishop. On August 2, 1844, Isaac was received into the church by Bishop McCloskey in the Old St. Patrick's Church on Mott Street in New York. Since Isaac had been baptized as a child, the bishop administered the sacrament conditionally.

In the wedding of his understanding of the Church with his understanding of the Spirit, Hecker attained the synthesis he was seeking. A synthesis was created between his own inner aspirations and external objects, between his personal religious experience and the experience of the community of believers, between his ideal view of the Church and the real, historical Catholic church. This synthesis, this deep sense of unity resonated in his soul. He wrote:

> It is with perfect ease and gracefulness that I never dreamed of that I will unite with the Church. No external realizations, events or objects can disturb this unreachable quietness, not any event breaks this deep repose . . . ."[42]

In looking back at his spiritual journey in July 1844, he realized that he had come into a place where, to a greater extent than ever before, the ideal and the real had been united. He spoke of plans to write a spiritual autobiography narrating the three stages of his pilgrimage. The first he would call the "unconscious period," the second, the "beholding of the ideal," and the third, the "identity of this ideal and the real."[43]

This was how Isaac understood his conversion. It was the consummation of all that had come before. God who had created him and placed within him a desire for truth and a hunger for a fuller participation in the divine life had providentially led him.

VII

CATHOLIC!

After his conversion to Catholicism in August 1844, Isaac continued his spiritual journey, seeking how, as a son of the church, to grow in his awareness of God. Becoming a Catholic opened to him a new range of possibilities. At his disposal now were the riches of age-old tradition, the treasury of the church's understanding. He had had a taste of these prior to his conversion. They had proved so appealing that they had drawn him to convert. Now he thirsted for more. To immerse himself in Catholic tradition, Catholic thought, Catholic culture became his main desire. As this desire grew, it caused him to consider the religious life and to long for the Catholic old world.

NOURISHING OLD TIES

Yet Hecker the Catholic was still Hecker the American. After his conversion he continued nourishing the relationships with his Transcendentalist friends that had become so meaningful to him over the past three years. Isaac's decision to become Catholic had not yet alienated him from these romantic seekers who prided themselves on their open-mindedness.

Isaac's relationship with George and Burrill Curtis remained especially cordial. His friendship with the Curtis brothers had begun at Brook Farm where the handsome and vivacious brothers won the

84

hearts of all. Isaac was particularly friendly with George. Their correspondence during 1844 was lively. They exchanged opinions on the current literary scene, providing one another with choice reading materials and recommendations. Later that same year and early the following year, Curtis discussed current tastes in poetry and literature with him. [1] Curtis spoke of his own enthusiasm for Keats, his interest in Voltaire, and the poetry and Lyceum lectures of Emerson. In March 1845 alone, Curtis wrote at least four letters to the young convert in which he gave his opinion of Shakespeare's works and Shelley's translation of Plato's *Banquet,* as well as samples of his own poetry. [2] And in April he and Hecker began a long series of discussions on a favorite Transcendentalist theme, the nature of genius. [3]

Despite the fact that Hecker had committed himself to Catholicism, Curtis still felt that he and his former Brook Farm friend were moving in the same direction down two different but parallel tracks. "You are indeed Catholic," Curtis wrote, "and while I feel the difference, I feel that there is no difference." He continued, "Let me believe that the difference of outward expression is but that of two natures, individual, but centered upon the same truth." [4]

The idea that Catholicism was merely a different outward expression of the same truths toward which Isaac aspired during his Transcendentalist days was shared by others among his friends. The mystically–inclined Charles Lane, whose effusive utterances on Eternal Spirit had held a certain fascination for Hecker, wrote Isaac a long letter in June 1845 from the Shaker community in Harvard, where he had been living after the demise of Fruitlands. Lane took delight in referring to his old friend as " 'Catholic' . . . not overlaid by the 'Roman.' " For Lane, the question of what was the true church was displaced by a concern that the individual soul be filled with the Spirit. "Does my friend yet find himself in the bosom of the true Church," he began his June 1845 letter, "as surely as his bosom is the true church?" [5] Lane was ready to view all outward forms as basically irrelevant to the Spirit's working. He agreed with Hecker that the Spirit could flow through old forms as well as new, but he implied that whatever was the form through which the Spirit flowed "spontaneously," that form was the true one for him. [6]

Soon after deciding to become a Catholic, Isaac was taken with the idea of making a pilgrimage to Europe. Toward the end of July 1844, he shared his plans with Henry David Thoreau in hopes that the young sage would join him on his journey. A more romantic adventure could hardly have been planned by any of the starry-eyed Brook Farmers than that proposed by young Isaac. He told Thoreau, "We desire to go without purse or staff, depending upon the all-embracing love of God, Humanity, and the spark of courage imprisoned in us."[7] Thoreau declined, though, as might be expected, not because of the impracticability of the scheme, but because he had himself determined to pursue a Brahman-like existence, cut off in large measure from social intercourse.[8] The stillness of Walden Pond beckoned more than the lure of far-off lands.

Even after his decision to join the Catholic church, Isaac continued to search for a more suitable environment in which to seek out the higher, richer life he had begun to taste. He was still given to following the inward leadings of the Spirit, however radical a course they might dictate. He was still an idealist who sought for the concrete realization of his dreams. And he was still a sensitive, mystically-inclined young man who believed that God's leadings could be direct and explicit and who had not yet fully defined the calling to which he felt drawn. George Curtis' brother, Burrill, rebuked him for this very tendency. Unimpressed by Isaac's plans concerning Europe, Curtis suggested that the indefinite impulses he was given to following were in fact aspirations that were not meant to be gratified. "Perhaps you will break from any desire to settle and follow always a mysterious power," Curtis wrote.[9]

By October 1844, Hecker had abandoned plans for a European trip. Doubtless his inability to find a companion and the discouraging advice of his counselors deterred him. But while he decided against a European pilgrimage, he did not heed Burrill Curtis' advice to discard the tendency to "follow always a mysterious power." In writing to Brownson, he told of his decision against Europe in favor of remaining in the United States and reviving his study of classical languages in preparation for the ministry. The reason he gave for this choice indicates, however, that he was still bent on following the inner leadings of the Spirit. "Submitting myself to this power which has guided me thus far," he told Brownson, "I am led to the determination of recommencing the study of the languages."[10] Isaac believed that the failure of his plans for a European trip was providential.

CHOOSING A WAY OF LIFE

During the period immediately following his conversion, Hecker was moved by his own deep spiritual hunger to consider entering the religious life. In his letters to his beloved mentor, Brownson, he expressed his conviction that a contemplative way of life would provide the necessary setting for his growth. He felt increasingly the need for the help of others in directing his spiritual life. Brownson, as both men realized, could offer Isaac sound advice and abundant insight on philosophical issues, but was no spiritual director. Isaac, convinced that the church was the channel of the Spirit, desired to submit his inner life to the church's discipline. His desire to serve God had become joined to a desire to serve the church. At the beginning of 1845, he wrote a letter to Brownson that began with a statement of his commitment to Jesus: "I see and feel one thing before me and that is the cause of Jesus." He continued in the same letter to tell of his zeal for the church: "Oh for the Church, the Church, the Church. My heart burns to realize the Catholic Church."[11]

One month after his confirmation in May 1845, Hecker decided to become a religious. He had heard of the Redemptorists through a conversation with a German Redemptorist in New York City and had read a book on the religious vocation by the Redemptorist founder, Alphonsus Liguori. The order, which had been established in 1732 by Alphonsus, offered a number of attractions. The ideal of blending the contemplative life with the life of the missionary was appealing. Though he delighted in contemplation, Isaac was enough attached to the active life to agree in some way with George Curtis' judgment that to be a monk closely bound to the cloistered retreat would not do justice to the outer world.[12] The Redemptorist practice of spending part of the year in prayer and part in active missionary labor appeared as an ideal balance. A second reason why the Redemptorists appealed to the German-American Hecker was the strongly German character of the congregation. The New York house was, like the other Redemptorist houses in America, mainly given to ministering to the masses of German immigrants that filled the cities. Brownson had even at one time suggested that Isaac might well serve God as a priest devoted to working with German-Americans.

The fact that the Redemptorists were a thoroughly European institution involved in American mission work appeared to Hecker to be a perfect combination. Before deciding to join the Redemptorists, Isaac, who had not abandoned his hopes of seeing Europe, wrote to Brownson, suggesting that if he joined the Redemptorists, he might be able to go to Europe for training and then return to his homeland for active service. The thought of going to Europe was attractive because, as he put it, "I feel the need of being under stronger Catholic influences than are so far as my experience goes, in this country."[13] Brownson had suggested the Jesuits, but Isaac's tour of the Jesuit seminary at Fordham left him unimpressed. The Redemptorists, it seemed, could better provide him the blend of old and new worlds that he desired.

During June and July, as Hecker dealt with the question of finding the religious order best suited to him, he grew in an awareness of his own sinfulness and of the need for self-mortification. Old and forgotten sins came afresh to his memory. A keen sense of the fruitlessness of his own efforts gripped him. "Recent actions," he told Brownson, "that I thought not sinful, seem now to me full of sin."[14] He desired more than ever to "be consumed by God" and sought for the "speediest means" to do this. Acutely aware of the distance between himself and God, he wanted desperately to separate all in himself that was unclean from that which was godly. He wanted to do only and always God's will in every situation. As zealous souls are wont, he desired and expected God's direct guidance in even the most minute affairs. "I would not move a finger," he wrote, "not draw a breath, not speak, nor eat . . . unless moved or commanded by God so to do."[15] Yet he was instantly cognizant of the difficulties involved.

Oh who has this assurance and how shall we obtain it? If we reckon how much in one day which we do interiorly and exteriorly that . . . we are neither commanded nor called to do, not to say how much more we do contrary both to the commands and inspirations of God, surely it is enough for to cover us with confusion . . . .[16]

The only solution he saw was to place himself under a spiritual director where he then felt he would be freed from himself. "I feel the need of being met," he wrote. "If I am deluded then I need something to be laid upon me to show up my delusion." He was ready to let others function as God's instruments. He went on in his usual intense fashion, "I want someone to kill me stone dead, or make me cry out enough, enough."[17]

Brownson, in a letter postmarked two days after Hecker had decided on July 29 to join the sons of Alphonsus, obliged him in his request for that precious oil of correction. In a straightforward, unrelenting style, Brownson, the master critic, informed him of what he saw as his dangerous tendency to mysticism.

> You have a very lively and active imagination, more so than you are aware, which joined to a quick sensibility and a warm heart and ardent temperament exposes you to many dangers against which you are not likely to be on your guard. Your danger is on the side of Mysticism.[18]

Brownson, who had told him one year before that he must become either a Catholic or a mystic, was not well disposed toward Hecker's penchant to be both. To the stolid Vermonter who had been led to Rome by sound reasoning, "Mysticism" denoted a vague, subjectivistic, emotional religiosity. He had little knowledge of mysticism being anything else. His critique of Isaac's character was, nevertheless, on target, and was echoed at various times in Hecker's life by others. What Brownson felt was most dangerous in Hecker's tendency to mysticism was a liability to "receive the truth under a form too subjective, and to mingle too much of sensibility with the objective forms of faith." He warned that Hecker might thus be deceived into following his own will under the guise of denying the self and seeking God's will.[19] This precise problem had been the one which, in germ form, Hecker presented to Brownson during one of their very first meetings, when he asked how one might know that his own thoughts corresponded to objective realities. In addition to correcting Hecker's tendency to subjectivism, Brownson urged Isaac to remember that the circumstances of life do not determine one's ability to obey God. "Our great business," he maintained, "is to do what God commands us now and where we are."[20] This corrective, too, was, in light of Isaac's past history of utopia-seeking, well founded.

But the enthusiastic Hecker was, in the final analysis, of no mind to hear such hard advice. He still longed to wander in search of adventure. He savored the unfamiliar, the challenging. Recently he had met two young men who were about to begin the type of odyssey he desired. Clarence Walworth and James McMaster were, like Hecker, converts who had been attracted to the followers of St. Alphonsus. On August 1 they were scheduled to set sail for the Redemptorist novitiate in St. Trond, Belgium. The thought of joining them on the *Prince Albert* when it sailed intrigued the impetuous Isaac.

He quickly obtained the blessing of his bishop in New York, John Hughes, who, though wishing that Hecker would choose the diocesan priesthood, recognized his attraction to the life of a religious. Only one obstacle remained in Isaac's path. The American Redemptorists at that time were part of the Belgian Province, under the charge of Father Frederick de Held, whose approval Isaac needed. On Friday night, July 31, Isaac decided to journey by train to Baltimore, speak with Father de Held who was visiting the Redemptorist house in that city, and return in time to make the *Prince Albert*'s departure. Unannounced, Hecker turned up at the provincial's home at 4:00 A.M. His enthusiasm and the good graces of Father de Held combined in winning for him an audience later that morning. After satisfying the provincial of his fitness to enter the congregation, Isaac rushed back to New York and somehow managed to get himself aboard ship en route to Europe and the adventures of the Redemptorist novitiate.

A THOROUGHLY CATHOLIC ENVIRONMENT

Hecker rather easily fitted into the regimen of the novitiate house in the small Belgian town about thirty-five miles southeast of

Antwerp. The discipline and the long hours given to prayer and meditation for the most part pleased him. "The conditions here are perfect," he wrote to Brownson soon after his arrival. "All that can hinder me from gaining the end for which God gave me being is a non-compliance on my part."[21] Around the same time, he received the habit of a novice and began observance of the Redemptorist Rule for a one-year period. His delight in the world he had entered is succinctly conveyed in the words written to his family in that same month: "All my seeking is now ended."[22] The spiritual pilgrim had at last found a situation that seemed to suit him perfectly. What he was unable to do at home and at the various Transcendentalist communities, he could do to his heart's content at St. Trond, namely, devote himself fully to the spiritual life and do so under the guidance of skilled directors who he believed would understand what he was experiencing.

As it turned out, however, his early experiences with his spiritual director were somewhat disappointing. The novice master seemed, in Hecker's view, not to understand the young American convert. Disclosing his interior life to him was one of the sorest trials of his novitiate. After a number of months, however, his rapport with the novice master improved considerably. He began showing more confidence in Hecker and even granted him the special privilege of daily communion.

After the end of his novitiate year, when Hecker was ready to leave St. Trond for the studentiate at Wittem in southern Holland, a general satisfaction with religious life was evident. On October 15, 1846, he took his vows as a Redemptorist and that same day wrote to his friend Bishop John McCloskey of Albany, summing up his attitude while at St. Trond. Since his sole desire had for some time been to "attain the most intimate and perfect union with God that is possible," and since this was the primary goal of the discipline of a religious order, he had been very happy and content.[23]

While at the novitiate, Hecker's spirituality—in fact his entire way of thinking and feeling about God—underwent a thorough catholicizing process. He had gone to Europe hoping to imbibe the ancient Catholic traditions in a way not possible in the new world. Given the opportunity to do so, he drank deeply, so much so that his vision of certain things that had been valuable to him became temporarily blurred. His letters to his family during this time were filled with inopportune pleadings and exhortations for his loved ones to immediately join the Catholic church or face damnation. So clearly did he now see the excellency of Catholicism that the Protestant churches to which his family members belonged seemed pale and vapid. He denounced Methodism as a heresy and Anglicanism as schismatic. The Roman church alone he saw as the true Church, outside of which there is no salvation.[24] Like Augustine's rejection of the Manichees, or Luther's denunciation of the monastery, Hecker's critique of Protestantism was the statement of one thoroughly persuaded by the power of his present convictions. He had seen a new light, the brilliance of which blinded him to all else.

While he was at the Redemptorist house of studies at Wittem, Isaac's knowledge of the rudiments of Catholic theology grew. He quickly used these new intellectual tools to demonstrate the superiority of his new persuasions. His notes were preoccupied with contrasting Protestantism with Catholicism. In his writings the young zealot wrote off Protestantism as "offensive to humility, reason, and the natural aspirations of man."[25] His defense of Catholicism centered upon the doctrine of infused grace. The doctrine of grace as formally impressed on the soul by a certain internal gift which is united and intrinsic to it appealed immediately to him. The Catholic doctrine of justification, which flows from this, seemed entirely preferable to the Protestant notion of alien righteousness that did not fully appreciate the operation of the Holy Spirit in the soul truly sanctifying the believer. Hecker also defended the Catholic doctrine of the sacraments along similar lines, arguing that they are the channels by which grace is most efficaciously conveyed to the soul. The Catholic church and it alone, as the Body of Christ, was likewise viewed as the great source of this grace to the world.[26]

One of the most significant aspects of this catholicizing process that Isaac underwent while in Europe centered upon his study of the writings of Catholic spiritual masters. Although he mentioned reading certain Catholic mystics prior to his conversion, his contact with them had not been as penetrating as that which took place within the cloisters of St. Trond. At the novitiate, the main emphasis was on spiritual discipline rather than the academic study of philosophy and theology. Thus encouraged by the surroundings, Hecker read with great delight a number of works on mystical theology and discovered in them a kindred spirit. He could identify from his own experience the various dynamics of the spiritual life that the masters discussed in their works. The explanations of spiritual growth and development that he found clarified elements of his own past experience and gave him the tools with which to share the dynamics of his spirituality with others.

The first with whom he wished to share was his mother. At last he felt that he could offer a reasonable explanation for his past behavior which he knew had caused her considerable anxiety. He wrote to her in October 1846 during his last week of novitiate: "It is by the life and writings of certain holy men and women in the Catholic Church, and with the grace of God, that my experience has become of late intelligible to me . . . ."[27] Isaac went on to describe three stages of development through which he had come. The first he termed, reflecting the influence of Catherine of Genoa, "the first purgation." In it, the defects which were grossest and most exterior, such as those associated with the physical appetites, were purged as the soul aspired to God, who infused it with a desire to seek him. The second purgation he described as resulting from a "more subtle and penetrating" infusion of love for God into the heart. This infusion entered to "despoil the soul of its will, its judgments, its memory," in fact, all of its own faculties, in order to teach the individual his great need for radical dependence upon God. The first of these stages began while he was at home, and climaxed, joined by the second, while he was at Brook Farm. But God had now, Isaac assured his mother, turned all his sufferings into joy by bringing him into the third stage, that of enlightenment. In this stage God infused gradually into the heart all the Christian virtues and graces. He enlightened the soul with "a hidden light." This occurred while he was at Concord in 1844 and was the cause, he said, of his sudden return home and entrance into the church.[28]

In a letter two weeks later to Brownson, Hecker again attempted to explain his spiritual pilgrimage in the terminology of the mystical writers. This time he was more detailed both in his explanation and in his citing of sources. The writings of St. Catherine of Genoa and St. John of the Cross were listed as his chief sources of instruction. He cited Catherine's *Treatise on Purgatory* and *Dialogues* and a three-volume edition of the complete works of John of the Cross.[29]

In addition to the writings of Sts. John of the Cross and Catherine of Genoa, Hecker encountered the work of a seventeenth-century French Jesuit, Louis Lallemant. Lallemant's 1694 *Spiritual Doctrine* served an important function in Hecker's catholicizing process. *Spiritual Doctrine* was actually the work of J. J. Surin, Lallemant's disciple, who took notes on the lectures that his master gave in the early 1600s. Surin later became involved in an extreme form of Quietism, which won him the dubious honor of being silenced by Rome. The teaching of *Spiritual Doctrine* stresses fidelity to the guidance of the Holy Spirit and dependence on his gifts. Using the principles of St. Ignatius Loyola's *Spiritual Exercises,* it instructs the individual on discerning the action of God in the heart and in the external events of everyday life. It posits a dynamic interrelationship between contemplation and action and concludes that concern for the welfare of others and for the spreading of God's Kingdom is the mark of the spiritually mature.

Isaac was attracted by Lallemant's doctrine with its sensitivity to the inward workings of the Spirit in the soul and its concern to harmonize such workings with the working of the Spirit in the Church and through providence. *Spiritual Doctrine* presented him with a spirituality that was warmly personal yet turned outward enough to leave room for the active virtues. In Lallemant he found a succinct statement of the synthesis between the Spirit's internal work and its work in the Church. He told of his delight in discovering the French master:

> When I was not far from being through with my noviceship, I was one day looking over the books in the library and I came across Lallemant's *Spiritual Doctrine.* Getting leave to read it, I was overjoyed to find it a full statement of the principles by which I had been interiorly guided. I said to Père Othmann: Why did you not give me this book when I first came? It settles all my difficulties.[30]

94

What the *Spiritual Doctrine* did more than anything else was to assure Isaac that his confidence in the inner guidance of the Spirit could be reconciled with Catholic teaching. Had he not believed this, he would never have become a Catholic. Now, however, he could adduce the respected Jesuit mystical theologian in support of his own doctrines. Characteristically, Hecker absorbed enough Lallemant to buttress his own position. Particularly useful was Lallemant's third article of the first chapter of his first principle, in which he defended his doctrine of the interior direction of the Holy Spirit in the soul against various objections.

During his later days at St. Trond and after he had moved to the Redemptorist house of studies in Wittem, Isaac was beset by an old problem. He could not study. He felt instead the inner Spirit leading him to cease entirely from his own activity. This inability brought with it certain hardships and anxieties. His fellow students thought him the fool. His superiors were confronted with three alternatives: make him a lay brother, send him to a contemplative order that did not require advanced studies, or allow him to move along at his own pace in his studies unfettered by the demands of the classroom. They chose the last alternative. Near the close of 1848, permission was granted Hecker to move from Wittem to a newly-established Redemptorist house in Clapham, England. He hoped that another environment might better enable him to study. In the new setting, he was able to study enough theology to convince Bishop (later Cardinal) Nicholas Wiseman to ordain him to the priesthood in 1849. Thus it was that Hecker was commissioned in the ministry of the church without ever having had a formal course of instruction in theology.[31]

In theology, as in the arts, Isaac was largely a self-educated man. He never was taught the rigors of Scholastic logic, never was made to memorize formulas and pat answers to the criticisms leveled against Catholic doctrine. His thinking drew on the many sources that he had encountered in his wide experience. When confronted with new challenges to his Faith, the speculative American turned not to a sealed corpus of doctrines and tradition, but to a process of reflection. He scrutinized the present situation, convinced that God in his providence had brought it about for a purpose. With the eyes of a contemplative, he endeavored to see God's hand in the present situation; he searched the signs of the times for the Spirit's action. As a result, his thought penetrates with a freshness and vigor characteristic of an original thinker. When he studied the past, he did so for the sake of the present. Antiquarian revelings were as foreign to him as was a lack of enthusiasm for the present moment. It was there that his experience of God centered, there that his life was focused.

But this originality, as we shall see, was accompanied by its share of liabilities. There would be times in Isaac's life when his solitary voice would go unheard and other even more vexing times when his voice would be heard, but not understood.

While at Clapham, Hecker submitted a thorough account of his spiritual life during his time at St. Trond and Wittem in a twenty-one page letter. In the letter, he appeared concerned with giving the very best account of himself possible—a disposition that is understandable in light of his unusual behavior in regard to study. His method of defense was based on his knowledge of mystical writings. He adduced quotations from a host of mystical writers to establish the validity of his own experience. He told, for instance, of being led into a period of cessation of activity: "My faculties were recollected inwardly to such a degree that I could make no use of the prayer book and for better than six months I did not even recite the breviary or say the rosary." In defense of this behavior he cited, in addition to John of the Cross' *Ascent of Mt. Carmel,* Teresa of Avila's twenty-eighth chapter of *The Way of Perfection* and Giovanni Scaramelli's first chapter of *Oratio Recollectionis.* To this list he added such authorities as St. Alphonsus Liguori, founder of the Redemptorists, the Angelic Doctor St. Thomas Aquinas, and the current pope, Pius IX. A similar strategy was followed in describing his devotion to the Holy Eucharist, his experience of supernatural prayer, and his periods of "spiritual sleep." He also told of his extreme acts of asceticism: sleeping on boards, wearing a hair shirt constantly, and taking the discipline five times a week for over fifteen minutes at a stretch, until the blood would often flow from the effects.

Aside from these more bizarre practices, Hecker centered on the main principles behind his spirituality while at Wittem. He named three: "resignation and conformity with the will of God, an entire fidelity to the inspirations and attractions of the Holy Ghost, and a to-tal abandonment of myself to the conduct of Divine Providence." These notions were by 1848 inextricably bound in his spirituality. To do the will of God, not his own will, was his constant aim. That will was revealed in the soul by the Holy Spirit—whom he called "the only true master in the Spiritual life"—and by divine providence in the external affairs. God's intimate touch on the soul and his hand in history both worked toward the same end—the revelation of the divine will.

Increasingly, however, Isaac was learning that it was not possible for him to fulfill God's will by his own devices. The more perfectly he saw the divine will, the more thoroughly he realized how far short of it he fell. It appeared so far beyond his reach that he cried: "The distance . . . is infinite. The will of God and my will are opposed to each other." The divine will appeared as the composite of the divine attributes. It was the sum of perfection and beauty, of sanctity and purity. He told of the lasting effect that this vision of the divine will had had on him: "This impression has remained with me. Its effect has been to separate me from all things else and to place me in entire dependence upon it."

Despite his attempts to demonstrate the soundness of his spiritual experiences, not all who heard of them approved. One who was well familiar with the young American and who was one of Isaac's favorites among his older Redemptorist brothers wrote to him in the early part of 1849, warning him, as had Burrill Curtis and Brownson, of certain tendencies which needed correcting.[32] Father Michael Heilig, former rector of Wittem, functioned as Isaac's spiritual director after leaving Wittem for a position as Provincial of the Redemptorists in Belgium. In counseling Isaac he assured him that he was destined to arrive at a great love of God and to do a great deal for the salvation of souls. Yet he feared that, were the impetuous youth not under the care of experienced directors, he would fall into serious faults. Heilig believed that Hecker's present state of "impression" was unbefitting to an individual desirous of healthy spiritual growth. Unfortunately, the director continued, Hecker had passed too quickly from the lower to the higher degrees of the spiritual life. He must immediately begin to rid himself of his present condition.

This could be done, Heilig suggested, by first putting aside all notions that he was traveling any extraordinary path toward perfection. He was to believe that his was merely a *via ordinaria*. Second, he urged Hecker to "despise all these impressions that he was being led in a special way, however holy and strong they may be." He, like Brownson, suggested that by attending to these extraordinary experiences, Hecker might in fact be feeding self-love, rather than defeating it.

But in the final analysis, Isaac was not interested in the *via ordinaria*. His experience of God was built around the belief that God was working in an extraordinary way and had destined him to perform a special task. These convictions continued to burn within the young man's heart.

THE CALL

During his years with the Redemptorists in Europe, Isaac never lacked concern for his homeland. He kept abreast of developments in the religious scene there by reading issues of the *Brownson Quarterly Review* which his family sent him.[33] Throughout his time in Europe he continued writing to Brownson and other old friends like Thoreau and George Curtis. In April 1849 he was still carrying on the discussion he had begun with George Curtis, before leaving for the continent, on the nature of genius.[34]

Central, though, to his interest in America was his desire to return to missionize the land. As he grew in his conviction that Catholicism was the highest, fullest, most comprehensive religion in existence, he grew in the belief that the masses of his fellow countrymen who were earnestly seeking, as he had been, something more in their religious experience would respond enthusiastically to Catholic truth if it were presented to them in the proper way. As early as January 1846, Isaac, in a letter to his brothers, stated his intention to return to the States to labor for "the conversion of our country."[35] In May 1848, when writing to the beloved Father Heilig, he envisioned a call to missionize America as that for which providence had destined him.[36] All that he had experienced among the Transcendentalists, all that he had learned of the concerns and aspirations of some of America's keenest minds he viewed as preparing him to bring good news to his land. Though he had been preoccupied with the contemplative life, he had never lost sight of the active life, but one he described as "supernaturally active."[37] His action had to spring from deep prayer and waiting upon God. His action had to be God's will, not merely his own, and had to harmonize with God's work in the world at large. Attuned to the Spirit's working in his soul and in the world, he would be able to act effectively. All that he had suffered through the suspension of his own abilities to do something for God, all that he had learned of the absolute necessity of God's assistance had functioned to convince him that, in his words, "this work will not be mine. . . . I shall be only the mean instrument for the accomplishment of His designs."[38] Though he felt for good reason that he needed an ample measure of intellectual sophistication to speak to those American Brahmins who made up the Transcendentalist movement, he had been unable to seriously study. This too, he now reasoned, had been providential. He wrote to Heilig: "Contrary to my first previsions He has unmistakably shown me that it is neither [by] learning nor eloquence that he calls me to convert others, but solely by His grace and power."[39] Thus he felt ready to return to America convinced that God was calling him. When he got the chance in 1851 to go to New York with Clarence Walworth in a missionary band headed up by the American vice-provincial, Father Bernard Joseph Hafkenscheid, he saw the hand of God leading him on to his destiny.

The young American convert whose conversion to Catholicism had represented a synthesis of the ideal and the real returned to his homeland seeking to complete this integration. For it to be complete, his Catholicism had to make place for his Americanism. In his youthful zeal he had gone off to Europe to find an environment in which he could deeply drink of Catholic life. So long he had been an anomaly; so long he had been vexed by his inability to share his inner life with others. When he had at last found a community of kindred souls in the Catholic church, he had wished to be identified with it completely.

But even as he sat in the Redemptorist student houses at Wittem and St. Trond, he could not forget his homeland. He could not put out of his mind the notion that he was by God's doing an American and that his native land was a place of God's special providence. So firmly had these ideas been impressed on Hecker from his youth that now in his manhood he longed to synthesize them with his Catholicism. This longing gave birth to a grand vision of a Catholic America.

the mission Hecker was assigned the morning instruction and the evening explanation of the rosary, Hewit and Walworth shared the task of giving the major sermon, and all joined in to hear the confessions of the multitudes who flocked to the sacrament at the close of each session. The first New York mission was warmly received. It was the beginning of a successful series of such missions that took the Redemptorist band to ten dioceses throughout the Northeast, South, and Midwest during the next five years.[2]

The Redemptorist missions begun by Father Bernard were among the first of their kind in American Catholicism. In their use of the protracted meeting and their emphasis on repentance, the Redemptorist missions resembled the evangelical revival meetings that Charles G. Finney and the numerous Methodist holiness preachers popularized in the 1830s, 1840s, and 1850s. Like the revival meetings, the Redemptorist missions provided the people with an exhortation to lead holier, more perfect lives and offered the means of grace to all those who would heed the call. In place of the mourner's bench and altar call used by the Finney revivalists, the Catholic missions provided the sacraments as the means of grace.[3] The penitent, when pricked in his heart by the dramatic preaching of a skilled orator like Clarence Walworth, could immediately after the sermon enter into the confessional to recite his sins and receive forgiveness. The next morning, the supreme benefit of the Eucharist was made available to all those in a state of grace. Combined with the emphasis on preaching and on the individual's response to the Word was ample opportunity for prayer and worship provided by the Mass and recitation of the rosary.[4]

THE METHOD AND THE MESSAGE

When Hecker traveled about the country in the 1850s with the mission band, he was then using a format that had certain similarities to one popular among the Methodist holiness advocates he had known in his youth. Though this similarity existed, it did not result from the fact that the two groups drew on a common source. The Redemptorists were looking for their inspiration and methodology directly to their eighteenth-century Italian founder, St. Alphonsus. For

Hecker, any similarity that might have existed was overshadowed by what he saw as the vast differences between Catholicism and Protestantism. The differences were for him so great—the former eclipsing the latter so totally—that he felt he could not only defend the validity of Catholicism but demonstrate its clear superiority.

In the early years of the missions, Hecker and his fellow evangelists directed their efforts almost solely toward the throngs of Catholics that crowded their services. This Isaac viewed as expedient, since it was, he reasoned, necessary to first renew those within the Catholic fold as a prelude to the future large-scale conversion of the American non-Catholics. He wrote to Brownson in 1851: "Until we have a higher tone of Catholic life in our country we shall do nothing."[5] What was needed was more enthusiasm among Catholics. This enthusiasm was not merely excess emotionalism, but rather "the activity of the passions supernaturalized." It was to be brought about by a "thorough discipline—an ascetic life." Only Catholicism was capable of giving people a permanent enthusiasm that would motivate great deeds of zeal.[6]

During this time Isaac had not forgotten his words to Father Heilig concerning his conviction of a call to present Catholic truth to that class of individuals with whom he had been associated in his religious odyssey—the non-Catholics. It was not until a series of missions in March 1856 at Norfolk, Virginia that Hecker and the band decided to make special efforts to reach the non-Catholic. At the close of the mission Father Hecker gave a series of lectures addressed specifically to Protestants. He lectured on the need for faith, the Bible, tradition, and the role of the Church. He argued for the superiority of Catholicism from an appeal to both reason and the religious needs of mankind. The next month he wrote to Brownson about the series, contending that he had broken new ground by putting the Protestants on the defensive and by appealing to human nature for support.[7]

Hecker's desire to address non-Catholic America had been developed prior to the 1856 Norfolk mission through the written word. While busily involved in the work of itinerant preaching, Hecker had nevertheless found time in the latter half of 1854 to write his first major apologetic work, *Questions of the Soul*. Before finishing the book, Hecker put forth its leading arguments in a September 1854 letter to Brownson. The leading idea, he said, was "to expose the wants of the heart and demand their proper objects, rather than a logical defense of the Church."[8] As Hecker was himself aware, this approach was novel to American Catholic apologetics of his day. The standard seminary manuals of the time put forth a three-part division of apologetics based largely on nineteenth-century Jesuit theologian Giovanni Perrone's *De vera religione adversus incredulos et heterodoxos* (Rome, 1840). The first division, *demonstratio religiosa*, was a study of religion in general and the grounds for theistic belief. The second, *demonstratio christiana,* examined revealed religion and the Christian claims. The third, *demonstratio catholica,* investigated the Church and the grounds for Catholic belief. American Catholic apologetics were preoccupied with *demonstratio catholica* and seldom got down to the other two more basic types of apologetic.[9] Americans looked to works such as John Milner's *The End of Controversy* (1818) and John England's *The Calumnies of J. Blanco White* (1826–28), which vindicated Catholic teaching by demonstrating that the Catholic church was identical with the church of the Apostles. Even Moehler's *Symbolik,* which was more irenic in tone than many of the apologetic works of the time, focused entirely on *demonstratio catholica.* In addition to vindicating Catholic teaching, American apologists like Francis P. Kenrick and Martin John Spalding attempted to show that there existed no disharmony between Catholicism and American institutions—a point that needed to be made in the face of accusations that American Catholics had a double alliance, to Rome as well as to their homeland.

Hecker's agenda in *Questions of the Soul* was to argue for Catholicism beginning with "the wants of the heart." The preface to the work asserted: "The question, Has man a destiny and what is it? agitates the souls of all men."[10] He proceeded to argue that man has a destiny, short of which he can never be happy. This point was profusely illustrated, as were many that followed, by references to what could pass for a favorite authors list of many a Transcendentalist. Carlyle, Goethe, Plotinus, Channing, Emerson, Plato, Pythagoras, Buddha, Alcott, Schiller, Tennyson, Longfellow, and Dryden, to name only some, were cited. To those who sought, as he had, for a higher, richer life, Isaac brought good news. The strivings of the soul for a better life and the dim sense of a noble destiny are not groundless. They are not merely the results of the Fichtean Ego positing itself. There are substance and reality to the soul's longings. "To those who feel within their hearts the strivings of a noble enterprize, we have a word of hope. . . . 'These are not dreams for laughter. Now but shoots, these trees hereafter shall with fruit refresh us' (Goethe)."[11]

That destiny is, Hecker continued, to know, love, and serve God. It is only through Jesus Christ that that destiny can be obtained. Christ is "the complement of man—the restorer of the race" who enables man to become all that he was created to be. This Jesus, Hecker then argued, is manifested to humanity in his fullness only by the Catholic church, which is "the organ by which Jesus Christ perpetuates his life upon earth and the organ of restoration, and nature's restoration through man."[12] In the church an individual can become fully Christian "without violating the laws of his reason, without stifling the dictates of his conscience." Catholicism, he concluded, is, unlike Protestantism, "adequate to all the wants of the human heart."[13]

Isaac found it necessary to begin with *demonstratio religiosa,* work through to *demonstratio christiana,* and then, and only then, culminate with *demonstratio catholica.* His interest was clearly with the fundamental questions of religion—with the hunger of the soul for God, with the nature of belief, with human destiny. In his own spiritual journey he had turned away from the Methodism of his childhood because it failed to provide him with a satisfactory treatment of the nature of religious belief, or, if you will, it failed to provide a cogent *demonstratio religiosa.* Transcendentalism supplied what Methodism lacked in this regard but it in turn failed to appreciate the importance of Christ and the life of grace. It did not give a satisfactory *demonstratio christiana.* Isaac then, in arguing for Catholicism, realized the importance of dealing with these first two levels of apologetics.

Although Hecker's emphasis on fundamental theology was novel within American Catholic apologetics of the 1800s, it was by no means unique to him. Concern with the basic religious nature of man was central to Transcendentalism. Brownson himself had popularized Benjamin Constant's theory of religious sentiment chiefly because he was delighted to find a theory that demonstrated that the religious sentiment was indigenous to man. The whole emphasis on the turn within, which characterized the Transcendental movement, rested on the belief in the inherent capacity for transcendent religious experience. The discussion on the importance of miracles which saw men like Ripley and Parker opposing Andrews Norton and others is another indication of how important were questions of fundamental theology to Hecker's Transcendentalist friends. They rejected the argument for the supernatural character of the Faith from the evidence of miracles because it ignored the internal evidences and stressed the external. The truth of Christianity, they insisted, had to be established by looking within at human nature's capacities and needs for the divine. Hecker, in arguing for the validity of Catholicism on the basis of the religious aspirations, was merely extending this method. Whereas the Transcendentalists often stopped with *demonstratio religiosa*, Hecker, like some of the less radical New Englanders, extended it to *demonstratio christiana*. But even in this final step he was not alone.[14] Brownson's *a priori* argument for Catholicism was certainly an application of the same method.

Hecker's book *Questions of the Soul* was, if one can judge from its sales, a success, running through three printings of one thousand copies each between February and June of 1855. Among the many favorable responses was one by the famous historian, George Bancroft. Bancroft hailed the volume as one of the signs of the time "that men are beginning to look inward and desire with loftier earnestness to solve the great problems of existence."[15] Brownson warmly welcomed the work, citing particularly the author's positive, irenic tone as proof that Catholic apologetics need not be offensive to be effective.[16]

By March 1855 Hecker was already discussing plans for a follow-up volume. In it he wished to show "how the dogmas of the Church answer, in a way, to the demands of the intellect, as the sacraments do to the wants of the heart."[17] He was still talking about the book to Brownson and to Richard Simpson in June 1856. While a student at Oriel College, Simpson had been influenced by the Tractarian Movement. After leaving the Anglican priesthood for Rome, he began promulgating his fresh, innovative brand of Catholicism throughout England in his magazine, *The Rambler*. Hecker had been struck with the similarity between his own thought and that of Simpson as put forth in a may 1856 article on original sin in *The Rambler*. "Have you been looking over my shoulder or I yours?" Hecker asked.[18] In the same letter Hecker outlined his dissatisfaction with Aquinas' arguments in proof of the necessity of revelation. He feared that they could be twisted to appear to favor rationalism. Instead he preferred the argument based on Leroux's theory of life by communion. Simpson responded enthusiastically, "I think the proof of the necessity of revelation is capital."[19] He liked the idea that contact with God is necessary for the exercise of man's godlike nature. He urged Hecker to stress clearly the notion of human nature as "really a Godlike nature capable of receiving God [and] incapable of absolute satisfaction by anything else by God." When Simpson spoke of man being satisfied by God he meant not only by teachings, by "mere revealed words and revealed knowledge," but by "a mystic hold, by an actual union with [and] partaking of Divine nature."[20]

Hecker also discussed plans for his second book with his theologically astute fellow Redemptorist missionary, Augustine Hewit. Hecker wrote to Hewit of his conviction that there was in America "a class of minds who by nature are inclined to asceticism and mystical life." But Protestantism, Hecker was convinced, could not meet the needs of these people since it was "deficient in Christian asceticism and [the] mystical life of sanctity."[21]

In 1857 Hecker published his second work, entitling it *Aspirations of Nature*. In the preface, the young missionary described three classes of people to whom his book appealed. First, those born and raised without any definite religious belief, in whom "the religious aspirations of the soul are awakened," who then seek a religion which does not "gainsay the dictates of Reason." Second, those who, after having received religious instruction, turn away from their beliefs as soon as "the eye of Reason opens." And third, those who, having discarded all formal institutional churches, "betake themselves to the different movements of the day in hopes of obtaining the solutions of the dark enigmas of life."[22]

Hecker then proceeded to argue that the religion toward which the aspirations of the heart pointed was one that was also compatible with reason: "The time is gone by, when men can easily be made to believe that that is Religion which leads its votaries to contradict the dictates of Reason."[23] "Human intelligence" must be retained as the "only stable ground for Religion."[24]

Having thus established the importance of reason, Hecker searched for the religion that would satisfy both the aspirations of the heart for a higher, richer life and the dictates of reason. In a section that sounds as if it could have come from his own diary, Isaac put forth what he called "The Confessions of an Earnest Seeker." Surveying the topic of the Church, he concluded that a church which corresponds to both man's religious aspirations and the dictates of his reason must be of divine origin, must be infallible in teaching religious truth, and must yield mankind assistance in its spiritual life.[25]

Hecker then reviewed various philosophical systems to determine whether or not they could meet the criteria which, as he saw it, were set by man's religious sentiments and by reason. Ancient philosophy and modern German and French philosophy, he argued, did not suffice. He concluded: "It is therefore on the plain, positive, and unimpeachable testimony of the philosophers themselves, that we are furnished the basis of the affirmation of the need of a light superior to that of Reason to answer its own demands."[26] The natural light of reason brought man, Hecker contended, to the realization of the need for divine light to fulfill his noble destiny. Thus reason and faith worked hand in hand. Reason preceded faith but did not contradict it.

Isaac next compared the teachings of Protestantism and Catholicism to determine which better gave answer to the "enigmas of Reason." He examined the topics of reason, free will, human nature, and justification, drawing on quotes from Luther, Zwingli, Calvin, and Charles Wesley and arguing that only Catholicism gave reasonable accounts of each. He quoted Abbé Louis Bautain and Pope Pius IX to illustrate the compatibility of reason and Catholic teaching.[27] Catholicism could, Hecker believed, encompass within itself all that was noble in the human community. All the truths of science, all the beauties of the arts, all the achievements of human nature's noblest abilities could be affirmed and complemented. In the Catholic church men could find that union between the natural and the supernatural for which they sought.

Hecker was convinced that Catholicism was the timely answer to the needs not only of various individuals, but of the whole nation. As the individual must resolve the questions of his soul in order to fulfill his destiny, so too a nation must eventually embrace a religion suited to its aspirations and needs before it could attain its destiny. He argued that Catholicism was not only compatible with American institutions but was in fact the religion best suited for the country. The newness and vigor of America offered an opportunity for a fuller acceptance of true religion than had been known in the past. The belief in America as a land in which a brighter, more excellent brand of Christianity would dawn was foundational to Hecker's message.

> Our civilization is young, fresh and in the vigor of its manhood. New elements are at work in it. We cannot repeat the past if we would. The new world promises a new civilization. And in this unfettered civilization, true Religion will find a reception it has in vain looked for elsewhere, and a development of unprecedented glory.[28]

Here was a catholicized version of the belief in the manifest destiny of America that motivated the New York Methodist preachers, the Mormon apostles, and, before them, the Puritans who came to the new world to establish a society in which the glories of the Reformation would attain greater brilliance. Hecker had set an old song to a new tune. With indefatigable enthusiasm he urged America to take steps toward realizing her destiny, which hung on "this moment."[29] Not until the nation embraced true religion could she progress. The young missionary called the nation to a unity of faith not around the standard of the Reformation but around that of the universal Church: ". . . in proportion to the intenseness of the unity of a people in a common religious belief so will be their energy. In proportion to the universality of the principles of their religious belief will be the grandeur of their development."[30]

Isaac's bold vision of the conversion of America to Catholicism motivated him to actively pursue plans for the establishment of an English-speaking Redemptorist house in the country. The idea of founding a house given primarily to the task of American missions had originated with the evangelically-minded Father Bernard. The Redemptorists had been primarily engaged in the work of pastoring the large numbers of German immigrants living in the United States. The demands of this work often left little time for missions. An English-speaking house wholly given to missionary work would provide, it was thought, a basis for a sustained evangelical effort.

The plans for American missions, however, encountered increasing resistance from the Redemptorist hierarchy. In June of 1850, America had been established as an independent province. A year later, Father George Ruland had replaced Father Bernard as the American provincial. Father Ruland and his second consultor, Father Gabriel Rumpler, were not impressed with the whole notion of missions—especially missions to non-Catholics. They favored instead the expansion of pastoral work among German-Americans.

By the end of 1856 a serious difference of opinion had developed between the band of American missionaries and their Redemptorist superior, Father Ruland. Hecker and his cohorts were convinced that their immediate superior possessed erroneous opinions of the American character, as well as of their intentions, which he was passing on to the rector of the Transalpine Redemptorists, Nicholas Mauron. In July 1857 the Americans received a severe reprimand from Father Ruland for pursuing plans for an English-speaking house. When it appeared that plans to establish a Redemptorist house in Quebec would destroy the Americans' hopes and split their band, the decision was made that one of their company must travel to Europe to appeal to Father Mauron in person. In accordance with Redemptorist disciplines, Hecker requested Father Ruland's permission for his journey. Father Ruland refused, arguing that a recent circular from the rector forbade any trip to Rome without the rector's explicit permission. The Americans reasoned, nevertheless, that the Constitution of the congregation had not been nullified by the circular, and that they, therefore, had the right to petition the rector in person.[31]

Obtaining money for his trip from his ever-generous brother George, Isaac quickly made plans to sail for Europe. Before leaving, he and his followers obtained letters of introduction from American bishops McCloskey, Hughes, and James Bayley. Hecker and his friends reasoned that if they encountered opposition from their superiors, they would need the help of some sympathetic persons in the Vatican. When Isaac departed aboard the *Asia* on the morning of August 5, he had with him letters to the powerful prefect of the Propaganda Cardinal Alessandro Barnabo, his secretary Archbishop Cajetan Bedini, and the rector of the Irish College, Monsignor Kirby, who was an expert in Vatican protocol.

As things turned out, the young American Redemptorist found himself in need of all the help he could get. His rector, having received word from Father Ruland that Hecker and company were acting against his will in a spirit of rebellion and self-interest, had little patience with Hecker and his grand vision for an American house. Instead, all that Father Mauron saw was the apparent insubordination of the Americans. After calling in his consultors, who were no more disposed than he to hear Hecker, he issued Isaac a letter of expulsion.

In disbelief Isaac repeatedly read over the shocking letter in his room at the Villa Caserta in Rome. He had come to Rome seeking the good of the congregation, sincerely convinced that once the rector had heard of the situation in America—of the rich opportunities and of the providential circumstances that favored the immediate establishment of an American house—he would gladly bless the project. Instead he had been condemned as an ambitious rebel. Even his effort to save the congregation the expense of his trip was misinterpreted. Receiving money from his brother without having obtained the written permission of his provincial was seen by the Redemptorist hierarchy as a violation of the vow of poverty.

Dejected, Hecker pondered his alternatives. Spurred on by the conviction that his cause was just, he decided that he would appeal his case to the Vatican. As a young man, unfamiliar with the ways of the Vatican, he knew that he faced an uphill battle. Every effort would be made, he was certain, to uphold the rector's decision. How could he convince anyone that Father Mauron had dealt unfairly with him?

Despite the difficulties, Hecker was encouraged by the belief that if Pius IX were to hear his story, he would move to redress the wrongs done in a way which only the pope could. Isaac had been converted to Catholicism through the conviction that the Spirit worked through the church. Surely the Spirit would guide him now. Try as he might, he could not stop believing that God had inspired his vision for American missions. The Spirit's work in his soul could not be contradicted by the church, which was animated by that same Spirit.

Hecker prepared himself for the difficult task ahead. He moved from the Villa Caserta to a more centrally-located apartment on the Piazza di Spagna and immediately began seeking out those influential persons to whom he had letters of introduction. Among those who gave him the most favorable hearing was Cardinal Barnabo. Barnabo, as prefect of the Propaganda, had a concern for missions and a vested interest in the most prolific of his charges—America. He perceived Hecker's sincerity and the importance of his cause for the future of the church in the United States. The Cardinal prefect was free from many of the anti-American prejudices that European hierarchs entertained. He could question the prudence of Hecker's impetuous trip to Rome, however, and he could not doubt that its outcome was most unfortunate. Still, during the next nine months he, more than any other, was Hecker's advocate and guide in his efforts to appeal his case. Through Barnabo's influence, Isaac was able ultimately to plead his cause before Pius IX who, impressed with the young priest's holiness and enthusiasm, granted in March 1858 a cancellation of Hecker's expulsion.

During his time in Rome, Hecker had become convinced through his discussions with Barnabo and others that the situation in America called for a new congregation, constituted specifically with the purpose of missionizing America. Pius IX responded positively to this suggestion, granting Hecker an annulment of his and his American cohorts' Redemptorist vows, plus his papal blessing on the new congregation.

Prior to the resolution of the conflict, Isaac had decided to put his case for American missions into writing. He prepared a two-part series for *La Civiltà Cattolica,* an influential Roman newspaper that had begun in 1850 with the encouragement of Pope Pius IX. Because of the pope's interest in it, its pages were carefully studied by the many clergy who constituted the various Vatican congregations. Although not an official organ of the Holy See, it was widely granted a semi-official status. Hecker had been able to convince *Civiltà*'s editor of the importance of the American cause. His two-part article, translated into Italian, was published anonymously because of his status as a suspended religious.[32]

The article's main thesis was that the time was now ripe for America to embrace Catholicism, which is the religion best suited for that nation. The argument was based on Hecker's analysis of the religious situation in America, which contended that there existed a widespread spiritual hunger that provided a providential opportunity for Catholicism, which alone would fill that hunger. Hecker began his article by asserting that nations, like individuals, are granted special seasons of God's favor to which they must respond if they are to attain their destiny. The church must, Hecker continued, know when such times are occurring in order to cooperate with God's dealings. "The Church is called to employ all her zeal, to set all her energies, to put in operation all her means to second the work of grace and so to aid in the realization of God's great designs."[33]

Hecker then proceeded to list the signs of the times illustrating that America was ripe for Catholicism. After discussing the American form of government and social institutions as favoring true religion in their championing of reason, freedom, and truth, he went on to argue that neither Calvinism nor Unitarianism could "suffice for the aspirations and needs of man's religious nature." He mentioned Brook Farm and Fruitlands as examples of widespread efforts to meet those spiritual longings. America was at present, he contended, a land where many were "serious-minded and dissatisfied with the life around them." "The longing after a more spiritual life" was, he contended, "one of the principal characteristics of the American people." This was illustrated by the great success of the Methodists. Hecker in his *Civiltà* article showed an awareness of movements within mainline churches that countered traditional Calvinism. His mention of Methodism was matched by a discussion of Henry Ward Beecher's *Conflict of Ages* and Catherine Beecher's "Common Sense Applied to the Gospel." Both writings, in Hecker's view, showed the dissatisfaction with the Calvinist doctrine of human nature and were examples of the enlightened mind "working its way up to the discovery of Catholic truth." In addition, Hecker cited the American response to the Oxford movement as another indication of the movement toward deeper spirituality and Catholicism.[34]

Thus did Hecker present to the European Catholic audience his vision of a Catholic America. In seeing the magnitude of his vision, however, we are left wondering how a man like Hecker, who was raised in America, could ever really think that a nation that from its beginnings had been firmly rooted in one of the most staunchly anti-Catholic sectors of Protestantism would suddenly renounce her heritage and embrace the oft-despised religion of Rome. The reasons can be found in Isaac's view of Protestantism and ultimately in his spirituality.

"PROTESTANTISM"

Protestantism, in Isaac's view, was a movement that had seen its day. It had accomplished its purpose and was now effete. Since it lacked the foundation for sustaining true religious belief, it therefore could not meet the demands of the age. One of the chief errors of Protestantism was its doctrine of human nature that asserted its "utter worthlessness."[35] The Lutheran doctrine of the Fall resulted in an understanding of sin as essential to human nature. As Hecker quoted Luther: "Sin is not an act or a phenomenon of our nature, it is our very nature."[36] Calvin's doctrine of total depravity painted the picture even more clearly in Isaac's mind. The 1827 Presbyterian Confession of Faith's condemnation of good works was an outgrowth of this negative view of nature. For Hecker, the "best compendium of these wretched tenets" was the popular proverb: "You'll be damned if you do, you'll be damned if you don't."[37] This view of human nature led to what he believed were inadequate doctrines of justification and sanctification, which denied the possibility of real participation in the divine nature.

When Hecker spoke of Protestantism in *Questions* and *Aspirations,* he spoke of it as a homogeneous entity. In drawing examples from Protestant theologians he centered on the Reformers—Luther, Calvin, Zwingli, Melanchthon. In a style that reflected the influence of Moehler's *Symbolik,* Hecker compared Lutheran, Reformed, and Catholic doctrine on basic theological issues: nature, justification, the Church, etc.[38] As his *Civiltà* article shows, however, Hecker was aware of movements within mainline American Protestantism that rejected the notion of total depravity. Yet, with what might be seen as either arrogance or astuteness, he interpreted such trends as movements toward Catholic truth, and, in that sense, not truly Protestant.

THE CORE OF THE VISION

Hecker's hope in the conversion of America to Catholicism rested in the final analysis on his own experience of God. His own search for God had brought him into contact with many hungry souls seeking a deeper spirituality. He felt sure that his own experience was not unique but typical of his day. He had plunged deeply into the currents of the age—an age that, he believed, was an age of the Spirit, in which concern for the spiritual dimension was paramount. His own journey had enabled him to see and appreciate this. Furthermore, he was certain that his discovery of Catholicism as that form of religion which best met his spiritual hunger and intellectual demands was also typical. He had discovered truth that was generally applicable, that was universal, that was catholic. Convinced that the inner light he followed was in fact a true light, Hecker believed that his own spiritual journey was a model for his countrymen. As he had been led by relying on his true self, following the inner leadings and aspirations of his nature, obeying the dictates of reason and striving to realize his destiny, so too could others. These qualities of his spirituality he saw as typically American. When rightly utilized, they led one to God and to Catholicism. There was no contradiction in being American and Catholic.

Central to his ability to see his own experience as typical was the belief that the Spirit guiding him was in fact the Spirit of God that animated the Church and ordered all things according to God's will. His first-hand, internal relationship with the Holy Spirit made it possible for him to recognize that same Spirit's dealings in the external world. In communing with that Spirit, Hecker's vision was

Orestes A. Brownson
(New York Public Library)

Parley P. Pratt
(New York Public Library)

George Ripley
(New York Public Library)

Dewey's Church of the Messiah
Broadway, New York City
(New York Public Library)

Junction of Broadway and Eighth Avenue, 1861

Church and Rectory of Missionary Society of St. Paul the Apostle, c. 1865
(Paulist Archives, New York)

Bronson Alcott
(New York Public Library)

Interior of Chapel at Redemptorist
Novitiate   St. Trond, Belgium
(Paulist Archives, New York)

Isaac Hecker, c. 1865
(Paulist Archives, New York)

The Young Isaac Hecker
(Paulist Archives, New York)

Scenes from Hecker's Nile Trip, Winter 1873–1874
Top: Riverboat *Sittina Miriam et Adra*, Bottom: Travelers
(Paulist Archives, New York)

thus extended beyond himself. It was universalized. It was catholicized in a twofold sense that involved a process of accommodating the doctrines and practices of Roman Catholicism and a process of taking on a universalized outlook.

With the commencement of mission work in 1851, Isaac became far more active and outgoing than he had been since the change of 1842 first set him on a spiritual search. His letters teemed with enthusiasm over the work and with a concern for the larger-than-personal dimension that was very much secondary in his earlier writing. His own spiritual experience had matured to the point where it was bearing fruits that could be shared with others. Hecker was no longer an introspective, self-effacing youth but a man with a message.

How shall we interpret Hecker's bold missionary vision? Was it the result of a keen ability to discern the signs of the times? Certainly the Oxford Movement had demonstrated that Catholicism could meet the questions serious men were asking about religion. In America, he and his fellow Redemptorists were not alone in their embracing of Catholicism. Had not the influential Brownson also seen the light, and were not a number of other New England intellectuals looking toward Rome with sympathetic eyes? Certainly there were grounds to believe that America would witness a number of conversions to Catholicism.

In moving beyond this to the vision, which never in any significant way materialized, of an America thoroughly catholicized, Hecker illustrated a weakness that was, as is often the case in a personality, the result of the unchecked expression of what was in and of itself an admirable quality. This weakness was associated with his tendency to see his own experience as paradigmatic, which stemmed from a deep faith in God's providence. When unchecked, however, it resulted in a certain myopia that too easily identified his own ways with God's ways.

At times, Isaac appears overconfident of his own convictions; one can even detect a hint of closed-mindedness. Later in life, in the face of pressing personal trials, this easy confidence disappeared, but in 1859 such troubles were as yet unknown to Isaac. These were the days of his strength. These were the times when he saw his dreams materialize, when he was full of expectation and hope.

IX

1858–1867

With the founding of the Paulists in 1858 Hecker entered upon
the central work of his life, the years from then through 1867 being
his busiest. They saw him laboring as the superior of the Paulists,
as pastor of a large urban parish in New York, as missionary and lec-
turer, and as crusader for the Catholic press. In the midst of his great
activity, however, can be discerned the same commitment to the inner life that characterized his younger days. He continued to be radically aware of God as the Holy Spirit dwelling within the soul,
moving in the world, and working in all the circumstances of his life.
His mature spirituality that developed during these years was the
product of the consistent development of earlier themes.

THE VISION TAKES SHAPE

After returning from Rome with the Pope's approbation to found
a religious congregation, Hecker wasted little time in pushing ahead
with the project. The idea of forming a community given to the work
of American missions had been very much in the minds of Hewit,
Francis A. Baker, George M. Deshon, and Hecker, all of whom
were, incidentally, converts from Protestantism. Walworth was from
the start somewhat of two minds about the idea, and he found himself
in again and out again during the following years.

By the summer of 1858 the group had begun to articulate their

118

ideas on the structure and function of their new Congregation, in July drawing up what they called the Programme of the Rule and Constitution of Missionary Priests of Saint Paul the Apostle. The Programme was intended to be a preliminary Rule for the new community until such time as a permanent one could be written. It was submitted to Archbishop John Hughes of New York, under whose jurisdiction the mission band had decided to place itself. The ideas put forth in the Programme clearly reflect Hecker's thinking, and the Congregation was the embodiment of a vision that had long been forming in his heart.

The main purposes of the Congregation as stated in the Programme were the promotion of the personal sanctification of its members and labor for the salvation of others, or, in other words, personal perfection and zeal for souls.[1] The first was to be advanced by living together in community and obedience, as well as by religious exercises including daily common prayer and examination of conscience. The private devotions of spiritual reading, visitation to the Blessed Sacrament and recitation of the rosary were also prescribed. In addition, a weekly chapter of faults and a conference relating to some subject of "theology, rubrics, the manner of giving missions, or some similar topic of common utility" were required. Acts of private and public self-denial were also enjoined. The spirit of mortification was, the Programme stated, "absolutely essential to solid Christian and Religious virtue." Hence members were permitted to "take discipline" in private on Wednesday and Friday evenings and to perform public penances and acts of humility in the refectory. Silence was required at all times in the oratory, refectory, kitchen, and corridors of the community house. The members were to "endeavor to practice a continual recollection, a constant and exact vigilance over themselves, an accurate observance of their spiritual exercises, a fervent and laborious zeal in performing the duties of their ministry and supporting the fatigue and hardships of the Apostolic life."

The second purpose of the Congregation, labor for the salvation of others, was primarily a statement of commitment to missions. Given the need for pastors in the burgeoning American Catholic church of the day, however, Hecker and his fellows knew that limiting themselves to non-Catholic missions would not please the bishops who had the interests of their own flocks in mind. Hence, although the Programme made clear that the second great purpose would be accomplished primarily through "misssions in the spirit of St. Alphonsus," they also opened themselves to taking parishes. The intention of avoiding participation in works that would "hinder or impede" missionary labor was clearly stated. Nevertheless, the tension between parish work and missions, evident even in the Programme, would plague the Congregation in later years.

The more novel aspects of the newly-formed Congregation are not evident from the careful language of the Programme, which was written, it must be remembered, primarily to obtain official episcopal sanction for the new community. Understandably, the ordinary aspects of the community were stressed. The idea that the Paulists' life would be similar in all essential respects to that of the traditional men's congregation was made clear in the opening section of the Programme. In fact, the Paulists differed from other congregations in a number of ways. Isaac's own spirituality formed the basic framework for the conception of the Paulists, and the novel characteristics of the Congregation flowed from it: its understanding of contemplation and action, its emphasis on freedom from external controls and structures, its accent on individuality, and its view of perfection.

The active dimension of the Christian life was most prominent in the band of busy missionaries, who were to travel widely throughout the land. But the outward activity of the Paulist did not mean that he was unacquainted with the contemplative life. On the contrary, Hecker held that contemplation must be the seed of action. True apostolic zeal had to be motivated by the Spirit, not by human ambition. Writing in 1859, Hecker explained the importance of devotion to the Spirit in the life of the Paulist missionary. He maintained that the contemplative life held first place in his esteem. "No man can be successful," he wrote, "without in some degree the gift of contemplative prayer." "All depends," he continued, "on the Holy Ghost being at the bottom and [being the] instigator of our enterprises. This made certain, all else follows, provided we remain faithful, humble, brave."[2]

The Paulists chose not to emphasize external controls and governing structures. They replaced the traditional vows with promises—promises of poverty, chastity, and obedience. But such freedom from external structures was not license to follow one's own fancy. It rested, rather, on the conviction that such external apparatuses were of limited value to men who knew the inner guidance of the Holy Spirit. The Paulists promised obedience to their superiors and to the episcopacy, but these elements were not stressed. To the degree that the individual was faithful to the Spirit's leadings, to that same degree would he be in conformity with the authority of the church. Hecker's belief that the same Spirit that inspired the individual was also the one that animated the church is evident here. He felt that there was no need to place primary reliance on anything but the chief teacher himself, the Holy Spirit. As he expressed it later in life, "What a member of another religious community might do from that divine guidance which is external, the Paulist does from the promptings of the indwelling Holy Spirit."[3]

The freedom that characterized American culture should be put to good use in the religious life, Hecker believed. Greater individual liberty, rather than posing an obstacle to spiritual growth, could promote spiritual health, if purged from the taint of selfishness and rebellion, by providing greater opportunity for cooperation with the Holy Spirit's guidance. Through his own experience Hecker had learned to grow in holiness by a continuous process of yielding to the inner solicitations of the Spirit. He knew the gentleness of the Spirit's work in the soul. Such a disposition could never result from coercion or force but only from a free act of the will.

The emphasis on individuality that characterized Hecker's idea of the Paulists was also grounded on his understanding of the Spirit's work. The notion of a religious community as a unique expression of the Spirit was basic to him. Even as a mature man he was still gripped by the idea inscribed in his early diary that "the Eternal-Absolute is ever creating new forms of expressing itself."[4] In emphasizing the work of the Spirit, he stressed the dynamic, active nature of the godhead. He experienced God's action within his own soul, and he saw it in God's providential dealings throughout the world. As God had inspired him to become part of his action in the world, and had called him to be a channel for divine life, so also God had called a Congregation of men to this same task. Each individual had, Hecker

121

believed, a special destiny; each had a unique part to play in God's grand scheme. Coming together to lead a common life should in no way prevent the individual from attaining that special destiny, but should, rather, be an aid. As he later wrote: "A Paulist is to emphasize individuality." It is to be an "internal and conspicuous element in the life of a Paulist."[5] So much must individuality be prized that one should "prefer to suffer from the excesses of liberty rather than from the arbitrary actions of tyranny."[6]

SPREADING THE GOOD NEWS

From the latter part of 1858 until the spring of 1865, Hecker and his fellow Paulists carried on parish missions similar to those undertaken while they were Redemptorists. There was scarcely a city of any size in the United States and Canada that the Paulist mission bands did not reach, including Southern cities before the War made it impossible.[7] From the start, however, the missions were hindered by a lack of manpower. Hecker was particular in admitting men into the Congregation. Convinced that the life of the Paulist was a special vocation, he sought men of quick mind and spiritual character suited to the group's style. He wanted men who were already attuned to the inner guidance of the Spirit, men whose thirst for personal holiness was deep and who had a zeal for souls. Such stringent criteria were not easily met. With the death of Baker in 1865, the Congregation was forced to suspend parish missions because of a shortage of personnel.

Although the work in parish missions was thus curtailed, Hecker's desire to missionize non-Catholic America found other channels. One such channel was the public lecture. During the 1860s, Hecker came into demand as a featured speaker. The public lecture format provided the chance to address the non-Catholic in precisely the fashion Isaac desired. He chose provocative topics aimed to arouse the interest of his audience. He sought to present Catholicism as the religion best suited for the Republic, to demonstrate the compatibility of religion and the highest aspirations and capacities of man, and to show the superiority of Catholicism to Protestantism. His approach was positive and optimistic. He spoke in a flowing, extemporaneous style, captivating his hearers with his quick wit and pithy aphorisms. By 1867 Hecker's reputation was winning him invitations to lectures throughout the nation. Between 1867 and 1869, his busiest years, the Paulist missionary delivered more than fifty-six lecture series. From Boston's Tremont Temple to Chicago's Liberty Hall, in Hartford, Providence, and St. Louis, Isaac found those hungry souls for whom he had long been concerned. During an 1868 tour to the West, he traveled more than 4,500 miles, lecturing twenty-five times to more than 30,000 people, two-thirds of whom were non-Catholics.[8]

Despite the hardships of travel, Isaac found special enjoyment in these missionary labors. Speaking to non-Catholic Americans was his chief joy; nothing was nearer to his heart. He felt a warm affection for his Protestant countrymen, sympathized with their concerns, and was at ease in their company. Yet he was straightforward in his defense of Catholic teaching, and some who heard him were offended by his boldness. The Chicago Congregationalist magazine, *The Advance,* described Hecker's lectures as sheer "effrontery."[9] But others, in fact most others, were charmed by him. His affectionate manner, his common-sense approach, and his frequent allusions to his own experience made them willing to hear from him ideas that in the mouths of other more contrary souls they would never have tolerated. Walter Elliott recorded his first impression of Hecker on the lectern:

We never can forget how distinctively American was the impression of his personality. We heard the nation's greatest men then living, and their type was too familiar to be successfully counterfeited. Father Hecker was so plainly a great man of this type, so evidently an outgrowth of our institutions, that he stamped America on every Catholic argument he proposed.[10]

Hecker was a Catholic counterpart to the Protestant princes of the pulpit who, especially after 1865, engaged in an effort to defend the claims of Christianity in the face of the new ideas that threatened the Faith. The rise of historical biblical criticism, the new theories concerning the origin of the species and creation, the growth of cities and the unchurched masses within the metropolises—all presented new challenges to the Church. Hecker attempted, as did preachers like Henry Ward Beecher and Phillips Brooks, to reconcile Christianity with the modern world.[11] An article in an 1868 issue of the *Atlantic Monthly*, written by the Protestant James Parton, remarked, "It is he [Father Hecker] who is putting American machinery into the ancient ark and getting ready to run her by steam."[12]

Among Hecker's more effective lectures were "The Church and the Republic," "Luther and the Reformation," "How and Why I Became a Catholic," "The State of Religion in the United States," " A Search after Rational Christianity," and "The Church and Society." These lectures were especially popular with what one observer described as the "humanitarians, nationalists, indifferentists, and skeptics" of the day.[13] Hecker himself was heartened with the results. He wrote to his friend, Cardinal Barnabo, after one of his early lectures: "The interest shown by my audience was remarkable, and the effect was equal to my hopes. My experience convinces me that, if this work were continued, it would prepare the way for a great change of religion in this country . . . ."[14]

THE PARISH ON 59TH STREET

Under the patronage of Archbishop John Hughes, the Paulists were given charge of a parish on 59th Street and 9th Avenue. In the late 1850s this section was sparsely populated with squatters' shanties and an occasional farmhouse. The suburban character of the parish pleased Isaac who found time in his busy schedule to cultivate a little garden patch on the church grounds. As he tilled his patch, which rested in the shadow of the convent and large church, his thoughts ran back to the gardens he had cultivated at Brook Farm. All around him stood the embodiment of his own unique vision, so different from the one that motivated the Transcendental utopians, but yet—in its idealism, in its search for truth, in its goal of improving society—so similar.

Despite the remoteness of the 59th Street church, its fast-growing reputation for first-rate liturgy began drawing a rather sophisticated membership. Quality preaching and congregational singing, both a heritage from the Protestant backgrounds of the early Paulists, gave the church a lively, provocative appeal to converts and non-Catholic inquirers. Like his Methodist counterparts, Hecker was also quite interested in establishing a Sunday school for children. He especially delighted in this work, frequently visiting the children's classrooms and affectionately embracing his tiny parishioners.

Each Sunday at the High Mass a major sermon was preached by one of the Fathers. During the 1860s Father Hecker took his turn on the pulpit. By now a seasoned public speaker, this man whom some described as a "born orator," treated his parishioners to the same brand of persuasive, stimulating discourse that was earning him a national reputation. His sermons generally followed a similar pattern. Each began with a text from Scripture, often but not always from the Gospel reading for the day. In a direct, straightforward manner, Hecker then proceeded to draw out one main point from the text, which he then embellished with numerous illustrations and reinforced with abundant Scripture references. The Scriptures were dealt with carefully and used to supply authority to the various assertions. Repeatedly, Isaac revealed his high estimate of the inspired nature of the biblical text, describing it with such phrases as the "voice of the Holy Spirit."[15] Each sermon ended with a practical application of the spiritual truth being expounded in which the listeners were often given rather concrete suggestions on how they could apply the principles they had heard to their own lives. The sermons reflected Hecker's optimistic view of human nature, his estimation of the importance of free will in the Christian life, and his love of action. They radiated with confidence and boldness and were clearly the productions of a man and a church that had come of age.

In one such sermon, entitled "Giving Testimony," Hecker urged his hearers to unashamedly give witness in word and in deed to their faith. He listed four classes of people who fail to give testimony. Hecker's missionary bent prompted him to castigate the "silent Catholic[s]," "the confessing Catholics who never go to church," the "occasional visitors," and the "rank and file sinners." In the last category he placed those involved in the sale and production of liquor. Hecker and his fellow Paulists, like many of their Protestant contemporaries, repeatedly spoke out against the abuses of alcohol, unrelentingly blasting those involved in the liquor trade. "The grog-shop keepers," Hecker declared, "are the worst enemies of our holy religion in this country, for they are not only a snare to Catholics but a bad witness to non-Catholics."[16]

GOING ON TO PERFECTION

The concern for reconciling the tasks of everyday life with the pursuit of Christian perfection, which Isaac had seen in Methodism and in Orville Dewey's preaching, surfaced in his own thought during the 1860s. His work as a pastor forced him to deal with the problems confronted by the laity in their quest for sanctity outside the monastery walls. Repeatedly he dwelt on this theme. His definition of perfection was in 1860 essentially what it had been in 1843: perfection was union with God. The more completely the individual participated in the divine nature, the more thorough the synthesis between human and divine, the more he progressed along the *via perfectionis*.

Soon after commencing his career as pastor he began expressing a desire to write his third book on the subject of perfection. As early as July 1860, he had begun writing a manuscript on spirituality for the laity that centered on the theme of perfection. The next year he began sharing his thoughts on this topic with his old friend, Richard Simpson. In a February letter to Simpson, Hecker stated his conviction: "There is no other way of perfection for the great mass of Christians than in the performance of the common duties of life with an eye toward God."[17]

In his fragmentary, yet pithy notes on Christian perfection, Hecker was concerned with correcting certain wrong ideas about the spiritual life. He stated his intention "to set aside any antagonism that has been created by heated imagination, false theology, and false philosophy between practical ordinary life, and true piety."[18] Characteristically, Hecker blamed Protestantism, especially Calvinism, for these wrong notions. He even was so bold as to assert that Protestant exaggeration of the role of private judgment had forced the Catholic church to insist upon external authority, and this in turn had its influence on the practice of asceticism. A basically Calvinistic

view of human depravity "crept into" Catholic asceticism, resulting
in an exaggerated notion of mortification which taught that one must
renounce the world, abandon reason, and uproot his passions. Asceticism rightly understood, however, had as its object "not the destruction of our nature but its restitution to its primitive relations
with nature and all things." If human nature is not essentially evil
and if grace in its working presupposes and perfects nature, then,
Hecker reasoned, the pursuit of Christian perfection and the discharging of the duties of the normal, everyday life should not conflict.
"Why is it," he asked, "that we seek to please God . . . by the performance of works or acts of devotion which are not required of us,
while neglecting those which He has enjoined, as those duties of our
condition of life . . . ."[19]

To the aspirant after the holy life Hecker said: Return to the
situation in which God by his providence has placed you and there
begin to work out your salvation. He wrote of the need to embrace
God in the present situation:

> One will be perfect when the other will convert—and al-
> ways that is to-morrow. . . . Are not the opportunities to-
> day to serve God as good as those of to-morrow? Is the grace
> of God not as powerful [today] as to-morrow? Since time be-
> gan was there a moment in which you could serve God bet-
> ter than the present one? Up! and be doing, seize hold of
> the great realities of life in the present . . . .[20]

Such a vision of the way to perfection rested on Hecker's ability
to see God as the Lord of all creation who ordered all things according
to his good pleasure. If God was the creator of the natural as well
as the supernatural order, if he not only made the world but sustained it with his life-giving Spirit, then one need not turn his back
on everything human to know the divine. "The internal life," Hecker
wrote, "requires more than renunciation." It required, in fact, what
Isaac had, namely, the ability to experience God in all things, to see
that, as Elizabeth Barrett Browning proclaimed in "Aurora Leigh,"
"Earth's crammed with heaven." As Hecker put it: "Genuine piety
calls upon all that is within, and all that is without to praise the

Lord. . . . For God is the ground of all created being."[21] This view of God as the ground of all being and of creation as a tool for the attainment of God's will reflects not only the speculations of Hecker's old Transcendental associates, but even more vividly an Ignatian view of all creation as tending to glorify God, which Hecker found in Lallemant's *Spiritual Doctrine*.[22] Hecker also drew support for this view from St. John Chrysostom. He cited the Greek Father in discussing the advisability of considering even irrational creatures to learn from them lessons in the spiritual life, and in contending that perfection may be attained outside the religious life.[23]

The best way for one to learn to see God's hand in all created things, Isaac believed, was by beginning to see God's work within the soul. "The great thing to be learned," he wrote, "is that the only great object in life is to live up to the light of God in the soul."[24] Unless one understood this, one was apt, Isaac thought, to set a false standard of perfection for oneself. A wrong standard was, in his view, the greatest obstacle to beginners in the spiritual life. They raise a standard of perfection that is beyond their power to reach, and after failing, they are disheartened.

A false standard of perfection along with an underestimation of natural powers to do good resulted, in Hecker's view, in "a false reliance on the power of God's grace which begets . . . pusillanimity which passes among some for humility."[25] An attempt to be thus delivered from the trials and sufferings of life caused one to miss the opportunity to learn to overcome by "resignation to God's holy will, by patience, confidence and other Christian virtues." Paradise, he urged, inspired by Philip Neri, "is not for cowards."[26] Instead Hecker put forth a doctrine of perfection that stressed the courageous, the joyous, the triumphant. "Some people think," he wrote, "that the practice of Christian perfection . . . necessarily produces a long face . . . this is not Christianity. . . . We read rejoice, rejoice, serve the Lord with gladness!"[27] He strove to get people excited about God and the prospects of sharing the divine nature. The holiness he preached was practical and positive, stressing the here-and-now merits of sanctity. "Let us not entertain," he wrote, "the folly that our perfection consists in floating on roses to clouds with trumpets in our mouths and swelling cheeks."[28] The heaven he sought was not an escape from the unpleasantries of the world, but rather the complement of the joy and happiness we find now on earth.

Two of Hecker's favorite models of this type of sanctity were St. Joseph and St. Catherine of Genoa. In 1863 Isaac preached a sermon on the former entitled "The Model Saint for Our Day." Joseph found perfection in the course of his everyday life as a father and laborer. The nineteenth century was, Hecker argued, one in which the prevailing type of Christian perfection was that which was worked out not in the monastery, but in the busy markets, counting rooms, and homes—in everyday life. Joseph used the elements of the common life as instruments for growing in grace. He was a many-sided man who could engage the world in a variety of ways and yet know a high level of holiness.[29]

THE CURE OF SOULS

In the first half of the 1860s, while deeply involved in pastoral labors, Hecker carried on an extended correspondence with Mrs. Jane King. Mrs. King, the widowed mother of two young children, at one time worked for James T. Fields on the staff of the *Atlantic Monthly*. She had sought out the Paulist founder as a spiritual director sometime in the early 1860s. He carried out a good deal of the pastoral direction in letters to her during years of correspondence between the two. From 1863 to 1865 the correspondence was brisk. In his letters to Mrs. King, Isaac made plain his ideas on spiritual direction and a number of topics concerning the interior life. From the volume of correspondence, as well as from Hecker's remarks, Mrs. King seems to have been an avid disciple whose teachableness pleased him. Hecker once wrote to her, "Could I only do for several others as I have done for you . . . my joy . . . would be complete."[30]

Hecker's technique of spiritual direction developed out of his experience of God. Although he drew on the work of certain spiritual writers, especially Lallemant, he always remained an original thinker. He read in the 1860s, as he had twenty years previously, for inspiration. When he found in others something that resonated with his own experience, he appropriated it. What he counseled Mrs. King to do was something he himself had done. When he explained to her a spiritual principle, it was one he had come to know through his own experience. Comparing Hecker's letters of direction with his own private writings of the time, one is struck with the fact that there is no disparity between his public and private statements. He did not hide the counsels of his heart from his disciple.

Axiomatic to Hecker's technique of spiritual direction was the belief that the Holy Spirit is the primary director of the soul. Father Hecker repeatedly made this point to Mrs. King. "Our primary study," he wrote in March 1863, "is to bring ourselves under the influence of divine grace, and the guidance of the Holy Ghost."[31] He stressed that the soul is cultivated for "the complete direction of the Holy Spirit, of God, of the Sanctifier," and that all external means— all practices of piety, spiritual reading, even the reception of the sacraments—are important only insofar as they lead to this end. So firmly did Hecker believe this that he attempted to give as much room as possible for the Spirit's work in the individual. His approach was never dictatorial. It was constantly gentle and encouraging, focusing on spiritual truths in an effort to bring individuals to a place where they could personally experience them. Hecker was not concerned with imposing his own experience on others. He wrote to Mrs. King:

Every day I feel more and more delicate about giving spiritual advice to others, lest I may interfere with the divine work of the Holy Ghost on their souls. . . . I feel jealous for the rights of God as the First and Supreme Director of Souls.[32]

Isaac saw his task as director primarily in terms of helping the individual to remove whatever hindrances existed to receiving the internal direction of the Spirit. This approach corresponded perfectly with his understanding of the capacities of the soul for divine communion. Once the hindrances of sin and lust were removed, the soul would instinctively respond to God. Asceticism functioned, as Hecker preached in his sermons of this period, to remove such hindrances, not to destroy nature. The doctrine of perfection that he expounded to Mrs. King corresponded with that put forth in his unpublished manuscripts of the time. He told his disciple that the primary means to perfection was fidelity to the Holy Spirit's inspirations. With each soul the Spirit worked in a personal, individual manner. "Every soul that is true to God," Hecker wrote in July 1863, "has something unusual." Isaac was still committed to the notion of the individual's worth that he had encountered in the Romantics. But he also remained convinced that grace was necessary for the individual to attain his special destiny. Thus he continued in the same letter, "Our nature is robbed of its truest and highest expression apart from grace."[33] The work of unfolding the fullness of the soul's unique nature was the work of the Spirit. Thus each soul must "study the way in which the Holy Ghost attracts it, be faithful to that *attrait*, and not depart on any account from it."[34]

The newness and vigor that Hecker saw as he traversed the nation in an age of unbounded optimism convinced him that in American spirituality there could be a synthesis between true piety and all that was good in modern civilization. The American Catholic, incorporating in his character a deep sensitivity to the divine reality with an openness to the very best that nineteenth-century man could attain, would stand forth, Isaac believed, as a model of a renewed Christianity. This was the type of character Hecker strove to produce through all his spiritual direction. If such a character were produced in the Catholics of the land, he felt it would be a compelling witness to Protestant America of the value of Catholicism. He wrote:

> This type of character will be superior to any that can be produced by a false or incomplete form of Christianity, hence attractive, and the means of bringing the truth of our religion to bear on the minds of our countrymen. Personal perfection is a means of the conversion of our country.[35]

As a laywoman, Mrs. King was the ideal subject for Hecker's doctrine of perfection as attained through the discharging of everyday affairs with an eye toward God. In counseling Mrs. King, Hecker indicated how his own spirituality had matured along these lines. His desire to do God's will, which from his childhood days had compelled him, now in his maturity was at the center of his heart. He wrote in 1864: "This is my daily, hourly, and only study, to surrender myself more completely to the guidance of God." What in fact God called him to—whether action or inactivity—was essentially unimportant. "God's will," he wrote, "makes all actions equally great . . . ."[36]

Over the years Hecker learned more fully the lesson that he had begun in 1842. He learned that God's will and his will were not always identical. He came to see that God's will was something much bigger than himself. It was something which required his submission. He realized that he had to wait upon God until the divine will became clear, and then resign himself to it. In a passage from a letter to Mrs. King, Hecker revealed how important this had become for him. "I do not know how it sounds in your ears," wrote the busy pastor, "that a man of such activity as I am supposed to be and really am, should talk constantly of waiting, of letting God speak in us and through us." Referring to his own internal history, in which, he said, this lesson was learned by "years of silence, humiliation, and inaction," he then concluded, "I would rather die alone in solitude, defeated in sight of the world on all points, than to move from this basis."[37]

LEARNING FROM THE MASTERS

Among the spiritual writers whose works Hecker and Mrs. King discussed were St. Francis de Sales, Augustine Baker, Catherine of Genoa, Julian of Norwich, Tauler, and Louis Lallemant. Hecker's three favorites were Catherine, Julian, and his old friend, Lallemant. After reading the *Revelations* of Julian, Hecker told Mrs. King that it was among the finest spiritual writings he had ever read. It commanded his full sympathy and assent. Catherine's *Purgatory* continued to claim its spot as one of the "chefs–d'oeuvre of the spiritual life."[38] But the highest praise was reserved for Lallemant's *Spiritual Doctrine*. Since being introduced to the French Jesuit's work in the novitiate, Hecker had often meditated on its pages. In a July 1863 letter to Mrs. King, Hecker revealed his indebtedness to Lallemant:

He has been my constant companion these twelve years past. I have but to think of his name and the contents of his book are present to my mind. . . . Appropriate his doctrines and sentiments, and I have nothing in addition to give or teach you.[39]

Hecker was convinced that Lallemant's doctrine was peculiarly well fitted for American converts. He suggested to Mrs. King that she rewrite an American version of the work and persuade James Fields to publish it with his publishing company, Ticknor and Fields. In January 1865 Hecker suggested how the work might be arranged, with the hopes that its doctrines might be thus rendered clear and more consistent.[40]

THE APOSTOLATE OF THE PRESS

Hecker's hopes for publishing an American version of Lallemant stemmed from his conviction that his country needed more good Catholic literature than was then available. Along with an edition of Lallemant, Isaac suggested that Mrs. King might urge Fields to also bring out Julian's *Revelations* and Catherine's *Purgatory*.[41] Hecker was becoming increasingly cognizant of the power of the press. From his childhood he was aware of the way in which the Methodists had been using the printed word to effectively spread their message. There was no American Catholic equivalent of successful magazines like the *Methodist Quarterly Review*. Neither was there any Catholic agency in the land that could produce and distribute low-cost literature to compete with the Methodist Book Concern or American Tract Society. Hecker's concern that this situation be remedied led him to promote the cause of the Catholic press in America.

By January 1865, Hecker had concretized plans for the publication of a monthly Catholic periodical devoted to current religious themes. The decision was made to begin with an eclectic review that would take its material from leading European Catholic theological journals. John Hassard was to function as editor, Edward Kehoe as the "businessman" and George Hecker as the "money-man."[42] The monthly was to be called *The Catholic World*, a name that suggests both Isaac's universal vision of the Church and his bold hope for the catholicization of the globe. The first issue was published in April 1865. After one successful year, the decision was made to begin soliciting original articles. In May 1866 *The Catholic World* carried Paulist Augustine Hewit's "Problems of the Age." During the ensuing months, the magazine was able to attract a number of original pieces whose literary merit equaled or surpassed that of the European articles. This was in no small measure due to the efforts of the master journalist, Orestes Brownson.

The relationship between Brownson and Hecker had remained cordial over the years. They regularly exchanged letters and held one another in the highest esteem. At Hecker's advice, Brownson had moved from Boston to New York when his views on the Irish character and his adaptation of Italian philosopher Vicenzo Gioberti's controversial ontological theories brought him into disfavor with certain Catholics. Isaac's love for his former mentor and high regard of his talents moved him in 1864 to establish an annuity for Brownson's support. Earlier that same year Brownson had been forced to suspend publication of the *Brownson Quarterly Review* due to the storm that had arisen around his ideas. With the establishment of *The Catholic World* in 1865, a new forum for Brownson was opened. He eventually became one of the chief contributors. By 1868, however, certain differences of opinion among Brownson, Hewit, and Hecker began to erupt. At certain points during the next year the relationship between Hecker and Brownson was severely strained, with Brownson objecting to Hewit's and Hecker's editing of his articles and criticizing what he deemed Hecker's liberal tendencies. Among the elements of Hecker's behavior that were disagreeable to Brownson was Hecker's willingness to emphasize the good side of certain religious movements outside the Catholic church. By the 1860s Brownson had become rather militantly conservative and had grown far less sanguine about the prospects of reconciling American life with Catholic principles. When Hecker spoke sympathetically about such movements as spiritualism, Brownson recoiled. Whereas Hecker saw this movement as a sign of the spiritual hunger of the age, Brownson could only deem it "bad, Satanic, on all sides."[43] Despite their differences, Isaac continued to esteem his old friend. In the 1880s he wrote a series of articles eulogizing Brownson in *The Catholic World* which are a clear statement of that esteem and admiration.

Hecker's involvement with the press was not limited to *The*

Catholic World. In 1866, he founded the Catholic Publication Society, and in 1870 a magazine for children, *The Young Catholic.* The Catholic Publication Society was designed to disseminate Catholic doctrine on a large scale, primarily to non-Catholics. It eventually issued more than seventy tracts which were distributed free of charge. The tracts were aimed at non-Catholics and dealt with elements of Catholic doctrine in a provocative manner. Hecker envisioned the establishment of local societies to distribute the material throughout the nation. The venture was not designed to be self-supporting and, therefore, relied on the contributions of the faithful. Hecker's efforts to raise support included a stirring address to the Second Plenary Council in Baltimore which in response wholeheartedly endorsed the Catholic Publication Society's activities. The more urgent concerns of the rapidly expanding church, however, prevented the enterprise from ever gaining the financial support it needed. The Society eventually became a conventional publishing house with George Hecker the prime backer. In 1874, the Society realized one of Father Hecker's earlier plans with the publication of *The Life and Doctrine of St. Catherine of Genoa.*

Although Isaac had certain Catholic models for the Catholic Publication Society in France and Germany, his vision was largely influenced by the Protestant publishing operations with which he was familiar. His willingness to adopt techniques used by Protestants was criticized by Brownson in a June 1868 letter to Catholic publisher James Sadlier. Hecker, Brownson complained, was "too much disposed to adopt and appropriate the machinery of the Sects."[44]

In 1867, Isaac was in the golden age of his active ministry. For years he had longed to realize the sense of divine calling that dwelt in him. With the founding of the Paulists, he had moved closer than ever to that realization. He was now the Superior of a band of men who, he hoped, shared his vision for a reformed America and a renewed Church. But even in the midst of the prosperity that surrounded his labors there lurked a certain uneasiness. He desired still more. Many of his bold visions and hopes were as yet unfulfilled. He was convinced that the circumstances were right for the success of his plans. The times demanded action; the fields were white with harvest. As Isaac looked about him he saw the hand of providence confirming what he heard the Spirit whispering to his heart. But still the imperfections of this life persisted, slowing progress. He still had to struggle to realize the ideal that burned in his breast. Little did he know as he busily labored in his 59th Street parish that the struggle would soon grow to unimagined intensity.

X

THE TRIAL AND THE TRIUMPH

The years 1867–1875 were a time of grand excitement, unexpected change, and severe trial for Hecker. In the late 1860s he was in the prime of his active ministry. His influence was spreading throughout America and across the Atlantic. He was thrilled by the progress he saw; he was inspired by the possibilities of the moment. The vision he had long pursued was slowly being realized. Yet not all was well. Beneath the surface there raged tensions that were taking their toll on Isaac's physical and psychological health.

THE COUNCIL OF MALINES

As early as the spring of 1867, Hecker began promoting the idea of a Catholic Congress.[1] Inspired by German and Belgian examples, he conceived plans for a national conference to be attended by clerical and lay delegates, which would discuss the present religious, political, and cultural situation in America in an effort to determine the most effective means for exerting a Catholic influence on the country. On the advice of Archbishop John McCloskey of Albany, Hecker decided to visit one of the more successful such congresses of this type in Europe in order to observe its functioning. His plans to attend the 1867 Congress of Malines received the support of his 59th Street congregation, which presented him and Father Hewit with three thousand dollars for traveling expenses. Prominent Catholic newspapers, the *New York Tablet*, the *Freeman's Journal*, and the *Pilot* of Boston all extended their good wishes.[2] The hope was voiced that Hecker would not only learn information profitable to the American church but would also present European Catholics with a bright picture of the progress of Catholicism in the United States.[3]

While attending the Belgian conference, Isaac was able to realize these two goals. He diligently studied the organization of the Council and heard addresses by some leading European Catholics of the day: Hecker's old Redemptorist teacher Victor Dechamps, then Bishop of Namur; Bishop Félix Dupanloup of Orléans; and the Carmelite Père Hyacinthe, whose keynote address on the final day was a defense of the workingman's rights. Hecker himself addressed the Council on the religious situation in the United States. His message reflected Hecker's abiding belief that the future of America was in the hands of Catholics. Protestantism, he argued in a style reminiscent of an earlier St. Simonian influence, had lost its power to be a positive force in American society. Catholicism, on the other hand, was able to provide the nation with the moral, intellectual, and spiritual resources necessary for continued progress.[4]

VATICAN I

Hecker's labors in the apostolate of the press, his lectures to non-Catholics, and his successful church at 59th Street earned him the respect of the hierarchy. In 1869, Pope Pius IX himself wrote to the Paulist founder praising his work, especially that of the Catholic press. Later that same year when Pius IX convened the First Vatican Council, the ailing Bishop Sylvester H. Rosecrans of Columbus appointed Hecker to go as his procurator. When the large attendance at the Council made it impossible for procurators to be admitted to the general sessions, Hecker was named by Bishop James Gibbons of North Carolina as his *peritus* theologian. In this capacity, Hecker was allowed to read the Council documents, learn what took place in discussions among the delegates, and attend meetings of the American bishops.

The great question of the Council was papal infallibility. It exercised the minds of Catholics and non-Catholics alike. Civil rulers feared that Rome would try to reinstate the temporal powers of the pope in an age when those powers had been severely limited. Church-men were curious to see the way in which the Council would define this ancient doctrine. Those in lands like America where there was a large non-Catholic population feared that the wrong definition would create new barriers between themselves and other Christians. The laity likewise was pensive. Would papal infallibility be declared as a dogma that must be accepted? What would one do if one found the definition unacceptable?

Such widespread curiosity had caused Hecker to address the question of infallibility before leaving for the Council. In his farewell sermon preached to his congregation at St. Paul's, he took up the question of what course of action the Council might undertake. The interest in the Council among the non-Catholic world Isaac found amusing. He saw it as a sign of an apprehension that the church might soon awake, as it were, from her slumber and begin exerting a powerful influence in the modern world's affairs. As to the question of what in particular the Council might do, Hecker had little else to say than to plainly state his conviction that the Council would do all that God the Holy Spirit willed—no more and no less.[5]

Because of his understanding of the church as the Body of Christ on earth perpetually animated by the Holy Spirit, Hecker did not object to the theory of papal infallibility itself. Whether or not he felt that a definition of infallibility was opportune for the time was, however, another matter. Hecker was friendly with some of the leading opponents of the opportuneness of the definition among the American bishops—Thomas L. Connolly of Halifax and John Lan-caster Spalding of Peoria. Like many of the inopportunists, Isaac left Rome before the final vote on the question was taken, but to draw inferences from these facts alone is perilous. What is certain, how-ever, from the many later references in his writings to the Council's work is that once the definition of infallibility had been made, he wholeheartedly embraced it. To do otherwise would have been out of line with his spirituality grounded on the belief that the ideal church, which was the channel for Christ's graces to humanity, was in fact the real, historical Roman Catholic church and that God's providential dealings in the world must be seen as a revelation of his will. Thus when the Council defined infallibility, Hecker saw it as an event that would function to advance God's Kingdom on earth.

After leaving the Council in the spring of 1870, Hecker spent some time visiting a number of shrines and memorials in Italy before returning home. At Rome he visited the tombs of the martyrs and was moved to tears while preaching a sermon in the catacombs. On April 28 he left Rome, journeying to Assisi. Seeing the town in which Francis had lived, he was inspired to speculate on the significance of Francis' work. "What Saint Francis did for his age," Hecker wrote in his journal, "one might do for our own. He touched the chords of feeling and aspiration of the hearts of his time, and organized them for united action."[6] What the age called for, Isaac reasoned, was not individuals attempting to relive the life of Francis, but individuals filled with Francis' genius who could freshly address their age as Francis had his.

From Assisi he traveled to Genoa and there viewed the body of St. Catherine. As he gazed in wonderment at the miraculously preserved body lying in the chapel of the hospital where Catherine had lived a life of sanctity and service, he thought of how well she had learned to reconcile fidelity to the interior direction of the Spirit with perfect obedience to the authority of the Church, at a time when the latter was particulary difficult. How relevant a lesson for his own age, he mused.

As Hecker traveled throughout Italy, he was strengthened in his conviction of the need for a spiritual revival within Christendom, and of America's special role in bringing about such a renewal. He saw a parallel between the political and religious movements of the day. As Europe was being politically renewed through the influence of American democratic ideals, so too, he speculated, could it be spiritually revived through the influence of the new world. Europe needed individuals who were free from effete traditions and loyalties and who were motivated by a "fresh view and contemplation of the truth." He wondered whether it would not be advantageous for communities based on the Paulist model to be established throughout Europe.[7] Looking forward to his return to New York, he was glad to leave the old world, more convinced than ever of the importance of his work at home. He wrote in February 1870: "No one of my previous convictions has been disturbed, but much strengthened. . . . I shall return with the resolution to continue them with more confidence, more zeal, more energy."[8]

THE SOUL'S DARK NIGHT

Little did Isaac suspect that less than a year and a half after his June 1870 return to New York, a serious breakdown of his health would greatly impair his ability to carry on his mission. By late 1871 Hecker's physical strength had been robbed by a disease that plagued him relentlessly until his death some seventeen years later. The malady was diagnosed by his physicians as a blood disorder that was compounded by acute angina pectoris. The effect was to make continued work as superior, pastor, and editor impossible. He spent the winter of 1872–1873 in the Southern states, but that failed to bring relief, and on the recommendations of his physicians he departed once again for Europe the following summer. Financed as always by his faithful brother George, he traveled to the health spa at Ragatz. The resort town in the Saint Gall region of Switzerland was famed for its hot mineral water baths. There, amid the breathtaking gorges and the ancient ruins of Nydberg, Isaac could forget the tensions of his busy New York routine. This was his fifth trip to Europe. Each time in the past he had journeyed with the hope of finding spiritual light and life; now he searched not only for those but also for his physical survival.

Hecker's physical suffering was accompanied by a deep inner struggle which the medicinal waters of Ragatz could not soothe. Seemingly cut off in his prime from the work to which he had so wholeheartedly consecrated himself, Isaac found the present turn of events difficult to understand. How was it that after bringing about the fruition of his past plans, God would now, when things were beginning to happen, when new horizons were opening, suddenly remove him from it all? All that he could comprehend was that God was trying him and that he must somehow have the fortitude to endure, but of the future he could offer no word of assurance. He told his Paulist brethren when leaving for Europe, "Look upon me as a dead man . . . . God is trying me severely in soul and body, and I must have the courage to suffer crucifixion."9

Along with the puzzling facts that he had been deprived of the physical ability to carry on his work, cut off from friends and country, and left to wander Europe in search of health, Isaac also experienced an added trial in his inner communion with God. Weakened in spirit and body, the once active and successful Paulist was becoming increasingly aware of his own feebleness before the Almighty. He told of his experience:

> There was once a priest who had been very active for God, until at last God gave him a knowledge of the Divine Majesty. After seeing the majesty of God that priest felt very strange and was much humbled, and knew how little a thing he was in comparison with God.10

He now felt the vanity of all things pressing down upon him as he struggled with the burden of a body that would no longer carry out the dictates of his still active mind. Gone was the easy confidence of the days when he stood before the crowds convinced that he was God's representative.

Despite the darkness, Isaac persisted in searching for the light. He had been ushered into a closer relationship with God some thirty years before by a period of trial and perplexity and had known anguish of soul in the long conflict with the Redemptorist hierarchy that resulted in the formation of the Paulists. Repeatedly he had studied the works of spiritual masters like Catherine of Genoa and John of the Cross, who spoke frequently of the purgative value of suffering. Desiring spiritual nourishment, his soul torn with grief, he came upon a work that, more than any other, spoke to him directly. As he read J. P. de Caussade's *Abandonment; or Absolute Surrender to Divine Providence,* Isaac found words of comfort that helped him make some sense of his present situation.

Caussade's book presented Isaac with two fundamental principles. The first was that nothing happens in the world that is not in some sense God's will. The divine action is everywhere and is always present. "All creatures," wrote Caussade, "are living in the hand of

God. The least moment and the smallest atom contain a portion of this hidden life, this divine action."[11] The second principle the work put forth was that God can will nothing, can permit nothing that does not correspond to the great end he purposed in creation, namely, his own glory.[12] All of creation is therefore God's instrument, functioning to ultimately advance this glory, and man's ultimate happiness as a creature is, then, to be found in submitting to God's designs. Thus in abandonment to God's providential dealings through the instrumentality of all creation, man has nothing to fear. Once the individual has surrendered himself to God, all that follows is the work of God and not man. In Caussade's words, "God asks nothing more of this soul than to blindly receive all that He sends, in a spirit of submission and universal indifference to the instruments of this will." He continued, "In all things we must love God and His order; we must love it as presented to us without desiring more."[13]

These principles were by no means novel to Hecker. The notion that all creation is tending to the promotion of the glory of God was basically the Ignatian principle that Hecker had seen in Lallemant and Surin. Caussade, like Lallemant, had been a Jesuit and had adapted Loyola's Principle 23 in his own spirituality. The emphasis on the passive dimension present in Caussade was one that resembled the Quietest notion of pure love—a notion with which Hecker had been familiar since his time at Fruitlands. But, doubtless, when faced with the situation that confronted him in the 1870s, this doctrine of absolute surrender to divine providence took on new appeal. He heard it with a depth of appreciation and understanding surpassing anything he had known before.

The doctrine became so attractive to Hecker that he encouraged Ella McMahon to do an English translation of Caussade's French original. Isaac, whose mind remained sharp, wrote a preface for this edition in which he recommended the work for those who had already "arrived at that stage of spiritual life where the immediate action of the indwelling Holy Spirit is or should be their main and immediate guide."[14] Caussade's book, Hecker indicated, could help individuals to discern better the action of the Spirit in their lives. The ability to see God's action in all things and to experience the conformity between his action in creatures and his action in the soul was the key to mature spirituality. In reading Caussade, Isaac was not at all willing to exchange his belief in the immediate guidance of the Spirit for a belief in a mechanical view of providence. A God who merely led by means of externals was unknown to Hecker, even in his most bitter moments. It was always, Hecker consistently held, in the synthesis of the internal with the external that God's will was fully revealed.

A NILE ODYSSEY

Yet, as much as these ideas helped in this moment of darkness, they did not relieve the pain. When on the better days the angina rested from sending torturous cramps through his chest, his mind could not rest from questioning. Knowing that God was calling him to a new level of self-surrender and abandonment was one thing; living through each day was another.

With the approach of the winter months, it was time to flee the bitter European cold, and a fascinating opportunity presented itself: Isaac could journey up the Nile River to the ancient port of Nibia. The dry climate would do him good, the doctors advised him, and the stimulation might help ease his troubled soul. Always hungry for an adventure, Isaac decided to go. As he boarded the river boat *Sittina Miriam el Adra,* he began an odyssey into the enchanting land he had so often read about in the Scriptures. The long, slow journey up the great river to Nibia consumed the winter of 1873–1874. It was a time of richness and revelation for the soul-sick priest. The easy pace of the people coupled with the majestic, timeless quality of the land provided a soothing background for meditation. He himself said of the journey: "This trip has been in every respect much more to my benefit than my most sanguine expectations led me to hope. It seems to me almost like an inspiration . . . ."[15]

As the Paulist Superior made his way up the Nile, he encountered for the first time the world of the East. Even as a young seeker after truth, Hecker had been intrigued by the great Eastern religions. Now, as an aged sojourner, he was encountering an Eastern culture face to face. The strange customs and the exotic people fascinated him and set him musing, reaching down into his heart in search of that small, still voice that he had heard so often. His mind raced back over the myriad of experiences that had filled his life. Through them all there seemed to run a thread. God had guided him. Isaac could not doubt it. Had he not often told those who filled the lecture halls of how God had led him? If only he could see more clearly what God wanted in this present moment!

Encountering a culture so radically different from what he had known in the past challenged Isaac to expand his already broad-ranging vision. By this time he had begun to include Europe as well as America in his vision of renewal. Europe, he hoped, would catch sight of the light that was beginning to shine in the new world, and would herself experience a spiritual renewal that would invigorate the Church and society and usher in a reconciliation between Christian truth and modern society. But now as Hecker sailed past the pyramids and saw the scores of faithful Moslems bowing in prayer toward Mecca, he began to envision a spiritual renewal that would encompass the East as well.

This broadening of his vision required no basic modification of his thinking, since the groundwork for such a universal vision was in place, indeed had been in place from the 1840s. He needed now only to expand his scope. From his earliest days Hecker had envisioned God in terms of universal Spirit—a life-giving, effective force that was the very action of God, creating and sustaining all things. Thus Issac wrote in his Egyptian diary: "The Spirit of the Lord fills the whole earth—let us rely more and more upon this fact."[16] This was an idea that he had heard affirmed by his former Transcendentalist friends, such as Bronson Alcott in his speculations on the "Universal Love Spirit," and that had been presented to him in the Ignatian-inspired visions of Lallemant and Caussade, who never tired of calling attention to the divine action in all creation. Why could he not now apply this understanding to encompass the world of the East, at whose fringe he stood? He continued: "The Holy Spirit is at work among Chinese, Moslems, and all nations, and tribes, in every rational soul."[17] Although weakened in body, Isaac was not diminished in his bold optimism. The Spirit's action in the world of his day was,

THE TRIAL AND THE TRIUMPH

he declared, a cause for great hope: "We may be nearer to the conversion of these races [the Eastern], and the unity of the race, and the triumph of Christianity than any one of us is aware of."[18]

Such would be the result of a universal renewal of religion. This was to be at its heart a spiritual renewal brought about not through reliance on secular means, but through the Church's "own inherent power, which was the indwelling Holy Spirit within her own Soul, her life, her strength, her wisdom, her recreator."[19]

Although Hecker believed in America's manifest destiny, he did not understand by the "triumph of Christianity" a christianization of the globe by means of the acculturalization of other peoples to American standards. He was far too keen a believer in the uniqueness of individual national characteristics to countenance such a course. Repeatedly he affirmed that there were certain forms of spirituality best suited for certain peoples. This notion was central in his theory of the compatibility of the American character with the personal guidance of the Spirit. The way to lead a people to Christian perfection was not to foist on them a foreign spirituality, but to encourage in them an experience of God that built upon and incorporated all that was good in their national character. Given the abiding principle that grace supposes and perfects nature, Hecker could affirm this position freely. "The Church in her doctrines," he later wrote, "can reconcile the Moslems, the Chinese, etc., without any violence to the primary doctrines which these hold."[20]

Hecker's understanding of Christianity, and, more particularly, Catholicism, was, at this time, essentially what it had been at his conversion. For Isaac it was unequivocally the fullness of truth toward which human reason naturally tended and for which the heart instinctively longed. The activity of the Spirit of truth in the world would lead people to the truth and ultimately culminate, Isaac was assured, in the triumph of God's glory. He wrote from Egypt:

> The Holy Spirit fills the whole earth, acts everywhere and in all things, more directly on the minds and hearts of rational creatures. . . . This all-wise, all-powerful action now guides, as He ever has and ever will, all men and events

to His complete manifestation and glory. Pentecostal days! were the promise of His universal triumph.[21]

In April 1874 after concluding his Nile odyssey, Isaac could not resist the urge to journey to the Holy Land. From Cairo he made his way to Jerusalem. His time in the Holy City confirmed the work that had begun while he was in Egypt. As he walked on the ground where Jesus had walked, he grew in his identification with his Lord. Seeing the places where Jesus had been scourged, crucified, and buried vivified the fact that Christ was truly a man who had suffered in the flesh. As Isaac preached one day to a small group of pilgrims at the grotto of the Garden of Gethsemane, he broke into tears as he spoke of the sufferings of the compassionate Jesus. His hearers perceived in him a familiarity with the subject about which he so movingly discoursed. His time of anguish had worked in him a contriteness and depth of character that had mellowed him. Like a refiner's fire, it had consumed some things and strengthened others. Gone was the impetuosity of his youth and the reliance on his own strength and ability, but the foundation of his faith had been shored up. Christ, who had truly suffered, had just as truly risen—of that Isaac was certain. His Spirit now filled the earth, carrying on God's plan to restore all things in Christ. More and more Isaac meditated on these things.

By the summer of 1874, he was anxious to share his thoughts with his friends in Europe. The old missionary again had a message—a grander, bolder message—which he was compelled to proclaim. He returned again to the Continent, where he leisurely toured for the next year and a half, visiting acquaintances in Italy, France, Belgium, and Switzerland. The physical malady which had plagued him held on, sapping his strength and necessitating long periods of bed rest each day. In the mornings, he would not awaken until 9:00 A.M. After taking some nourishment, he would attempt reading or writing in bed. He found that any concentrated work drained him terribly, yet, driven by a strong will that was accustomed to bearing pain, he persisted. At midday he would rise and spend as much time socializing as his health would allow. Some days he would feel quite well—well enough to think that he would soon be fully restored, but such total recovery kept eluding him; the good days continued to be offset by the bad.

Despite his illness, Hecker still was able at times to demonstrate in public that vigor and enthusiasm that were so much a hallmark of his earlier career. One such moment occurred at the International Catholic Congress held at Ferney, France. On the western shore of Lake Geneva, Ferney's Cardinal Gaspard Mermillod had summoned churchmen from throughout Europe to respond to the challenge of the *Kulturkampf*. The Paulist Superior, noted for his interest in the relationship between the church and contemporary events, was asked to address the Congress.

The suppression of the German church under Bismarck in the 1870s was to Hecker a perfect example of how enfeebled, timid Catholics had allowed a godless minority to rob them of their rights, and it caused his German-American blood to boil. Addressing the Congress, Isaac put forth what he believed to be the remedy for this detestable situation. It was essentially simple: renew the individual through the direct inspiration of the Holy Spirit. This was the means for empowering and enabling the Church to assume a leading role in society. This was the truth that had become so vital to Isaac during the last months. Though he spoke for only ten minutes in rather colorless French, the genuineness of his faith shone through. His virile, intense words brought spontaneous waves of applause from the large audience that had gathered, ironically, at the town where the great hero of the free thinkers, Arouet de Voltaire, had kept his famous chateau. Hecker challenged his brethren to respond manfully to the crisis of the day. Remarked one listener: "His words seemed to flash the very lightnings of the eloquence of St. Paul."[22]

THE PROGRAM FOR RENEWAL

Encouraged by the enthusiastic response his ideas had received at Ferney, Isaac determined that they should be written down and published. From the spring of 1874 until January of the following year, he worked intently on a manuscript, writing and rewriting outlines and notes into drafts slowly but surely. His illness did not in any significant way diminish his ability to think and write clearly, though it did prevent him from moving along as quickly as he had in the past. Nevertheless, in its final form, his essay on renewal was as cogent a piece of writing as he had ever produced.

In January of 1875 he completed his program for renewal, entitling it *An Exposition of the Church in View of the Recent Difficulties and Controversies, and the Present Needs of the Age*. Originally, Isaac had planned to publish the work in Rome. He submitted its contents to various church officials for their approval, which at first was granted. Then, at the last moment, the publication of the work was blocked by word from the hierarchy.

For over a year Isaac had been thoroughly immersed in the ideas put forth in the *Exposition* and he felt that it was the product of a special grace. After receiving word of the decision not to print the work, he mused over possible alternative explanations for the event. He considered the possibility that he had been mistaken about the views he expressed. He thought that perhaps he had been simply premature and not found the right opportunity. But reflecting back on his earlier struggle with the Redemptorist hierarchy, he was more inclined to believe that he was right and that perhaps opposition was necessary to keep him on the right path. He offered a final explanation which, in light of the storm that broke out over his ideas after his death, was somewhat prophetic. "One may be right," he reasoned, "and by contradiction and condemnation open the way to [the] success of the truth."[23]

After being urged by those identified by Hecker only as "prominent persons" to publish the work, he decided to do so without obtaining the advice of the Roman authorities. The question of publication hinged, as Isaac understood it, not on the soundness of his doctrines, but merely on the propriety of publishing them in Rome.[24] Early in February, Hecker accordingly sent his manuscript to London for publication. The work was brought out that same year by the Basil Montagu Company and soon was published in France and Germany, as well as in Hecker's own magazine, *The Catholic World*. The essay, essentially intact, was published in America in 1887 as the first chapter of Hecker's final book *The Church and the Age*.

The *Exposition* was a forceful statement of Hecker's views on the problems of contemporary society, the condition of the church, the need for spiritual renewal, and the timeliness of devotion to the inner work of the Spirit. His central point was that a renewal of society depended on a renewal of religion, which in turn hinged on "a greater effusion of the creative power of the Holy Spirit."[25] This greater effusion of the Spirit could be brought about by "the giving of increased attention to His movements and inspirations in the soul." Fidelity to the Spirit was, Hecker continued, "the radical and adequate remedy for all the evils of our day" and the "source of all true progress." The cure for the world's problems was Spirit-filled individuals.

> The age is superficial; it needs the gift of Wisdom, which enables the soul to contemplate truth in its ultimate causes. The age is materialistic; it needs the gift of Intelligence by the light of which the intellect penetrates into the essence of things. The age is captivated by a false, one-sided science; it needs the gift of Science . . . . The age is impious; it needs the gift of Piety which leads the soul to look up to God as the Heavenly Father and to adore Him with feelings of filial affection and love. The age is sensual and effeminate; it needs the gift of Fortitude . . . .[26]

The calling of the believers' attention to the divine action in their souls was, as Hecker saw it, the great work that awaited the church in the closing decades of the nineteenth century. Vatican I had prepared the way for the faithful to follow the inner guidance of the Spirit with greater safety and freedom. Rather than viewing the Council's definition of papal infallibility as inhibiting the turn within, Hecker saw the definition as encouraging it. He described the doctrine as "the axis on which turns the new course of the Church, the renewal of religion and the entire restoration of society."[27] The doctrine of infallibility, as he viewed it, represented the fullest development of the church's teaching on authority. Compelled by the Protestant Reformation, the church for the last three centuries had been forced to deal repeatedly with the authority question. After the Vatican I definition of infallibility, the church was free to move in other directions. She could now concentrate on encouraging an increased awareness of the Spirit's work in the soul. The external structures of the church, which had been more firmly set in place by the Council, were to function as an aid to spiritual growth. Hecker criticized those groups like the Old Catholics for rejecting the doctrine of infallibility in the name of spiritual freedom.

> Stupid Döllingerites do not see or understand that what they pretend to desire, the renewal of the Church, can only be accomplished by the reign of the Holy Spirit throughout the Church, and that this can only be brought about by those whose primary attention and fidelity to His inspirations is accompanied with a filial submission to her divine external authority.[28]

The *Exposition* concluded with a challenge to the church to take up this work of religious renewal.

TO THE UTTERMOST PARTS OF THE EARTH

In Hecker's writings during 1875 and 1876, two sentiments appear repeatedly. On the one hand, he continues to express a deep perplexity over his present state of affairs. On the other hand, he shows a growing conviction of the importance of religious renewal and of the special part he was to play in promoting it. The incomprehensibility of his present condition tried him severely, and the constant pain caused by his physical maladies augmented his mental anguish. While in Turin in the fall of 1874, he cried out from the pit of despair: "Death invited, alas, will not come! What a relief from a continuous and prolonged death."[29] Isaac's pain was real enough for him to utter such a statement in the bleak moments he experienced. Like the dark creatures that had tormented him thirty years earlier when he had left home searching for meaning in life, these demons of doubt and frustration now racked him from head to foot. Still, a disposition that resided deeper in the character of the aging Paulist ultimately dominated his behavior—an optimism and faith that would not die. His confidence in God's providence was too great to allow him any

151

lŏng-term despondency. Hecker's writings are filled with statements indicating his ability to see even in his present difficulty the hand of God working all things for the good. Just one month after he uttered his death wish he wrote in the same journal: "The mind quiet both to past and the future, contented with the present moment."[30] Though seemingly cut off from all past relationships, he was content to wait on God.

Increasingly he grew in the ability to see his present sufferings as redemptive. Though incomprehensible, the hardships he had been forced to endure were spoken of as the "secret ways of Divine love" ultimately intended to aid in his sanctification.[31] While residing in northern Italy, he was inspired by Catherine of Genoa's understanding of the purgative value of suffering. He was comforted by Catherine's statement that God, in bringing man from good to better, brings him into even greater ignorance of his situation.[32]

Looking back at his past life, Hecker drew courage and hope. He saw a parallel between his own present situation and that which he had confronted in 1857 in founding the Paulists. Then he had submitted his plans for counsel to those given spiritual responsibility in the church; now he would do the same. The *Exposition*, he hoped, would promulgate his vision of renewal. In 1857 an entire act of faith in the personal guidance of the Holy Spirit and a complete confidence in the Spirit's action in all things had seen him through. Now also he was willing to trust that the Spirit had led him to his present condition and would open a way for the future. He resigned himself to be "above fear, doubt, hesitation or timidity, but patient, obedient, and stable."[33]

As his past experience in America had fitted him for the task of bringing the Gospel to non-Catholic America, so too, Isaac believed, was his present suffering fitting him for a new ministry. What else had his exile from home and his travels to Europe, Egypt, and the Mideast been for if not, in his words, to "prepare my soul to make my life-experience applicable to the general condition of the Church and the world in its present crisis"?[34] As he had in the past seen his own experience as a model for America, he now began to view his new experience as a model for the world. In the late 1840s he had journeyed to Europe and been catholicized. Now he had journeyed abroad and been led one step further. He was now no longer merely a Catholic, but, as he put it, "an International Catholic."[35] His vision was no longer primarily on the American church, but on the global church. Providence, he reasoned, had cut him off from his past to expand his horizons. He wrote: "The eyes of my soul are fixed on another phase of the Church, on a different future which makes the present fade and become of little interest except as the basis of that which is to come . . . ."[36]

Hecker had long speculated over the idea of American Catholicism, once renewed, becoming the model for the universal Church. Even in 1870 he thought of establishing communities in Europe infused with the inspiration that generated the Paulists. He again reiterated this idea in the spring of 1875 and shared it with the bishop of Salford, England, Herbert Vaughan, and his old Redemptorist friend and newly-created cardinal, Victor Dechamps. But there was one important difference in the 1875 version of this idea. In 1870 Hecker had been interested in seeing such communities established, but felt called to return to New York and labor more vigorously than ever in his native land. Five years later, however, he considered remaining in Europe and, as an International Catholic, working to establish such communities and promote his program for renewal. He was willing to see himself as a kind of first fruits of the harvest of blessing that America was to bestow on the world. Was it not fitting, he mused, that the American church should in gratitude repay her parents during this time of crisis? "In former days," he reasoned, "the Holy Spirit inspired souls with the vocation to go into the wilderness of America and plant the Church. . . . Why, in our day, should he not inspire souls with the vocation to aid the Church to recover Europe?"[37] Should Catholics who knew the fullness of faith stand by idly, he asked, as men like Moody and Sankey spread their deficient brand of Evangelical revivalism throughout Europe?[38]

RESPONSE TO THE PROGRAM ON RENEWAL

During his stay in Europe between 1874 and 1875, Hecker widely discussed his program for renewal. Part of his strategy, as he stated in his journal from the time, was to make known his ideas through discussions with influential people. Hecker's previous visits to Rome in 1857 and 1869 had gained him the acquaintance of leading persons in the church. In addition, his involvement in the Catholic press had provided a good relationship with the editors of European Catholic journals. As he journeyed throughout Europe, he sought out his old acquaintances to discuss his ideas on renewal. Even before completing the *Exposition* late in November 1874, he had begun to discuss its contents with prominent Catholics and Protestants in Geneva and Turin. His program, which he described to his brother George and George's wife as "nothing less than a general outline of a movement from without to within," received wholehearted encouragement from many.[39] Peter Rossi, an Italian Lazarite priest, assured Hecker that his enterprise was sure to succeed. "A great number of souls support the venture," he wrote. No one could reject such a picture of religion as the well-balanced synthesis of all that was good in both the natural and supernatural orders, Rossi reasoned.[40] In January 1875, Hecker met with the newly-appointed prefect of the Propaganda, Cardinal Alessandro Franchi, who expressed interest in his ideas. Around the same time, Hecker had his work translated into French by Cardinal Gaspard Mermillod, the convener of the International Conference at Ferney. Mermillod was heavily involved in Catholic social reform movements and had been active since the 1850s in the apostolate of the press, founding *Les Annales Catholiques* and *L'Observateur.*

The decision to publish the *Exposition* in London, despite the last-minute move to block publication in Rome, apparently had not incurred any ill feelings on the part of Propaganda.[41] Hecker had been careful to submit a copy of his essay to two influential English churchmen—Henry Manning, bishop of Westminster, and John Henry Newman—before giving the go-ahead on publishing the work. In February 1875 Manning sent an encouraging reply:

> In the general outline I heartily agree. And I especially hold that the low state of mind in respect to the Office of the Holy Ghost in the Church has caused most of our modern

errors; and forgetfulness of His presence in us has made us unspiritual and merely natural.[42]

Manning went on to inform Hecker that he was just bringing out a volume himself on the work of the Spirit in the soul.

In March 1875, Hecker also had sent a copy of his *Exposition* to Newman, asking for his opinion of the work. Newman's response was not as favorable as Manning's. He disagreed with both Hecker's analysis of the present situation in the church and society and with his proposed solution. As Newman saw it, the desperate state of affairs in the world did not necessarily mean that a renewal was about to spring forth. He could not share Hecker's optimism. Things could, he reasoned, get worse rather than better. He likewise did not agree that a greater effusion of the Holy Ghost was the basis for reform. Instead, he reminded Hecker that the Pope had been insisting for years that the maintenance of the Pope's temporal power was the key to society's well-being.[43]

Response to the *Exposition* on the Continent was encouraging. In Paris support for Hecker's work centered upon Augustus Craven and his wife, the former Pauline Marie Armande Aglae Ferren de la Ferronnays. Mrs. Craven, the descendant of an old French aristocratic family, was a successful novelist whose latest book, *Fleurange*, had become a best-seller in France and had been published serially by Hecker in *The Catholic World* during 1872. Early in 1875 Mrs. Craven did a French translation of Hecker's *Exposition*. Augustus Craven, a British career diplomat stationed in Paris, supervised publication of his wife's translation in the spring of 1875. He wrote to his friend Isaac: "I need not tell you what we think of it or attempt to express the sacred delight its perusal and study have caused us. *It must be made known.*"[44] The Parisian newspaper, *Le Correspondant*, for April 25 carried a favorable review of the French edition of the *Exposition*. In the fall, *Le Monde* praised it as the product of "a great philosophical mind and a profound theologian."[45]

Hecker's work also met with some success in Germany. Cardinal Dechamps warmly received the *Exposition* and urged publication of a German edition. Benjamin Herder, himself warmly disposed toward

Hecker and his ideas on renewal, brought out a German edition in Fribourg in 1875. In Italy as well, interest in the *Exposition* ran high. Another of Hecker's influential friends, Joseph Burone of Turin, vowed to make the work known through the *Ateneo Religioso* of Turin and the Florence journal, *Revista Universale*.[46]

Not all response to the *Exposition* was favorable, however. One frequently-made criticism was that the work, in the final analysis, failed to offer any real concrete solutions for the problems of the day. A Parisian priest wrote to Hecker: "When I read you, my reason follows and says to almost everything, Amen. But my Latin and Western mind always asks for a *quomodo* and looks for ways and means." Hecker, he thought, was, in his idealism, too German, too oriental.[47]

The most thorough critique that Hecker received was from the mouth of one who personally agreed wholly with him but felt the responsibility of briefing him on the criticisms being leveled by some against the work. Xavier Dufresne summarized the objections under two headings. The first centered upon Hecker's contention that Catholics were, generally speaking, in an enfeebled state because of the church's emphasis since the Reformation on submission and passivity. Dufresne explained that some interpreted this to suggest that obedience to authority engenders feebleness—a position that no good Catholic could countenance. The second objection concerned Hecker's view of the Holy Spirit's work. "Many good Catholics say," he told Hecker, " 'Oh, it is nothing but mysticism and illuminism. It is a Protestant theory.' " The notion of the Holy Spirit's new reign on earth smacked, he continued, of the erroneous doctrines of the Millennialists. Dufresne warned Hecker that the influential French prelate Monsignor de Richmont had found his doctrines bearing traces of an exaggerated, non-Catholic mysticism.[48]

Hecker was, however, aware of such objections even before his friend Dufresne mentioned them. He looked to the writings of Lallemant for a defense against such charges. This move was expedient, since, as Isaac well knew, the Jesuits had been influential in bringing about the Council's definition of infallibility. The vigorous efforts of the Society of Jesus to strengthen papal powers made them a likely threat to Hecker's program, which emphasized the turn within. By adducing the Jesuit Lallemant's work on the harmony between the internal guidance of the Spirit and Church authority, Hecker could parry the Jesuit onslaughts with an appeal to a master of Ignatian spirituality. In addition to Lallemant, Hecker discovered in the spring of 1875, after publishing the *Exposition,* the works of Joseph Marie DeMaistre. DeMaistre's predictions of a bright future for the Church appealed to Hecker. The Frenchman's understanding of the organic unity of society and the centrality of the Church as the pillar and groundwork of truth and true progress paralleled Hecker's, and the fact that DeMaistre was a French traditionalist who favored the strengthening of papal power made him attractive as a further means of answering critics who felt that Hecker's notions militated against Church authority. All in all, however, Hecker's claim that the idea of the *Exposition* and the answers to objections made against it could be found in DeMaistre reflects the work of the "American Scholar," picking and choosing those elements which resonate with his own intuitions and ignoring the rest. Hecker was thus able to remain unaffected by the fact that although DeMaistre held positions that Hecker favored, he was also vigorously anti-democratic, convinced that Christianity could only flourish under a monarchy—a position to which the Paulist founder obviously never would have ascribed.[49]

Despite the objections, Isaac was encouraged by the overall response to his work, gladly noting that support had come from representatives of divergent parties.[50] He was aware that his ideas would be misinterpreted by many, especially those who, in his words, "receive and see things almost exclusively from the outside."[51]

XI

A DIFFICULT DECISION

During his 1873–1875 stay in Europe, the Paulist superior, in addition to promoting his ideas on renewal, was carrying on certain Community business. The thrust of Hecker's efforts on behalf of the Paulists was to gain official Vatican approval of the Congregation's Rule and Constitution. He acted as the chief liaison between the Vatican and the Paulists in the long, drawn-out process of obtaining approval. The business of writing an account of the Congregation's history and overseeing the drafting of the formal requests for approbation fell to Hewit, whom Hecker had appointed acting superior in his absence. Throughout his time in Europe, Hecker showed an entire willingness to serve his Community in the negotiations with Rome, but he appeared to be following the impetus of the New York group rather than taking an active leadership role. The majority of his correspondence with the Paulists was with Hewit, and the tone of the letters revealed the warm affection and admiration these two men held for one another. Hewit was, for the most part, kind and generous in his statements to the Paulist founder, demonstrating a confidence in his decisions and a concern for his recovery.[1] Hecker, on the other hand, while aware of the fact that his presence was sorely missed, seemed fully bent on doing God's will, not at all certain what that meant for the future. He felt that his present circumstances were leading him in a new direction to which he had to remain open. He wrote to Hewit from Turin:

I cannot break through what withholds me from speaking of the things you are doing at home. My whole past is a dream. . . . It seems to me that if God permitted one human or natural affection, or feeling of attachment, to enter my heart, I would fly back to New York with lightning speed. But He has sealed up all this. . . . When the end will come and what it will be I have no idea. . . . God's will be done.[2]

Isaac was not wandering through Europe whimsically ignorant of his responsibilities. As he wrote to his sister-in-law, Josephine Hecker: "I am unconscious of being unfaithful to my conscience, to the solicitations of God's grace, to my duties to the holy Church."[3]

As time went on, Hecker's willingness to remain in Europe increased, but the Paulists' ability to carry on without their founder was decreasing. In July 1875, Alfred Young, one of the ablest of the new additions to the Congregation, wrote to Hecker, "Your absence is a great trial."[4] Young closed his letter with a sincere statement of his and the entire Community's affection for their beloved superior. A number of problems were confronting the Paulists that many felt required immediate attention. The elections for superior were scheduled for September, and there was the question of where to locate the Paulist studentiate. Also, the 59th Street neighborhood was changing. The city had plans for building a huge abattoir at the foot of 59th Street just a few blocks west of the Paulist convent. In addition, the horrendous 9th Avenue elevated railroad was inching its way north and soon would be noisily belching out its sooty smoke right at the doorstep of St. Paul's Church. With the stench from the slaughter yard and the noise from the railroad, was 59th Street the best place for the Community house? On top of these concerns, there was the whole matter of the relationship between the Paulists and *The Catholic World* and the Catholic Publication Society. Should the Community continue direct involvement or sell out to others? There was also the question of a new church building. Growth had made it necessary to build a larger facility. But should they erect a low-cost structure, or attempt, amid the growing financial uncertainty of the 1870s, to produce a costly edifice?

These were the main issues that Hewit presented in two letters to Hecker, written during July 1875. Hewit, himself not in the best of health, was beginning to feel the strain of carrying a double load. Besides taking personal responsibility for providing a philosophical and theological education for Paulist seminarians, he was editing *The Catholic World* and laboring as acting superior at a time when the Congregation was trying to put its best foot forward toward Rome. He had come to the end of his strength and sincerely believed that the Community's affairs were at an impasse that only Hecker's presence could overcome. "It seems to me," he wrote, "that the will of God and duty call you to return, whatever the state of your health . . . ."[5]

During the same month Isaac was the house guest of his longtime supporter, Xavier Dufresne. For the summer months the Dufresne family resided in their chalet atop picturesque Mount Salève in Savoy. The alpine regions of southeastern France, northern Italy, and Switzerland had become especially dear to Isaac. In the cheerful atmosphere of the Dufresne home, he felt fitter than he had in some time. Between the times of quiet contemplation, Isaac busied himself with the children of the house. One of the Dufresne boys was so impressed with the old Paulist that he was able to write of him vividly over twenty years later when he had become an abbé. He recalled that Father Hecker had the appearance of one physically broken down and familiar with suffering. His bright piercing eyes portrayed, however, a keenness that adversity had not dulled. When he was with others, he was relaxed and affable, his abundant conversation filled with gaiety and wit. Overall he had an air of stability about him that made the various aspects of his character blend harmoniously.[6]

It was while visiting the Dufresnes that Isaac received the urgent request from Hewit that he return to New York immediately. Before receiving it, he had struggled with the idea of returning; after receiving it, the struggle redoubled in intensity. He had by this time become convinced that returning to the Community was impractical, given his physical condition and his conviction, buoyed by the response to the *Exposition,* that he was being called to work for renewal as an International Catholic. But, in addition, he felt that his intellectual interest in his former employments had ceased. Though it pained him to admit it, there was a conflict between his own ideal of the Paulists and the direction in which the Community had, against his better judgment, developed. The conception of the Paulists, as Isaac saw it, was one in which "the elements of self-control, conscience, and internal guidance of the Holy Spirit should take lead over the control of discipline, Rules, and external authority."[7] All his companions, however, had demonstrated over the years a tendency to increase discipline, fix rules, and stress external authority. This sorely vexed the sensitive Isaac. A conflict raged between his own vision of a religious community and theirs. His, he maintained, was in the spirit of St. Philip Neri's Oratorians, while theirs was in the spirit of St. Ignatius' Jesuits. Neri had tended to minimize external authority; Ignatius, on the other hand, emphasized strict, militaristic authority structures. It was this inner struggle that had, in his opinion, broken down his physical health.

After illness had necessitated his leaving New York in 1871, the development in the Community of his companions' tendency increased. At the same time, while he was abroad, Hecker's own convictions in the opposite direction had also intensified. As he said in 1875, contemplating his new vocation, "My whole soul is alive to this great work."[8] To return and live in the Community would rekindle this conflict of interest, Isaac speculated, and would probably result again in his physical breakdown. Life in the Community, he said, would "stifle my own convictions [and be] a thing impossible morally and physically—a slow consuming martyrdom."[9] As an alternative to returning, Hecker thought that he could remain in Europe and engage in a work similar to that of the American Paulists. If he were free to follow his *attrait,* he would gladly offer the Paulists his fullest cooperation, counsel, sympathy, and love.

Isaac's perplexity over returning to the Paulist community stemmed from his keen awareness of the conflict between the ideal and the real. His ability to perceive the ideal clearly and to desire and dedicate himself fully to its actualization was one of his greatest strengths. But in his longing to see the ideal perfected, he sometimes lost patience with the imperfect world around him. When it pushed in and seemed ready to inflict mortal wounds on his ideals, he would snatch these from the fray and, with his ideals held safe within his bosom, soar like an eagle to some new height, far above his foes.

This impatience with the imperfect, coupled with a courage in pressing on to new horizons, had functioned in the past in Hecker's favor. Had the young earnest seeker not been willing to leave family and friends in search of the ideal that motivated him, his life would have obtained little notice. Had he not been willing to sacrifice all in an effort to realize his sense of divine calling, he never would have had the charisma to inspire so many to a life of faith. But when a conflict developed between Hecker's vision of the Paulists and that of the other members of the Community, the perplexity was excruciating for him, because the Paulists were, more than anything else in the world, the embodiment of his ideals. These American missionaries were the actualization of his hopes. They were the special agents God had raised up to convert the land and the first fruits of a new kind of Catholic—one who would incorporate all that was good in modern society with all that was precious in the past. They were to be American and Catholic. "American"—what better symbol of modern society, of the new world, of the bright future, of the rich experience of the present which Hecker so cherished; and "Catholic"—the perfect symbol of the synthesis, harmony, and unity that he sought.

When, however, the Paulists became not merely a vision, but an institution, Hecker became, as it were, locked into a struggle from which he could not flee. The ideal which he had fathered had become wedded with an imperfect world. The effects of that union were often bitter to him. Going to Europe in the early 1870s had removed him temporarily from the fray. Returning would be agony, he felt, precisely because, as he said, it would "stifle" his convictions.

But as he read Hewit's letter in late July he was moved by a love for his Paulist brethren that despite the conflicts was still warm and compelling. He had always believed that God would lead through the providential ordering of situations. Now it appeared that God was asking him once again to deny himself and do the divine will. As much as Isaac would have liked to do otherwise, he knew he must once again be open to God's call. The day after receiving Hewit's letter he replied:

> The past has not given any grounds for suspicion of my willingness to sacrifice myself for the good of the Community, and as for the present, it is in its hands. Let the Community deliberate and decide, and if it be for immediate return—send me a telegram—it will find me indifferent to my health or what physicians may say. [10]

His decision marked a crucial point in Isaac's spiritual development. It was the ultimate expression of his willingness to deny himself and accept the present situation as a manifestation of God's will. By returning, he chose to remain in the fray and to deal with the struggle involved in actualizing his ideals. His illness had forced him to accept the limitations and the frailty of human existence to a greater degree than ever before. In returning to the Paulists, he did not abandon his ideals or conclude that they were wrong because they were not being actualized in the way he wished. Rather, he held on to his hopes and continued to believe that his ideals would find their expression. But how and when they would find expression, he could not say. More than ever, he bowed in reverence to the Lord whose inscrutable designs are known only imperfectly by men.

XII

GOING HOME

By the first week of August 1875 Hecker had received a response to his offer to submit himself to the Community's decision. Hewit requested that he be back in New York by November 1. The Community's decision did not surprise Isaac who had expected that they would ask for his immediate return and had committed himself to abide by their decision. After receiving the request for his return, he determined to begin traveling in the autumn. The closing weeks of the summer he would spend resting and preparing for the trip in the peacefulness of the Dufresnes' alpine retreat.

After making the decision to comply with his colleague's request, the Paulist superior experienced a certain degree of relief from the intense inner trials that had beset him since the onslaught of his illness. He wrote to his brother George: "With the help of God's grace I have, I trust, got through the greatest of my struggles and my soul is now quiet and tranquil."[1] He was able to accept the present situation as God's will. He thus continued in his letter to his brother: "My mind is not at all distressed at the turn of events. On the contrary, it seems to me the best."[2] While he remained aware of the potential conflicts that awaited him in New York, he believed that they could be overcome. Although he felt that his physical condition, as well as his internal disposition, would not allow him to resume his former role in the Community, he was sanguine about working out a new relationship with the group. Writing to Hewit, he spoke en-

164

couragingly about his future: "All, I feel sure, will come out right—
let us keep our minds free from all agitation."[3]

In October Isaac journeyed home. He was going back at last to
his country and to the beloved city of his birth where he would spend
the final thirteen years of his life. At other times he had longed to
return, longed to recommence his labors to missionize America. Now
that he was finally going, he went not with the contagious enthusiasm that he had lavished on so many of his past actions, but with
a tranquil resignation. He was resigning himself to do what duty and
piety called him to do but that was as much as he could fathom. He
was not able to understand why God would will such a thing. Lacking
this insight, he was unable to see the bigger picture. An awareness
of his own smallness and of the ultimate inscrutability of God's ways
that had grown during his years of suffering remained branded on his
heart. It motivated him now that the cockiness of his youth had per-
ished in the fires of tribulation. He had learned, in his own words,
to "love suffering and to ask God, if it be His Divine Will, never to
let me be a moment free from suffering until the moment of my leaving the body."[4] Rather than reject the imperfections of the present,
Isaac was learning to embrace them, believing that in their midst the
will of God would ultimately be done.

Upon returning, Hecker resumed, in a limited fashion, some of
his former duties. He was still the superior of the Paulists, and although as consultor Hewit continued to bear much of the load, Father Hecker was looked to for direction. Father Alfred Young, the
pastor of the Church of Saint Paul the Apostle at 59th Street, asked
Hecker for advice on the construction of a new church. Isaac had
specific ideas for the design of the mother church that he wanted im-
plemented. He took part in the project, consulting personally with
the first architect, Jeremiah O'Rourke, and engaging the service of
three eminent American artists: Augustus Saint-Gaudens, John La-
Farge, and Stanford White.[5]

In addition to involving himself with the construction project,
Isaac resumed the business of spiritual direction. He became involved
in counseling two nuns who were in New York attempting to found
a house of Poor Clares. His direction to them radiated with his devotion to the Spirit. "May the Holy Spirit," he wrote to the Poor

Clares residing in Manhattanville, "be your guide. . . . May God bless you both with the fullness of His Spirit."[6] Hecker had made the acquaintance of Sister Mary Constance of Jesus and Sister Magdaline during his recent European stay. In October of 1876, he received a letter from another European friend, H. S. C. Noteware, recommending the work of the Poor Clares to him. "How true are your words," Noteware told Hecker. " 'The Holy Spirit will bring all things to the right end if we trust and follow Him.' Sometimes I think that this is, par excellence, the Age of the Holy Spirit. He is working silently, imperceptibly beneath all the chaos and darkness of the external world."[7]

After his return to New York, Isaac also became involved once again with editing *The Catholic World*.[8] The Panic of 1873 and the severe economic depression that followed for the next four years were having their effect on the publishing business. By 1876, the situation had become critical enough to force Hecker into issuing a circular to the American bishops urging them to appeal to clerics and laity to support the Catholic press.[9] The Catholic Publication Society was experiencing even more acute financial woes. The Paulists by the early 1880s had decided to lessen their direct involvement with the Society. By that time it had become the property of its principal financier, George Hecker. In 1882, George offered the enterprise to its business manager, Edward Kehoe, who was, however, unable to raise the cash for a down payment.[10]

Despite the financial headaches, *The Catholic World* continued publishing. Hecker dealt with editorial matters—soliciting articles, responding to readers' comments, and exchanging articles with editors of European journals. His correspondence with Xavier Dufresne, Augustus Craven, and Joseph Burone continued to be brisk.[11] In addition, Isaac did some writing for the magazine. Between 1875 and 1888, he wrote no fewer than twenty-one articles for *The Catholic World*, ranging from discussions of the spiritual life to treatments of social and philosophical issues of the day. In 1881 and 1882 he addressed the public school question. In 1884 he took up the matter of Antonio Rosmini and the Neo-Thomist revival of Scholastic philosophy. In 1887 and 1888 he did three brief pieces on the guidance of the Holy Spirit.

GOING HOME

Though plagued by physical feebleness, Isaac retained a sharp acquisitive mind; he studied the events of the time, as he had done for so long, searching them for the hand of providence.

NEO-THOMISM

In *The Catholic World* for April 1880 Isaac published an article entitled "The Intellectual Outlook of the Age." Leo XIII had recently issued the encyclical *Aeterni Patris*. American prelates such as Bishop Michael Corrigan of New York were concerned that some reply be made to the interpretation given the encyclical by Dr. Samuel Alexander in *The Princeton Review*.[12] Hecker, even before hearing of Corrigan's concern, had already produced an article that not only lauded *Aeterni Patris* but interpreted its doctrine as that for which nineteenth-century Protestants were, in effect, seeking.

According to Hecker, Thomism, the philosophy of St. Thomas Aquinas, offered a useful model of the synthesis between faith and reason such as the nineteenth century required. Protestantism, with its basic tendency to oppose such a synthesis, was unable to meet the valid demands for a reasonable faith. Returning to an old theme, Hecker insisted that Catholics needed to present their faith in a way that would satisfy men's inner needs—both their questions and their aspirations. The Liberal Protestant rejection of Calvinism, the Neo-Thomist revival, the new interest in science, and Leo XIII's declaration of "Christ as the Restorer of the Sciences" all indicated that this approach was more appropriate than ever.[13]

Sometime after February 1886, Hecker tried his hand at composing a presentation of the Faith utilizing this method. The work, entitled "God and Man," was never published, though Isaac intended it to be his last word to the public.[14] It was his most serious attempt at apologetics. In it appeared his mature statements on a number of issues that had long occupied his attention.

The work began with a discussion of epistemology and worked its way in twenty-one sections through the topics of God, Christ, the Church, and the Sacraments. Hecker aimed his barbs at current trends on the intellectual scene that he saw as erroneous attempts at synthesis. Unitarian Edward E. Hale's doctrine of the Fatherhood of God was castigated by the aged Paulist as the product of a "spurious mysticism" that blurred the distinctions between God and man and eliminated the necessity for grace. Francis E. Abbot's "scientific deism," which attempted to reconcile Christianity with Darwinism, was rejected for the same reason.

AMERICAN PROTESTANT PERFECTIONIST MOVEMENTS

During his last fifteen years, Hecker was keenly aware that his emphasis on the internal, immediate work of the Spirit in the individual was a truth highly prized by Protestants in general. In addition, he knew that increasing interest in perfection and in the sanctifying work of the Spirit had been present among a broad range of American Protestants between 1842, the year Hecker began writing his journal, and 1888.[15] He was aware of the work of two men who were deeply involved in perfectionist movements, Asa Mahan and Thomas Upham.

Mahan was one of the chief spokesmen of the Oberlin perfectionist school. Together with the renowned evangelist Charles G. Finney, he defined a doctrine of perfection that stressed a distinct second experience of grace. The second work was a special endowment of divine power that rendered the Christian better able to lead a life of holiness. In 1854 Mahan published a succinct statement of this doctrine in a book entitled *The Baptism of the Holy Ghost*.[16]

Hecker was interested enough in Mahan's volume to solicit H. J. D. Ryder of London to write a review of the 1872 edition of *The Baptism of the Holy Ghost*. In presenting the request to the Englishman, Hecker stated, "The subject is one of vital interest and of greater importance than is commonly supposed. It involves a great Catholic Truth—a Truth which I believe, that instead of diminishing, will increase in importance."[17]

Hecker himself made reference to Mahan's book in an article originally written late in 1877 and reprinted in 1886 in *The Church and the Age*. The article was a review of John W. Nevin's essay, "The Spiritual World," which appeared in the *Mercersburg Review* for October 1876. Hecker noted that Nevin's interest in the supernatural world was one indication of a hunger for a deeper spirituality among Protestants. As another example of this tendency, Hecker mentioned Mahan's work and quoted from *The Baptism of the Holy Ghost.* Hecker thought it remarkable that Mahan had acknowledged in his book that certain Catholic saints, in particular, Thomas à Kempis and Catherine Adorna (St. Catherine of Genoa), were examples of those who had received the "unction of the Spirit." Hecker went on to note that a "desire for a closer union with God finds expression among all Protestant denominations. With the Methodists and Presbyterians it is known by the name of 'perfectionism,' or 'the higher life,' or 'the baptism of the Holy Ghost.' "[18]

In the same article, Hecker made mention of another important figure in Protestant perfectionist circles, Thomas C. Upham. The work of Upham that interested Hecker most was one that dealt with one of Hecker's favorite saints, Catherine of Genoa. In 1845 Upham published *The Life of Catherine Adorna; Including Some Leading Facts and Traits in Her Religious Experience; Together with Explanations and Remarks, Tending to Illustrate the Doctrine of Holiness.* The book went through numerous editions, one of which was published by the American Tract Society. It was the first study published in America on Catherine and predated the first Catholic publications on the Italian saint by some twenty-nine years. Hecker's conviction that Catholic spirituality offered Protestants the richness they were seeking found one of its best evidences in Upham's *Life of Catherine.* By means of Upham's work, knowledge of Catherine was promulgated among Protestants involved in perfectionist movements.[19]

Hecker's awareness of Protestant interest in Catherine of Genoa had prompted him to push for the publication of an 1874 Catholic Publication Society edition of *The Life and Doctrine of St. Catherine of Genoa.* The work was the first English translation of Cattaneo Marabotto's *Vita e Dottrina,* and was done, with Hecker's encouragement, by Mrs. George Ripley, who had, since the days of Brook Farm, converted to Catholicism. Hecker himself wrote the preface for this volume in which he mentioned the American Tract Society edition of Upham's work as an indication of the irresistible attraction which Catherine's type of Christian perfection held for certain Protestants. In recommending the Catholic Publication Society's edition of Catherine's *Life*, he pointed to a number of the same things that Protestants found attractive in the saint. For Hecker, Catherine was a laywoman whose practical orientation in the world made her an apt model for those seeking perfection in the context of everyday life. She was a woman who found freedom of action in the Church. And, primarily, she was one who knew the inner, sanctifying work of the Holy Spirit in her soul. [20]

During his final years Isaac began adopting a more irenic posture toward Protestantism than he had prior to 1875. Although he remained convinced until his death that Protestantism was an error that had seen its day, he was more willing in his later years to stress the points of agreement between Protestants and Catholics. Thus he was willing to acknowledge Protestant interest in perfectionism as a good thing, stressing that Mahan and Upham were pursuing a worthy aim.

This desire to emphasize the positive grew during Isaac's old age. Mellowed by nearly seventy years of service, he put forth in 1888 one of his strongest statements of this theme in a *Catholic World* article entitled "The Things That Make For Unity." In this article Isaac noted a statement made by the *Christian Union* that advocated stressing the points of agreement between Protestants and Catholics, rather than the points of difference. To this he gave his complete support. He observed that many Protestants were in fact desirous of unity and were people without guile who believed, as earnestly as did Catholics, in the Gospel of Christ, though they lacked the fullness of Catholic truth. They could be described as "fair men whose truth is fragmentary, honest minds in partial obscurity . . . rather non-Catholics than anti-Catholics."[21]

ONGOING CONFLICTS

Despite his rewarding involvement with some of his former occupations, all was not well with Isaac. Since returning from Europe in October 1875, he had been living with his brother George at his New York home and his summer retreat across the river in Orange Hill, New Jersey. Isaac had purposely chosen to avoid the busy at-

170

mosphere of the Paulist Community's 59th Street house. It was not until 1879, after rather constant, though courteous, insistence by Hewit and other Paulists, that Isaac recommenced living with his confreres.[22]

In addition, Isaac's physical condition remained about the same as it had been while he was in Europe. His lack of energy prevented him from becoming too involved with the affairs around him. Even his correspondence lacked the spunk and luster of his earlier days. He was unable to find the strength to make the public appearances he had once so cherished. He declined an invitation to the consecration of his good friend John Keane to the bishopric of Richmond in September 1878. He likewise was prevented from traveling to Rome in the early part of 1879 to attend a ceremony in honor of Leo XIII.

Besides the physical affliction, Isaac still had to contend with some of the inner conflicts that had tormented him while he was in Europe. As his illness hung on year after year, he painfully confronted the possibility of death. Though he had for so long loved those things which are unseen, he was now filled with fear at the thought of encountering the unknown realm of the dead. In 1876 he wrote in his journal, "My soul is driven hither and thither with the desire to die and dread of death."[23]

The situation with the Paulists, like his health, continued to be a problem. Before returning from Europe, Isaac had been concerned about his ability to rebuild a relationship with his fellow Paulists, given the trend of the Community's development in recent years. Members of the Community, soon after Isaac's return, began voicing the opinion that what was needed were more clear-cut principles and rules. Hewit described the situation to Hecker in a letter of 1878: "The great difference at present consists in a distrust of our having any divine vocation or sufficient principle of unity and growth. Some desire a rule more distinctively religious . . . ."[24] A segment of the Community felt the necessity of concretizing the Paulist vision and hoped that this could be done by the writing of a Rule and Constitution that encapsulated the spirit of the Community. The absence of such statements left them puzzled, unable to move ahead with confidence.

The uncertainty that since 1871 had disturbed Hecker about his own future had tormented the Community as well. They had been waiting and hoping that things might soon return to normal. As a result, Hewit's administration as acting superior had been marked by reticence. He felt that Hecker was the man God had called to found and lead the Paulists, and he had not been willing to define new directions until his hand was forced by impending necessities. Hewit had hoped that Hecker would return and supply the direction and leadership needed to further the Congregation's development. When Hecker returned, however, he was not inclined, either physically or mentally, to assume such a leadership role. Though active in some ways, Hecker took a low profile and cut his public activities and priestly duties to a minimum. Besides, there were the questions about the nature of his illness. Often there was an undertone of suspicion, voiced by Mrs. Julia Beers, who had hosted Hecker in Rome, that the illness was more mental than physical. [25]

The tension caused by this situation came to a head in 1884. On September 4 the small community of Paulists gathered together at their 59th Street house to hold a Chapter meeting. The central task that confronted them was the election of a superior for a new term. Some of the more influential members of the Community favored the reelection of Father Hecker. Among them was one of the brighter lights among the young Paulists, Walter Elliott, who left a vivid narrative of the proceedings. He reported that Hewit, George Deshon, and he fully expected Hecker to be reelected on the first ballot. When the votes were counted, however, Elliott experienced one of the greatest shocks of his life. The count was eight votes for Father Hewit and five for Father Hecker! Despite the commotion, Hecker seemed entirely undisturbed. Elliott remarked, "It was the greatest proof of his virtue I ever saw. He was the most unconcerned man in the room." [26] Hecker calmly left the meeting and let his brethren proceed. Since a two-thirds majority was needed for election, a second ballot was necessary. Again the vote was in favor of Hewit, but lacked the necessary margin. The turn of events prompted Hewit to address the Chapter and state his unwillingness to accept election. He then proceeded to present a moving tribute to the Paulist founder. In Hewit's eyes, God had called Hecker to found the Congregation and had endowed him, and him alone, with the grace of leading it.

The fact that Hecker was enfeebled did not change things in Hewit's mind.

Still the deadlock persisted. The day after Hewit's speech, the opposition party presented its case. George Searle, John Robinson, Edward Brady, Aloysius Nevins, Clarence Woodman, and Thomas McMillan sided against Hewit, Deshon, Young, Elliott, Michael Smith, Alexander Doyle, and Henry Wyman in opposing Hecker's reelection. The argument of the opposition stated that Father Hecker's infirmity made him unable to discharge the duties of superior. Resistance to Hecker's reelection, they stressed, was not based on any lack of esteem or affection for their founder. The Paulists were, in their eyes, moving into a new era and needed visible, active leadership if they were to carry on their ministry.

The deadlock lasted until the afternoon of September 8. Hewit's unwillingness to compromise, along with the personal remonstrances of the pro-Hecker party, at last triumphed. The final vote was Hecker, eleven; Hewit, two.

In their desire to concretize the Paulist spirit, the opposition party interestingly enough had chosen the Church of St. Paul the Apostle as the sign of a new era for the community. The era they foresaw was one that, like the new church building, would be characterized by clear-cut lines and rigid structures. It would also be one that was centered in parish work. Hecker's vision for the Paulists was far different. It was wedded to the overriding concern of his last fifteen years: spiritual renewal.

"THE RENEWAL OF THE CHRISTIAN LIFE"

In December 1875, after returning to his Community in America, Hecker had attempted to draw out the ramifications of his vision for religious communities. In a manuscript entitled "The Renewal of the Christian Life," he discussed the ways in which new religious institutions such as the Paulists could best carry out this mission of reform. He began by stating a position that had been basic to his spirituality for over thirty years. "The renewal of the Christian life," he wrote, "depends on a fresh recourse to primary truths."[27] That was the great need of the age. It was the recourse to fundamental theology, the move to an internal apologetic. Also it was the way of greater sensitivity to the inner life and of increased awareness of the Holy Spirit's work in the soul. New religious institutions must consist of individuals who possessed a clear insight and firm grasp of "the great primary truths of both natural and revealed theology" and would see more clearly than others the omnipresence of God.

These ideas, which had been part of Hecker's thinking prior to the 1870s, now were articulated with an awareness of a new enemy. Isaac's barbs were no longer directed primarily at Protestantism, as they had been before the Civil War, but toward the challenges to the Christian faith produced by the flood of new ideas that broke loose on America during the Gilded Age. Hecker, who was well aware of the intellectual climate of both Europe and the United States, foresaw a growing conflict between infidelity and true religion and believed that Christians must respond to the intellectual challenges with mental acumen. His spirituality, stressing as it did the value of human reason, could in no way adopt an anti-intellectual polemic, and he was critical of Protestant revivalists such as D. L. Moody for taking this approach. In addition to being able to refute the intellectual errors of the age, the members of the new religious institutions that Hecker envisioned would also be able to sympathize with the valid intellectual movements of the day and to "collect all elements of truth from various sources."[28]

As the work of the Holy Spirit was central to Isaac's vision of renewal, so was it also central to his view of new religious institutions. "It is a fresh infusion of this Spirit which," he insisted, "must inform these new institutions and breathe in all the actions of their members."[29] As he looked out from his study in his brother's house on the booming metropolis of New York, built by men who like himself were convinced that the future would bring bigger and better things, he was transfixed by a glorious vision of the future, which he recorded at the end of his manuscript.

> The prediction of the triumph of the gospel upon earth will receive a more literal fulfillment. The day of Pentecost will become more characteristic of the whole Church. The note of sanctity will be developed as hitherto it has not been

within the Church. In cooperating in this way, new religious institutions will fulfill their special mission . . . .[30]

How different was this vision of the Paulists' function from that of those who opposed Hecker's reelection in 1884! Whereas their vision was centered on the external Church, symbolized, as it were, by the massive, fortress-like building on 59th Street, Hecker's was centered on the internal Church, on the beauties of the sanctified soul in union with God and in harmony with the rest of creation.

It is no wonder that Hecker complained that "the direction toward which things are turned is one that differs from that which my interior spirit can concur with." Isaac was disturbed that involvement in regular parish duties rather than the apostolate to the non-Catholic was becoming central to the Paulists. Vexed, he considered possible alternatives to this painful situation. The first alternative was to continue to wait on divine providence, "with constant prayer for light and strength," and to continue in his present course, doing all he could for the Community, trusting that God would change things when he pleased. The second was to alter in some way his relations with the Community, and to be left "entirely alone with no one but God." That he was willing to do, should it be necessary, to obey the divine will and carry on the ministry he envisioned.[31] As real as these alternatives were, Isaac never committed himself to either. Instead he held them in tension until his death, and the tension continued to perplex him.

The decision he had made to return to the Community needed constant reaffirmation because of his tendency to strike out on a new course when the actualization of his ideals was impeded. He was, nevertheless, willing to resign himself, despite the difficulty, to the present situation and wait for the opportunity to pursue more fully the desires of his heart. His resignation was true. His statements of discontent with the course of the Community are so few and far between that it is clear that Hecker did not often express the dissatisfaction that was part of the cross he had chosen to bear. On the other hand, his hope for a new opportunity to advance his vision was also real, but the new opportunity never came in a large-scale way. Neither his health nor the situation in the Paulist Community ever improved enough to make that possible. But Isaac persisted, doing what he could and resigning himself to what he understood to be God's will. As a romantic hero, he never forsook the yearnings of his heart, and he battled to realize his dreams in the midst of an increasingly pragmatic age. As a disciple of Christ, he chose to bear the imperfections of this world, seeing through them God's more perfect plan and experiencing in the midst of them the redeeming presence of his Lord.

But at last the tensions ended, and the constant battle against the illness that had long plagued him ceased. On December 22, 1888, while residing at the 59th Street Community, Isaac Hecker died.

AFTERWORD

What is the picture of Hecker's spirituality that emerges from his life? In closing, I would like to summarize the main characteristics of his spirituality and offer some thoughts on their significance.

In surveying the spirituality of this man who made so much of being both Catholic and American, one is compelled to attempt to describe the uniquely American character of his experience of God. Sydney Ahlstrom has pointed to two distinguishing characteristics of American theology that are also helpful in isolating the main characteristics of American spirituality: its derivativeness and its diversity.[1] If we apply these categories to Hecker, it becomes evident that his spirituality was typically American in that it was derived from a number of diverse sources. Like the land of his birth, Hecker's piety was a blend of Protestant and Catholic, traditional and contemporary influences that he shaped and styled into a unique whole.

The American character of his spirituality also is evident in its stress on God's special providence. Like his Protestant fellows, he believed that America was to be a city set on a hill.[2] But from it was not to shine the further light of the Reformation, as they thought, but the glories of a renewed Catholicism. His belief in America's manifest destiny will perhaps be seen by some as an example of nineteenth-century American cultural imperialism. However, as tempting as it might be to describe Hecker's thought in these terms, to do so ignores the man's motives and guiding passions. He was not interested in the triumph of American customs, nor did he hopelessly confuse them with Christian values as did some of his contemporaries. If other nations saw America move ahead by embracing a re-

177

ligion that perfectly met its emotional and intellectual needs, then they would be enabled to do likewise, he believed, in their own unique way. It should also be remembered that as his vision for renewal broadened during the last fifteen years of his life, he modified the role that America was to play. In his later years, he was less inclined to insist that the revival he foresaw must take place first on a large scale in America, and then be exported to other lands. He came to believe that it could happen anyplace where people would begin becoming more sensitive to God's presence in their souls, in the church, and in the world.

We have seen that Hecker applied an understanding of special providence to himself, as well as to his homeland. His conviction that God had destined him for some special, extraordinary role is one of the most fascinating and perplexing aspects of his spirituality. At times it seems to be out of line with reality. To some he may appear as a self-styled messiah with grandiose delusions about his own importance. But such is not the impression he made on his contemporaries. People did not perceive this man to be full of himself. He was chastised often, by friend and foe alike, as a dreamer, but never as a proud dreamer. Though his visions were grand, he had at the same time a sense of his own littleness. His plans were big because his idea of God was big. He could believe that he had been called to do great things for the same reason that a Joan of Arc or a Catherine of Siena could believe she had a special task. In this regard he takes his place in the mystical tradition that holds that "divine fecundity" follows the death of the false self.[3]

Hecker's mysticism is not only manifested in this regard, but also in a more fundamental aspect of his spirituality—his radical awareness of God, who was primarily conceived of as the omnipresent Spirit at work in all things.[4] Although asceticism had a place in his spirituality, it clearly received less emphasis than did the mystical dimension. After becoming a Redemptorist, Hecker learned of the classic three-part division of the spiritual life into the illuminative, purgative, and unitive ways. But though he found this somewhat helpful in describing his past experience, it never became a central part of his mature teaching. For him the keen sense of God often spoken of as the dominion of the unitive state was a far more accessible

178

reality. Here the influence of Hecker's Methodist and Transcendentalist backgrounds are evident.

From this mystical awareness flowed Hecker's fascination with the inner life and his desire for synthesis, harmony, and communion. Because of his belief that the Holy Spirit could reside in the soul, he optimistically viewed the capacities of the individual. It was this belief that formed the basis for his emphasis on individual liberty, for his apologetic that appealed to man's religious nature, and for his doctrine of perfection as union with God.

Hecker's desire for synthesis, harmony, and communion motivated him to seek for the reconciliation of forces within modern society with traditional understandings of the Faith. This vision of a synthesis between the church and the modern world was as clear a foreshadowing of Vatican II's *aggiornamento* as one will find in the nineteenth century. That Hecker's ideas could have been seen after his death by critics like the French monarchist Abbé Charles Maignen as opposed to Catholic doctrines of the Church and the sacraments reflects the shallowness of these attacks.

As has been seen, Hecker's hope for a more perfect world made the imperfections of the present all the more painful. It is ironical that a man with such a vivid perception of a more perfect world was so beset with the imperfect, especially during his final fifteen years. Perhaps there is truth in the statement that appeared in the *New York Tablet* at Hecker's death that suggested that in his zeal he had "actually burnt himself out before his time."[5] But any attempt to describe the mature Hecker as "burnt out" has to keep in mind that it was during the 1870s, just when he was, physically speaking, least able to effect his own desires to do good, that he articulated his most universal and optimistic vision of renewal. Here we see Hecker not only as a romantic visionary, but also as a Christian who learned from the example of his Lord how to draw redemptive value from suffering.

The study of Hecker's life makes it clear that his vision of the ideal, his vision of God, was his central motivation and that his life story makes little sense unless his experience of God is given a salient role. But was it not the case that few of his grand schemes materialized? The Paulists were never the dashing forerunners of a new church he had hoped they would be. America was never catholicized, and Vatican I, instead of ushering in an age of the Spirit, initiated an era of triumphalism and regression. Doubtless his hopes ran ahead of reality. Though they contained important insights, they were at points too idyllic, and perhaps even naive.

Hecker's greatest value is not as the architect of a new theology or the founder of a school of speculative spirituality. His thought was never systematic or comprehensive enough for that. Rather, he can be for us what so many things in his world were for him—an inspiration. He dared to believe that God was actively involved in creation, bringing all things to a harmonious end, and that he was destined to be part of that process. Wholeheartedly, and at times recklessly, he ordered his life according to those beliefs. If his vision strikes us as too quixotic, we should keep in mind that visions of a better world are part of the Christian and, indeed, human traditions. They point us to the possibilities of the moment and challenge us to be all that we are capable of being. Hecker had this effect on scores of men and women of his own time, and, if we let him, he can do the same for us.

NOTES

INTRODUCTION

1. *The Concise Sacramentum Mundi,* s.v. "Spirituality," by Josef Sudbrack.

2. Louis Bouyer, *Introduction to Spirituality* (Collegeville, Minn.: Liturgical Press, 1961), pp. 1–4.

3. Walter Elliott, *The Life of Father Hecker* (New York: Columbus, 1894).

4. Vincent Holden, *The Early Years of Isaac Thomas Hecker* (Washington, D.C.: Catholic University, 1939); *Yankee Paul* (Milwaukee: Bruce, 1958).

CHAPTER ONE

1. New Haven *Daily Palladium,* November 7, 1862.

CHAPTER TWO

1. Walter Elliott, *The Life of Father Hecker* (New York: Columbus, 1894), p. 14.

2. Carl W. Schlegel, *Schlegel's German American Families in the U.S.* (New York: American Historical Society, 1916), p. 44.

3. *Ibid.*

4. Georgiana Bruce Kirby, *Years of Experience* (New York: Putnam's, 1887), p. 4.

5. Elliott, p. 3.

6. Quoted in A. Emerson Palmer, *The New York Public School* (New York: Edwin Hill, 1908), pp. 35–36.

7. William O. Bourne, *History of the Public School Society of the City of New York* (New York: Wood, 1870), p. 37.

8. *Ibid.,* p. 38.

9. Elliott, p. 14.

10. *Doctrines and Disciplines of the Methodist Episcopal Church,* 23rd ed. (New York: Methodist Printing Office, N. Bangs and J. Emory, 1825), pp. 3–4.

11. In Gordon Wakefield, *Methodist Devotion: The Spiritual Life in the Methodist Tradition 1791–1945* (London: Epworth, 1966), p. 41.

12. *Ibid.*

13. Kirby, quoted in Elliott, p. 4.

14. Methodist Church Records (abbreviation MCR), Forsyth Street Church, No. 76, "Members 1822–32," New York Public Library.

15. *Doctrines and Disciplines,* pp. 50–55.

16. *Ibid.,* p. 58.

17. MCR, General Records, "Classes 1825," No. 66.

18. MCR, Forsyth Street Church, "Minutes of Sunday School Union, 1827–1833."

19. *The Christian Advocate and Journal,* May 26, 1827. On September 5, 1828 this periodical merged with *Zion's Herald* and was called *The Christian Advocate and Journal and Zion's Herald* until August 23, 1833.

20. Hecker to family, January 19, 1843, Hecker Papers (abbreviation HP), Paulist Fathers Archives, New York, N.Y.

21. *Methodist Quarterly Review* 19 (1832): 346, in *Journals of the General Conference of the Methodist Episcopal Church, 1840* (New York, 1844), p. 161.

22. Frederick Norwood, *The Story of American Methodism* (New York: Abingdon, 1974), p. 50.

23. *John Wesley,* ed. Albert Outler (New York: Oxford, 1964), pp. 9–10.

24. John Wesley, "The Scripture Way of Salvation," in Outler, p. 272.

25. Matthew Simpson, ed., *Cyclopedia of Methodism,* revised ed. (Philadelphia: L.H. Everts, 1880), p. 856.

26. Timothy L. Smith, *Revivalism and Social Reform* (New York: Abingdon, 1957; reprint ed., Gloucester: Peter Smith, 1976), pp. 116–34.

27. In Elliott, p. 293.

28. Named after the Dutchman Jacob Arminius (d. 1609), Arminianism emphasized, in opposition to Calvinism, free will and universal atonement. In nineteenth-century America, Methodists clashed with those who,

like the followers of Connecticut's Samuel Hopkins (d. 1803), favored a strict interpretation of Calvin's teachings.

29. The five points were defined by the Synod of Dort as the doctrines of total depravity, limited atonement, double predestination, irresistible grace, and the perseverance of the saints.

30. Nathan Bangs, *The Reformer Reformed* (New York: Totten, 1819), p. 167.

CHAPTER THREE

1. Elliott, pp. 7–8.
2. Hecker to spiritual director, 1858, p. 1, HP.
3. See Dixon R. Fox, *The Decline of Aristocracy in the Politics of New York* (New York: Longmans, Green, 1919), pp. 229–71, cited in Holden, *Early Years,* pp. 28–29.
4. F. Byrdsall, *The History of the Loco-Foco or Equal Rights Party* (New York: Clement and Packard, 1842; reprint ed. New York: Burt Franklin, 1967), p. 15.
5. *Ibid.,* p. 28.
6. *Ibid.,* pp. 104, 140.
7. Schlegel, pp. 51–57.
8. "Dr. Brownson and the Workingman's Party Fifty Years Ago," *The Catholic World* 45 (May 1887): 203.
9. Hecker to spiritual director, 1858, HP; cf. "Dr. Brownson and Bishop Fitzpatrick," *The Catholic World* 45 (April 1887): 3.
10. Elliott accepts this three-stage interpretation of Hecker's early years uncritically (p. 31). Holden notes that Hecker's political interest continued past 1837 into Hecker's "social" stage, but he fails to realize that Hecker's social and religious concerns were also present during Hecker's "political" stage (*Early Years,* pp. 30–33, 42–43).
11. Holden, *Early Years,* p. 42.
12. Byrdsall, pp. v–vi.
13. *Ibid.,* p. 5.
14. *Ibid.,* p. vi.
15. *Ibid.,* p. 12.
16. *Ibid.,* pp. 41–42.
17. In Elliott, p. 14.
18. *Ibid.,* p. 4.
19. Schlegel, p. 50.
20. MCR, Forsyth Street Church, "Members 1839–73," No. 208.

21. "Dr. Brownson and Catholicity," *The Catholic World* 45 (November 1887): 231.

22. "Dr. Brownson and the Workingman's Party Fifty Years Ago," 205.

23. In Elliott, p. 12.

24. In Holden, *Early Years,* p. 44; Elliott, p. 31.

25. Orville Dewey, "A Discourse Delivered at the Dedication of the Church of the Messiah" (New York: Stationer's Hall, 1839), pp. 11–12.

26. *Idem,* "The Moral Significance of Life," in "Discourses of Human Life," in *The Theological Works of the Reverend Orville Dewey* (London: Griffin, 1854), p. 311.

27. *Idem,* "On Human Nature" in *Works,* pp. 15–16 and 23.

28. *Ibid.,* p. 23.

29. *Idem,* "Life Considered as an Argument for Faith and Virtue," in *Works,* p. 215.

30. *Works,* p. 315.

31. *Ibid.,* pp. 317–18.

32. *Ibid.,* p. 323.

33. *Idem,* "A Discourse Delivered at the Dedication of the Church of the Messiah," pp. 19–21.

34. Elliott, p. 133; Schlegel, p. 53.

35. Holden in *Yankee Paul* dealt with the Hecker-Pratt relationship only in a footnote (n 20, p. 48) in which he set the time of their meeting for the winter of 1843–1844. Hecker's May 31, 1844 diary entry and letter to his mother suggest, however, that Hecker had met Pratt prior to this time. By May 1844 Hecker referred to Pratt as "an old friend" whom he had not seen in a "great length of time." In an article which he wrote for the *Paulist News* dated January 27, 1938, Holden developed Hecker's relation with Pratt.

36. Diary, January 1844, HP.

37. Joseph E. Smith, "The Truth about Mormonism," *Out West,* September 1905, pp. 244–45, quoted in Robert C. Webb, *The Real Mormonism* (New York: Sturgis and Walton, 1916), p. 320; Holden's article, p. 2.

38. In Elliott, p. 23.

39. Webb, pp. 112–13.

40. Hecker to spiritual director, 1858; Webb, pp. 111–12.

41. David B. Davis, "The New England Origins of Mormonism," in *Mormonism and American Culture,* ed. Marvin Hill (New York: Harper and Row, 1972), p. 20.

NOTES

42. See "Mormon Doctrines," *Chicago Democrat,* March 1842, in William LaRue, *Foundations of Mormonism* (New York: Revell, 1919), p. 136.

43. *Voice of Warning,* 13th ed. (Salt Lake City: George Cannon, 1891), p. 181.

44. *Ibid.,* p. 188.

45. "Dr. Brownson and Catholicity," *The Catholic World* 45 (November 1887): 235.

46. In Thomas R. Ryan, *Orestes A. Brownson: A Definitive Biography* (Huntington, Ind.: Our Sunday Visitor, 1976), p. 102.

47. Brownson Papers, microfilm roll 10, in Ryan, p. 110.

48. Letter of Brownson's to George Bancroft, November 10, 1837, Brownson Papers, roll 9, in Ryan, p. 22.

49. "Dr. Brownson and the Workingman's Party Fifty Years Ago," 205.

50. Quoted in Holden, *Early Years,* p. 54.

51. Hecker to Brownson, Brownson Papers, I, 3, f., Archives, University of Notre Dame, South Bend, in Holden, *Early Years,* p. 49.

52. *Tribune,* January 17, 1812, in Holden, *Early Years,* p. 57.

53. Holden, *Early Years,* p. 62; Elliott, pp. 26–30.

54. Holden, *Early Years,* p. 65.

55. "Dr. Brownson's Road to the Church," *The Catholic World* 45 (October 1887): 6.

56. In Elliott, p. 18.

57. Diary, April 24, 1843.

58. *Ibid.,* May 18, 1843. See Chapter III for Lawrence McDonnell's observations on Hecker's dream-vision.

59. John Hecker to Brownson, January 7, 1843, Brownson Papers, I, 3, g., in Holden, *Early Years,* p. 74.

60. See Hecker's 1882 account of this period in Elliott, p. 34.

61. Neither Elliott (p. 32f) nor Holden (*Early Years,* p. 90) fully appreciated this.

CHAPTER FOUR

1. Clara Endicott Sears, *Bronson Alcott's Fruitlands* (New York: Mifflin, 1915), p. 35.

2. Ora Sedgwick, "A Girl of Sixteen at Brook Farm," *Atlantic Monthly* 85 (1890): 394–404; Kirby in Lindsay Swift, *Brook Farm* (New York, 1900: rpt. New York: Corinth, 1961), p. 98.

3. George Curtis to Walter Elliott, February 28, 1890, in Elliott, p. 55.

4. Sears, p. 21.

5. Alcott to Hecker, February 15, 1843, in Sears, pp. 12–13.

6. Diary, November 1, 1843.

7. *Ibid.,* July 27, 1843, p. 57.

8. *Ibid.,* August 9, 1843, p. 83.

9. *Ibid.,* June 13, 1843, p. 33.

10. *Ibid.,* June 26, 1843, p. 39.

11. *Ibid.,* June 26, 1843, p. 40.

12. *Ibid.,* p. 39.

13. *Ibid.,* July 12 and 13, 1843, p. 47.

14. *Ibid.,* July 17, 1843, p. 48.

15. *Ibid.,* July 17, 1843, p. 49.

16. *Ibid.,* p. 54.

17. *Ibid.*

18. *Ibid.,* July 22, 1843, p. 54.

19. *Ibid.,* August 16, 1843, p. 85.

20. *Ibid.,* September 28, 1843, p. 89.

21. *Ibid.*

22. *Ibid.,* July 27, 1843, p. 56.

23. Hecker to family, July 31, 1843, HP.

24. Diary, August 15, 1843.

25. *Ibid.,* May 19, 1844, p. 162.

26. *Ibid.,* June 6, 1844, p. 176.

27. *Ibid.,* August 9, 1843, p. 71.

28. *Ibid.,* December 6, 1843, p. 104.

29. Hecker to family, April 24, 1843, in Elliott, p. 33.

30. Diary, July 13, 1843.

31. I. T. Hecker, "Dr. Brownson's Road to the Church," *The Catholic World* 45 (October 1887): 7.

32. Hecker to family, February 22, 1843, in Elliott, p. 41.

33. *Ibid.,* March 6, 1843, HP.

34. Diary, July 17, 1843, p. 49.

35. *Ibid.,* January 10, 1843, p. 2.

36. *Ibid.,* February, 1843, pp. 5–6.

37. *Ibid.,* January 11, 1843, pp. 3–4.

38. *Ibid.,* August 9, 1843, p. 71.

39. *Ibid.,* March 25, 1844, p. 119.

40. *Ibid.,* January 10, 1843, p. 2.

NOTES

41. *Ibid..* August 24, 1843.
42. *Ibid.,* August 9, 1843, p. 64.
43. *Ibid.,* August 13, 1843, p. 84.
44. *Ibid.,* April 1843, in Elliott, p. 64.
45. *Ibid.,* August 2, 1843, p. 63.

CHAPTER FIVE

1. See Claude Welch, *Protestant Thought in the Nineteenth Century, Vol. I: 1799–1870* (New Haven: Yale, 1972), p. 180, fn. 8.
2. For a discussion of the various European and Oriental sources on which the Transcendentalists drew see: Kenneth Cameron, *Emerson the Essayist,* 2 vols. (Raleigh: Thistle, 1945); Donald Koster, *Transcendentalism in America* (Boston: Twayne, 1975); Rene Wellek, "The Minor Transcendentalists and German Philosophy," *New England Quarterly* 15 (1942): 652–80; and Arthur T. Christy, *The Orient in American Transcendentalism* (New York: Columbia, 1932).
3. *Boston Daily Advertiser,* November 9, 1836, in Perry Miller, *The Transcendentalists* (Cambridge: Harvard, 1950), p. 163.
4. *Ibid.*
5. *Ibid.*
6. Brownson Papers, microfilm roll 10, in Ryan, p. 110.
7. *New Views,* in Miller, p. 119.
8. See Stanley M. Vogel, *German Literary Influences on the American Transcendentalists* (New Haven: Yale, 1955).
9. *Ibid.,* pp. 157–160.
10. Lawrence McDonnell, C.S.P., "Isaac Hecker, a Man of Letters" (typewritten), p. 8.
11. Diary, January 10, 1843; McDonnell, p. 8.
12. McDonnell, p. 8.
13. Diary, December 31, 1843.
14. Ralph W. Emerson, "The American Scholar" (1837), in *The Complete Writings of Ralph W. Emerson, Vol. I* (New York: William Wise, 1929), p. 28.
15. Cf., Odell Shephard's list in *Peddlar's Progress. The Life of Bronson Alcott* (Boston: Little, Brown, 1938), pp. 258–9.
16. Emerson, p. 36.
17. Frederick Carpenter, *Emerson Handbook* (New York: Hendricks, 1953), pp. 128–29.

18. Bronson Alcott, Journal, September 21, 1835, in *Journals of Bronson Alcott,* ed. O. Shephard (Boston: Little, Brown, 1938), p. 65.

19. *Ibid.,* May 1833, p. 36.

20. Plotinus in *The Essence of Plotinus,* comp. Grace Turnbull (New York: Oxford, 1934), pp. 109, 113–14.

21. See Paul Henry in *Introduction to Plotinus: The Enneads,* 2nd ed. (London: Faber, 1956), p. xlix.

22. Alcott, Journal, December 5, 1839, in Shephard, *Alcott's Journal,* pp. 136–37.

23. Catalogue of the Original Fruitlands Library, in Clara F. Sears, *Bronson Alcott's Fruitlands* (New York: Mifflin, 1915), appendix.

24. O. A. Brownson, "The Philosophy of Cousin," *Christian Examiner* 21 (September 1837): 1f.

25. Review of James F. Clarke's translation of *Revelation of Specimens of Religion, Christian Examiner* 10 (January 1842): 363.

26. "Life of St. Bernard of Clairvaux; a Chapter Out of the Middle Ages," *Christian Examiner* 30 (March 1841): 1f.

27. See James Walker, "Reaction in Favor of the Roman Catholics," *Christian Examiner* 23 (September 1837): 1f.

28. Diary, August 2, 1843, p. 64.

29. Hecker to Brownson, April 6, 1844, HP.

30. Diary, May 23, 1844.

31. *Ibid.,* September 1, 1843; October 26, 1843; February 15, 1844; June 14, 1844.

CHAPTER SIX

1. Diary, February 4 and 5, 1843, p. 8.

2. *Ibid.,* April 17, 1843, p. 11.

3. Hecker to family, April 19, 1843, HP.

4. See J. A. Moehler, *Symbolism* (New York: Dunigan, 1844).

5. "Brownson and Catholicity," p. 225.

6. Hecker to family, March 1, 1843, in Holden, *Early Years,* pp. 107–08. Hecker does not indicate which Tracts he read.

7. Diary, April 18, 1843.

8. *Ibid.,* April 24, 1843.

9. *Ibid.,* April 28, 1843.

10. *Ibid.,* May 4, 1843, p. 21.

NOTES

11. *Ibid.,* May 24, 1843.

12. *Ibid.,* June 5, 1843.

13. Curtis to Hecker, September 3, 1843, HP.

14. Diary, November 1, 1843.

15. *Ibid.,* November 11, 1843.

16. *Ibid.,* October 17, 1843.

17. Brownson to Hecker, November 8, 1843, Brownson Papers, in Holden, *Early Years,* p. 190.

18. Brownson did not join the Catholic church until October 20, 1844, two months after Hecker.

19. Hecker to family, May 30, 1843, HP.

20. Ripley to Hecker, October 8, 1843, HP.

21. Cf. Brownson to Hecker, October 8, 1843, HP.

22. Hecker to Brownson, December 14, 1843, HP.

23. I. T. Hecker, "Dr. Brownson's Road to the Church," *The Catholic World* 46 (October 1887): 5.

24. *Ibid.,* pp. 9–10.

25. *Ibid.,* p. 6.

26. O. A. Brownson, *The Convert* (New York: Edward Dunigan, 1857), p. 304.

27. *Ibid.,* p. 293.

28. *Ibid.,* p. 313.

29. *Ibid.,* p. 333; also in "Brownson and Catholicity," p. 230.

30. Dana to Hecker, January 2, 1844, HP.

31. *Ibid.*

32. Hecker to Brownson, March 9, 1844, Brownson Papers, in Holden, *Early Years,* p. 198.

33. Hecker to Brownson, April 6, 1844, HP.

34. Hecker to Mrs. John Hecker, May 31, 1844, HP.

35. Hecker to Brownson, June 4, 1844, HP.

36. Brownson to Hecker, June 6, 1844, HP.

37. *Ibid.*

38. Diary, June 7, 1844.

39. Hecker to Brownson, December 14, 1843, Brownson Papers, in Holden, *Early Years,* p. 190.

40. Hecker to family, June 11, 1844, HP.

41. "Notes on the Holy Spirit," p. 64, HP.

42. Diary, June 13, 1844.

43. *Ibid.,* July 9, 1844.

NOTES

CHAPTER SEVEN

1. See George Curtis to Hecker, November 3, 1844, January 24, 1845, HP.
2. *Ibid.*, March 2, 5, 9, 21, 1845.
3. *Ibid.*, April 29, 1845; May 5, 1845.
4. *Ibid.*, June 2, 1845.
5. Charles Lane to Hecker, June, 1845, HP.
6. *Ibid.*
7. Hecker to Thoreau, July 31, 1844, HP.
8. Thoreau to Hecker, August 14, 1844, HP.
9. Burrill Curtis to Hecker, August 23, 1844, HP.
10. Hecker to Brownson, October 29, 1844, HP.
11. *Ibid.*, January 14, 1845, HP.
12. Curtis to Hecker, April 13, 1845, HP.
13. Hecker to Brownson, July 23, 1845, HP.
14. *Ibid.*, July 24, 1845.
15. *Ibid.*
16. *Ibid.*
17. *Ibid.*, July 23, 1845.
18. Brownson to Hecker, July 31, 1845, HP.
19. *Ibid.*
20. *Ibid.*
21. Hecker to Brownson, September 18, 1845, HP.
22. Hecker to family, September 18, 1845, HP.
23. Hecker to Bishop John McCloskey, October 15, 1846, HP.
24. Hecker to family, March 4, 1846; April 28, 1846; August 26, 1846; October 15, 1846, HP.
25. "Theological Notes," HP.
26. *Ibid.*
27. Hecker to family, October 15, 1846, HP.
28. *Ibid.*
29. Hecker to Brownson, November 1, 1846, HP.
30. Hecker in Elliott, p. 311.
31. Hecker to spiritual director, written in Rome, January 6, 1858, HP.
32. Heilig to Hecker, March 24, 1849, HP.
33. Hecker to family, September 20, 1847, HP.
34. Hecker to Thoreau, May 15, 1847, HP; Hecker to Curtis, April 15, 1849, HP.

35. Hecker to family, January 1, 1846, HP.
36. Hecker to Heilig, May 30, 1848, HP.
37. *Ibid.*
38. *Ibid.*
39. *Ibid.*

CHAPTER EIGHT

1. See Holden, *Yankee*, Chap. VIII, pp. 149f.
2. *Ibid.*
3. Finney promulgated the practice of calling those seeking the grace of conversion to the front of the church. There those awaiting grace would sit on a bench where they would mourn over their past sins.
4. See Jay Dolan, *Catholic Revivalism* (South Bend: University of Notre Dame, 1978).
5. Hecker to Brownson, September 5, 1851, HP.
6. *Ibid.*
7. Hecker to Brownson, April 12, 1856, Brownson Papers, in Holden, *Yankee*, p. 201.
8. Hecker to Brownson, September 14, 1854, HP.
9. See Joseph F. Gower, "The New Apologetics of Isaac Thomas Hecker (1819–1888): Catholicity and American Culture" (Ph.D. dissertation, University of Notre Dame, 1978).
10. I. T. Hecker, *Questions of the Soul* (New York: Appleton, 1855), p. 5.
11. *Questions*, p. 33.
12. *Ibid.*, p. 290.
13. *Ibid.*, p. 291.
14. Gower's statements on the originality of Hecker's apologetic (p. 90) would be modified by a fuller consideration of his Transcendentalist background.
15. Bancroft to Hecker, March 14, 1855, HP.
16. *Brownson Quarterly Review* 3 (April 1855): 215f., in Holden, *Yankee*, p. 192.
17. Hecker to Brownson, March 2, 1855, HP.
18. Hecker to Simpson, June 1856, HP.
19. Simpson to Hecker, July 28, 1856, HP.
20. *Ibid.*
21. Hecker to Hewit, June 29, 1857, HP.

22. I. T. Hecker, *Aspirations of Nature* (New York: Kirker, 1857), pp. 7–8.

23. *Ibid.*, p. 27.

24. *Ibid.*

25. *Ibid.*, pp. 40–43.

26. *Ibid.*, p. 87.

27. *Ibid.*, pp. 208–10.

28. *Ibid.*, p. 45.

29. *Ibid.*

30. *Ibid.*, p. 46.

31. See Holden, *Yankee*, p. 224 for details of the period 1857–58.

32. *Ibid.*, pp. 298–99.

33. Transcript of the original Hecker manuscript for *Civiltà Cattolica* as published (in Italian) in *Civiltà*, Nos. 184 and 185 (1857), series III, Vol. 8, pp. 385 and 513, HP.

34. *Ibid.*

35. *Aspirations*, p. 142.

36. *Ibid.*

37. *Ibid.*, p. 147.

38. E.g., *Aspirations*, Chapter XIX, pp. 141–51, and fn. on p. 151 citing *Symbolik*.

CHAPTER NINE

1. Programme, quoted in Joseph McSorley, *Isaac Hecker and His Friends* (New York: Herder, 1952; reprint ed., New York: Paulist, 1972), pp. 190–91.

2. Hecker to Abbé Roequet, December 27, 1859, HP.

3. Quoted in Elliott, p. 292. No source is given, but most likely it is from "Notes Concerning New Religious Institutions" which Hecker wrote sometime after April 1876, HP.

4. *Ibid.*, p. 290.

5. *Ibid.*, p. 294.

6. *Ibid.*

7. *Ibid.*, pp. 326–27.

8. Hecker to Bishop Chatard, February 2, 1868, HP.

9. *The Advance* (Chicago), May 28, 1868.

NOTES

10. Elliott, p. 342.

11. See Sydney Ahlstrom, *A Religious History of the American People* (New Haven: Yale, 1972), p. 738.

12. *Atlantic Monthly* (April and May 1868), in Elliott, p. 346.

13. Elliott, p. 341.

14. Hecker to Barnabo, July 1863, in Elliott, p. 338.

15. E.g., in "Fidelity to Conscience," *Paulist Sermons* (New York: Sadlier, 1864), p. 17.

16. "Giving Testimony," *Paulist Sermons 1861* (New York: Parys, Hugot, Howell, 1861), p. 73.

17. Hecker to Simpson, February 22, 1861, HP.

18. Manuscript A on the Spiritual Life, April 1860, HP.

19. *Ibid.*

20. Manuscript B on the Spiritual Life, p. 18, HP.

21. *Ibid.*, p. 7.

22. See Hecker to Mrs. King, July 12, 1865, HP.

23. Manuscript A, pp. 16, 21.

24. Manuscript B, pp. 11, 12.

25. Manuscript A, p. 8.

26. *Ibid.*, p. 9.

27. Manuscript B, p. 19.

28. *Ibid.*, p. 5.

29. "The Model Saint for Our Day," *Paulist Sermons 1863* (New York: Sadlier, 1864), p. 91.

30. Hecker to King, January 24, 1864, HP.

31. *Ibid.*, March 1863.

32. *Ibid.*, April 16, 1863.

33. *Ibid.*, July 27, 1863.

34. *Ibid.*, March 25, 1863.

35. *Ibid.*, January 18, 1864.

36. *Ibid.*, August 2, 1864.

37. *Ibid.*, February 4, 1865.

38. See Hecker to Simpson, February 22, 1861, HP.

39. Hecker to King, July 12, 1863.

40. *Ibid.*, January 4, 1865.

41. *Ibid.*, December 4, 1863; September 23, 1863.

42. *Ibid.*, January 26, 1865.

43. Brownson to Hecker, March 10, 1869, HP.

44. Brownson to Sadlier, June 3, 1868, HP.

NOTES

CHAPTER TEN

1. "Our New York Letter." *The Catholic Standard*, March 25, 1867.

2. *New York Tablet*, July 27, 1867; *Freeman's* Journal, July 20, 1857; *Pilot*, July 20, 1867.

3. *New York Tablet*, July 27, 1867.

4. Hecker's address was given in French and under the title "La Situation Religuese Des Etats-Unis," *Revue Générale*, October 1867, pp. 348–58.

5. "Farewell Sermon," *The Catholic World* 10 (December 1869): 289 f.

6. "Notes Made in Italy, 1869–1870" (abbreviation NI), HP.

7. *Ibid.*, February 24, 1870.

8. In Elliott, p. 370.

9. *Ibid.*

10. *Ibid.*, p. 380.

11. J. P. de Caussade, *Abandonment*, trans. Ella McMahon, with an introduction by H. Ramière (New York: Benziger, 1887), p. 69.

12. *Ibid.*, p. 380.

13. *Ibid.*, pp. 120–21.

14. Preface to Caussade's *Abandonment*, HP.

15. In Elliott, p. 274.

16. "Notes Begun in Egypt 1873 and Finished in Europe and the U.S. 1874, 1875," (abbreviation NE), p. 3, HP.

17. *Ibid.*

18. *Ibid.*

19. *Ibid.*, p. 3.

20. *Ibid.*, p. 28.

21. *Ibid.*, p. 3.

22. L'Abbé Dufresne, "Personal Recollections of Father Hecker." *The Catholic World* 67 (June 1898): 325.

23. "Notes on Interior States in 1874, '75, '76," (abbreviation IS), p. 8, HP.

24. *Ibid.*

25. *The Church and the Age: An Exposition of the Catholic Church in View of the Needs and Aspirations of the Present Age* (New York: Catholic Publication Society, 1887; reprint ed., New York: Catholic Book Exchange, 1896), p. 26.

26. *Ibid.*, p. 27.

27. *Ibid.*, p. 29.

28. "Notes on Holy Spirit" (abbreviation NHS), p. 41, HP.
29. IS, p. 5.
30. *Ibid.*
31. *Ibid.*, p. 1.
32. *Ibid.*, p. 6.
33. *Ibid.*
34. *Ibid.*
35. *Ibid.*
36. *Ibid.*, pp.6–7.
37. *Ibid.*, p. 12.
38. *Ibid.*, pp. 16–17.
39. Hecker to George and Josephine Hecker, November 13, 1874, HP.
40. Peter Rossi to Hecker, December 20, 1874, HP.
41. Julia Beers to Archbishop Bayley, March 11, 1875, HP.
42. Manning to Hecker, February 1, 1875, HP.
43. Newman to Hecker, April 10, 1875, HP.
44. Craven to Hecker, March 14, 1875, HP.
45. *Le Monde,* September 15, 1875.
46. Joseph Burone to Hecker, March 22, 1875, HP.
47. D. Chocarne to Hecker, August 8, 1875, HP.
48. Dufresne to Hecker, March 31, 1875, HP.
49. Hecker to George Hecker, March 4, 1875. See also *The Church and the Age,* p. 32. For discussion of DeMaistre, see Gerald McCool, *Catholic Theology in the Nineteenth Century* (New York: Seabury, 1977), pp. 37–40.
50. Hecker to Simpson, September 23, 1875, HP.
51. Hecker to George Hecker, March 4, 1875, HP.

CHAPTER ELEVEN

1. Hewit to Hecker, November 25, 1874, HP.
2. Hecker to Hewit, November 23, 1874, HP.
3. Hecker to Josephine Hecker, October 12, 1874, HP.
4. Young to Hecker, July 7, 1875, HP.
5. Hewit to Hecker, July 9, 13, 1875, HP.
6. L'Abbé Dufresne, "Personal Recollections of Father Hecker," *The Catholic World* 67 (June 1898): 325–326.
7. Hecker, IS, June 6, 1875, p. 15.
8. *Ibid.*, August 1, 1875, p. 14.
9. *Ibid.*, p. 16.
10. Hecker to Hewit, July 30, 1875.

CHAPTER TWELVE

1. Hecker to George Hecker, August 4, 1875, HP.

2. *Ibid.*

3. Hecker to Hewit, September 21, 1875, HP.

4. *Ibid.*

5. Joseph Malloy, *The Church of St. Paul the Apostle in New York* (New York: Paulist, n.d.), pp. 5, 11. See also Hecker to LaFarge, January 12, 1876, HP.

6. Hecker to Sr. Mary Constance of Jesus and Sr. Magdaline, September 16, 1865, HP.

7. H. S. C. Noteware to Hecker, October 4, 1876, HP.

8. See Hecker to Hewit, December 1875, HP.

9. See Hecker to Bp. McQuaid, August 15, 1876; Hecker to Bp. Foley, October 31, 1876, HP.

10. Kehoe to Hudson, June 18, 1882, HP.

11. E.g., Hecker to Burone, February 7, 1876; Craven to Hecker, February 29, 1876; Dufresne to Hecker, October 1877, HP.

12. Corrigan to Hecker, March 22, 1880, HP.

13. "The Intellectual Outlook of the Age," in *The Church and the Age*, pp. 181–206.

14. "God and Man," n.d., HP.

15. See for example, John Morgan, *The Scriptural Testimony of the Holy Spirit* (Oberlin: Goodrich, 1875), preface; L. R. Dunn, *The Mission of the Spirit* (New York: Carlton and Lahaman, 1871), preface; Amory Bradford, *Spirit and Life: Thoughts for To-day* (New York: Fords, Howard, Hulbert, 1888), p. 71; William Biederwolf, *A Help to the Study of the Holy Spirit* (New York: Revell, 1904), p. 7; and Timothy L. Smith, *Revivalism and Social Reform* (New York: Harper and Row, 1956).

16. Asa Mahan, *The Baptism of the Holy Ghost* (New York: Palmer, 1878).

17. Hecker to Ryder, January 18, 1877, HP.

18. "The Spiritual World and the Rule of Faith," in *The Church and the Age*, p. 262.

19. See George Peck, "Dr. Upham's Works," *Methodist Quarterly Review* 27 (1846): 248–65; Frederick Huntington, "Catherine Adorna," *Hours at Home* 1 (1865): 293–301; Dougan Clark, *The Offices of the Holy Ghost* (London: Haughton, 1878), pp. 27, 81–82.

20. *The Life and Doctrine of St. Catherine of Genoa* (New York: Catholic Publication Society, 1874), pp. 7–10.

NOTES

21. "The Things That Make For Unity," *The Catholic World* 47 (April 1888): 103.

22. See Hecker to H. J. D. Ryder, January 18, 1872; Hecker to Hewit, September 9, 1874; Hewit to Hecker, September 12, 1879, HP.

23. IS, August 3, 1876.

24. Hewit to Hecker, September 9, 1878, HP.

25. Julia Beers to Archbp. Bayley, March 11, 1875, HP.

26. Elliott's notes on the 1884 Chapter, HP.

27. "The Renewal of the Christian Life," p. 1, HP.

28. *Ibid.*

29. *Ibid.*, p. 4.

30. *Ibid.*, p. 8.

31. "The Spirit of the Paulist Community," n.d., HP.

AFTERWORD

1. See Sydney Ahlstrom's "Theology in America: A Historical Perspective," in James W. Smith and Leland Jamison, eds., *Religion in American Life*. Vol. I: *Religious Perspectives in American Culture* (Princeton: Princeton University Press, 1961), p. 234.

2. See Robert T. Handy, *Christian America: Protestant Hopes and Historic Realities* (New York: Oxford, 1971).

3. See Evelyn Underhill, *Mysticism* (London: Methuen, 1911), Part II, Chapter 10.

4. See the definitions of mysticism given by Underhill, Part II, Chapter 1, and Bouyer, p. 303.

5. *New York Tablet,* December 30, 1888.

SELECTED BIBLIOGRAPHY

The primary source for this study has been the Hecker Papers collection, located in the Paulist Fathers Archives, New York, N.Y. An annotated bibliography of the unpublished Hecker Papers which were of particular value in the study of his spirituality follows. Below are listed other sources which were especially helpful. Full references to all sources cited in the text may be found in the footnotes.

I. MANUSCRIPT COLLECTIONS

New York, N.Y. Paulist Fathers Archives. Hecker Papers.

>This collection contains all the extant works of Isaac Hecker, along with the papers of other early Paulists. It is the product of the diligent labors of Walter Elliott and those Paulist archivists who have succeeded him, the most prominent of whom has been Vincent Holden.

New York, N.Y. New York Public Library. Methodist Church Records. Forsyth Street Church Records.

>Useful source for information on Mrs. Hecker's church.

II. OTHER SOURCES

Ahlstrom, Sydney. *A Religious History of the American People*. New Haven: Yale, 1972.

Alcott, Bronson. *Journals*. Edited by Odell Shephard. Boston: Little, Brown, 1938.

Biederwolf, William E. *A Help to the Study of the Holy Spirit*. New York: Revell, 1904.

SELECTED BIBLIOGRAPHY

Bradford, Amory. *Spirit and Life; Thoughts for To-day*. New York: Fords, Howard, Hulbert, 1888.

Brownson, Orestes A. *The Convert*. New York: Dunigan, 1857.

————. *The Works of Orestes A. Brownson*. Edited by Henry F. Brownson. Detroit: Thorndike, 1882.

Bucke, Emory S., ed. *The History of American Methodism*. 2 vols. New York: Abingdon, 1964.

Byrdsall, F. *The History of the Loco-Foco or Equal Rights Party*. New York: Clement and Packard, 1842; reprint ed. New York: Burt Franklin, 1967.

Cameron, Kenneth W. *Emerson The Essayist*. 2 vols. Raleigh: Thistle, 1945.

————. *Young Emerson's Transcendental Vision*. Hartford: Transcendental, 1971.

Cushing, William. *Index to the Christian Examiner*. Boston: Cushing, 1879; reprint ed., Hartford: Transcendental, 1967.

De Caussade, J. P. *Abandonment; or Absolute Surrender to Divine Providence*. Translated by Ella McMahon. New York: Benziger, 1887.

Dewey, Orville. "A Discourse Delivered at the Dedication of the Church of the Messiah." New York: Stationer's Hall, 1839.

————. *The Theological Works of the Rev. Orville Dewey*. London: Griffin, 1854.

Elliott, Walter. *The Life of Father Hecker*. New York: Columbus, 1894.

Emerson, Ralph W. *Nature*. Boston: James Monroe, 1846; reprint ed., New York: Scholar's Facsimiles and Reprints, 1940.

————. "The American Scholar." Printed in *The Complete Writings of Ralph W. Emerson*. Vol. 1. New York: Wise, 1929.

Frothingham, Octavius B. *Transcendentalism in New England*. New York: Putnam's, 1876.

Gower, Joseph F. "The New Apologetics of Isaac Thomas Hecker (1819–1888): Catholicity and American Culture." Ph.D. dissertation, University of Notre Dame, 1978.

SELECTED BIBLIOGRAPHY

Handy, Robert T. *Christian America: Protestant Hopes and Historic Realities.* New York: Oxford, 1971.

Hecker, Isaac T. *The Questions of the Soul.* New York: Appleton, 1855.

———. *The Aspirations of Nature.* New York: Kirker, 1857.

———. Article on the prospects for Catholicism in America. *Civiltà Cattolica* (Rome), nos. 184, 185 (1857), pp. 385f., 513f.

———. "La Situation Religieuse des Etats-Unis," *Revue Générale* (Paris), October 1867, pp. 348–58.

———. "Farewell Sermon," *The Catholic World* 10 (December 1869): 289f.

———. "Dr. Brownson and Bishop Fitzpatrick," *The Catholic World* 45 (April 1887): 1–7.

———. "Dr. Brownson and the Workingman's Party Fifty Years Ago," *The Catholic World* 45 (May 1887): 200–07.

———. "Dr. Brownson's Road to the Church," *The Catholic World* 46 (October 1887): 1–11.

———. "Dr. Brownson and Catholicity," *The Catholic World* 46 (November 1887): 222–35.

———. *The Church and the Age.* New York: Catholic Publication Society, 1887; reprint ed., New York: Catholic Book Exchange, 1896.

———. "The Things That Make for Unity," *The Catholic World* 47 (April 1888): 102–09.

Holden, Vincent. *The Early Years of Isaac Thomas Hecker.* Washington: Catholic University, 1939.

———. *Yankee Paul.* Milwaukee: Bruce, 1958.

McDonnell, Lawrence. "Isaac Hecker a Man of Letters." (Typewritten)

McGiffert, Arthur C. *The Rise of Modern Religious Ideas.* New York: Macmillan, 1915.

McSorley, Joseph. *Father Hecker and His Friends.* New York: Herder, 1952; reprint ed., New York: Paulist, 1972.

Manning, Henry Cardinal. *The Internal Mission of the Holy Ghost.* New York: Sadlier, 1881.

SELECTED BIBLIOGRAPHY

Methodist Episcopal Church. *Doctrines and Disciplines of the Methodist Episcopal Church.* 23rd ed. New York: Methodist Printing Office, 1825.

Miller, Perry. *The Transcendentalists.* Cambridge: Harvard, 1950.

Outler, Albert, ed. *John Wesley.* New York: Oxford, 1964.

Plotinus. *The Essence of Plotinus.* Compiled by Grace Turnbull. New York: Oxford, 1934.

Pratt, Parley P. *The Voice of Warning.* 13th ed. Salt Lake City: Cannon, 1891.

Preston, Thomas S. *The Divine Paraclete.* New York: Coddington, 1879.

Rose, Earnest. *A History of German Literature.* New York: New York University, 1960.

Ryan, Thomas R. *Orestes A. Brownson: A Definitive Biography.* Huntington, Ind.: Our Sunday Visitor Press, 1976.

Schlegel, Carl W. *Schlegel's German American Families in the U.S.* New York: American Historical Society, 1916.

Shephard, Odell. *Peddlar's Progress. The Life of Bronson Alcott.* Boston: Little, Brown, 1938.

Smith, Timothy L. *Revivalism and Social Reform.* New York: Harper and Row, 1956; reprint ed., Gloucester, Mass.: Peter Smith, 1976.

Upham, Thomas C. *The Life of Catherine Adorna.* . . . 3rd ed. New York: Harper, 1858.

Wakefield, Gordon. *Methodist Devotion: The Spiritual Life in the Methodist Tradition 1791–1945.* London: Epworth, 1966.

Webb, Robert C. *The Real Mormonism.* New York: Sturgis and Walton, 1916.

Welch, Claude. *Protestant Thought in the Nineteenth Century.* Vol. I: *1799–1870.* New Haven: Yale, 1972.

Zardetti, Otto. *Special Devotion to the Holy Ghost.* Milwaukee: Hoffmann, 1888.

ANNOTATED BIBLIOGRAPHY

ISAAC T. HECKER'S UNPUBLISHED WORKS

Diary, Vol. I, January 10, 1843 through May 14, 1844; Vol. II, May 15, 1844 through December 18, 1844.

> Important source for Hecker's early spirituality. Many ideas articulated in the diary by the young Transcendentalist became important themes in Hecker's later writing.

"Theological Notes," c. 1850.

> Holden's note runs as follows: "From the context it would seem that these notes were written by Fr. Hecker as a Redemptorist student or early in his priesthood. They are more a contrast between Catholic and Protestant than 'theological.'"

Hecker Correspondence with Mrs. Jane King, March 25, 1863 through July 12, 1865.

> Letters of spiritual direction written to New York laywoman, Mrs. King. Subjects include: the role of the Holy Spirit as guide of the soul, Christian perfection, and the type of spirituality especially suited to the American character.

Manuscript I on the Spiritual Life, 1860.

> Holden identifies this booklet as the "ideas ITH had in mind when he told [Richard] Simpson he had plans for a book on spirituality for the laity." Hecker states his desire to "reconcile devotion with practical life—to set aside an antagonism that has been created by heated imagination, false theology, and false philosophy between practical, ordinary life, and true piety."

202

Manuscript II on the Spiritual Life (pp. 1–82), 1860.

>Apparently a continuation of the above work.

"Thoughts on the Spiritual Life," n.d., but after 1865.

>Stresses the familiar themes of perfection as attainable in the common everyday life, the importance of the direct guidance of the Holy Spirit, and the need for practicing virtue in the world.

"Views Relative to Past and Future," December 1875.

"The Renewal of the Christian Life," Vol. I (pp. 18–28), December 1875.

"The Renewal of the Christian Life," Vol. II (pp. 29–49), December 1875.

"The Organization of New Religious Institutions," originally pp. 1–6 of Vol. II of "Renewal of the Christian Life."

"Notes Concerning New Religious Institutions." Title given by Elliott. Supposedly is a revision of "The Renewal of the Christian Life."

>These five works represent various versions of what was apparently intended to be one work. Topics dealt with include: the role of new religious institutions in bringing renewal, the characteristics of such institutions, and the importance of the Holy Spirit's work in renewal.

"Notes on the Holy Spirit," n.d., most likely 1870s and 1880s.

>Notes on the Holy Spirit culled from various unidentified Hecker sources. Compiled by Walter Elliott. Deals with work of Holy Spirit in believer and in the Church.

"God and Man." Revised and edited by Walter Elliott, n.d., but after 1886.

>Intended by Hecker as his "last word to the public." The manuscript, which appears ready for publication, is an example of what Hecker thought was the type of apologetic especially well suited for the nineteenth century.

"The Spirit of the Paulist Community," n.d., but c. 1888.

>Hecker expresses discontent over the present direction of the Paulist community. Maintains that they have been turned to a direction which "differs from that which my interior spirit can concur with."

Hecker Correspondence, September 18, 1843–1888.

ANNOTATED BIBLIOGRAPHY

Of special interest for Hecker's spirituality are the Hecker-Brownson and the above-mentioned Hecker-King correspondences.

"Notes Made in Italy," 1869–1870.

Observations on Vatican I and the Italian character made by Hecker during the time of his involvement in the Council as *peritus* theologian.

"Notes in Egypt," begun in Egypt 1873, finished in Europe and the United States, 1875–1876.

Opens with diary which Hecker kept in Egypt beginning November 25, 1873. Includes discussion of future worldwide renewal of religion.

"Preface to Caussade's Abandonment," n.d., c. 1870.

Intended as a preface to McMahon's English translation of Caussade's work.

"Notes on Interior States in 1874, '75 and '76 While Abroad."

Notes made by Hecker during European and Egyptian tour. Describing himself as an "International Catholic," Hecker discussed plans for the promulgation of his scheme for Church renewal which he describes as his "programme."

INDEX

Abbot, Francis E., 168.
Absolute, The Eternal, 54, 67, 121.
Acculturalization, 146.
Adorna, Catherine. *See* Catherine of
    Genoa, St.
Advance, The (Chicago), 123.
Aeterni Patris, 167.
Aggiornamento, 179.
Ahlstrom, Sydney E., 177.
À Kempis, Thomas, 68, 169.
Alcott, Bronson: Alcott House, 49; as
    American Pestalozzi, 49; and
    asceticism, 49, 68; and English
    following, 49; and Fruitlands,
    49–50; and German philosophy,
    64, 67–69; and Hecker, 50; and
    social reform, 49; and Spirit,
    67–68, 145; and Temple School,
    49; and Transcendentalism, 50;
    and Universal Love Spirit, 145;
    mentioned, 58, 70, 105.
Alcott House, 49.
Alexander, Dr. Samuel Davis, 167.
Alexandria, St. Clement of, 17.
Allaire, James, 10.
Alphonsus Liguori, St., 87, 89, 90, 96,
    102, 103, 120.
America: missions to, 98–100,
    101–117.
——manifest destiny of: American
    Catholic vision of, 6–7; Christian
    Democratic vision of; 26–27;
    Hecker's vision of, 6–8, 98–100,
    101–117, 146, 165, 177; Loco-
    Focos' vision of, 26; Methodist

vision of, 12–13, 16, 110;
    Mormon vision of, 34–37, 110;
    Puritan vision of, 6, 110.
"American Scholar, The," 63–66, 69,
    157.
American Tract Society, 133, 169.
Americanism, 99, 123, 162, 177.
Anglicanism, 82, 92. *See also*
    Protestant Episcopal Church.
Annales Catholiques, Les, 154.
Apologetics: of John England, 105; of
    Hecker, 105–110, 167, 179,
    191n14; of Moeheler, 73; of
    nineteenth-century Catholic
    church, 105–107.
Apostolic succession, doctrine of, 79.
Aquinas, St. Thomas, 96, 108, 167.
Arc, St. Joan of, 178.
Arminianism, 19, 182n28.
Arminius, Jacob, 182n28.
Asceticism (self-denial, self-
    mortification): Alcott and, 49–50,
    68, 74; Catholics and, 127;
    Hecker and, 36, 49, 53–54, 88,
    89, 96, 104, 126–27, 130,
    162–63, 178; Paulists and, 119;
    Protestants and, 108.
Asia, The, 112.
Aspirations of Nature, 108, 115.
Assisi, St. Francis of, 140.
Astor, John Jacob family, 22.
Ateneo Religioso, 156.
Atheism, 52.
Atlantic Monthly, The, 124, 129.
Augustine of Hippo, St., 92.

INDEX

Aunt Alice, 4.
Avila, St. Teresa of, 96.

Baker, Augustine, 118, 122, 132.
Bancroft, George, 63, 107.
Bangs, Nathan: his *Errors of Hopkinsianism Detected and Refuted,* 19; and Forsyth Street Church, 15; and Holy Spirit, 19–20; and Methodist Book Concern, 16, 17; and Methodist Sunday School Union, 16; and perfectionism, 18, 19; and Phoebe Palmer, 18; his *Reformer Reformed,* 19; rejection of Calvinism, 19-20; mentioned, 29.
Barlow, Almira, 56.
Barnabo, Cardinal Alessandro, 112, 113, 124.
Barnum, Phineas T., 14.
Basil Montagu Company, London, 149.
Bautain, Abbé Louis Eugene Marie, 109.
Bayley, Bishop James, 112.
Beck, Carl, 63.
Bedini, Archbishop (Cardinal) Cajetan, 112.
Beecher, Catherine, 114.
Beecher, Henry Ward, 114, 124.
Beecher, Lyman, 5.
Beers, Mrs. Julia, 172.
Belief, nature of, 106.
Benedict, Rev. Abner, 19.
Bernard of Clairvaux, St., 69, 81.
Bible, The: Hecker and, 125; in Hecker home, 12; historical criticism of, 123; in Methodism, 12; in schools, 11.
Bismarck, Prince Otto von, 148.
Boehme, Jacob, 64, 66, 69.
Boston Reformer, The, 39, 63.
Boston Quarterly Review, The, 38, 39.
Bouyer, Louis, 2.
Bower, Samuel, 49.
Bradford, George, 48, 49.
Brady, Edward, 173.
Brevoort family, the, 22.

Bridget, St., 68.
Brook Farm: Course of study at, 49; *The Harbinger,* 64; Hecker's stay at, 48–50; the Hive, 48; origin of, 47–48; mentioned, 7, 30, 52, 53, 56, 57, 62, 64, 65, 70, 73, 77, 80, 84, 85, 86, 93, 114, 124, 169.
Brooks, Phillips, 124.
Browning, Elizabeth Barrett, 127.
Brownson, Orestes: and *Boston Reformer,* 39, 63; and *Boston Quarterly Review,* 38, 39; and *Brownson Quarterly Review,* 98, 134; Catholicism, 39, 60, 117, 134; and *The Catholic World,* 134–35; and *The Convert,* 79, 80; and Christian Democracy, 41; and *The Christian Examiner,* 62–63, 68; and Church of the Future, 60, 63, 76, 80; and Democracy, 39–40; doctrine of the Church, 75, 76–80; as early advisor to Hecker, 38, 42, 44, 45, 47, 50, 76–81; and eclecticism, 59; and French philosophy, 38–39; and Hecker family, 38, 40, 44; Hecker's correspondence with, 86, 87, 91, 93, 104–5; and human nature, 63; and idealism, 42; lectures of, 38–41; and mysticism, 81, 89; his *New Views of Christianity, Society, and the Church,* 38, 60, 62, 63; and politics, 39, 41; and progress, 39; and Protestantism, 39, 60, 134; and religious reform, 41; and social reform, 38–41, 63, 77–79; and Society for Christian Union and Progress, 38–39; and Transcendentalism, 45, 62–63, and Unity, 39; and Workingman's Party, 38; mentioned, 16, 46, 66, 68, 69, 73, 98, 107.
Brownson Quarterly Review, 98, 134.
Buddha, 105.
Burone, Joseph, 156, 166.
Burton, Warren, 48.
Byrdsall, F., 25–26.

Cairo, Egypt, 147.
Calvin, John, 109, 115, 183n28.
Calvinism: and Arminianism, 19,
182n28; and Catholicism, 73; and
doctrine of total depravity, 20,
31–32, 115, 126–27, 183n29; and
five points, 19, 183n29; and
Methodism, 19–20; mentioned,
167.
Carlyle, Thomas, 63, 105.
Catacombs, the, 140.
Catechism of the Council of Trent, The, 73.
Catherine of Genoa, St.: her *Dialogues,*
94; Hecker's admiration of, 129,
140; influence on Hecker, 93, 94,
142, 152; her life of perfection,
129, 169–70; Protestant interest
in, 169–70; her *Treatise on
Purgatory,* 94, 132, 133.
Catherine of Siena, St., 178.
Catholicism: in America, 103–4,
109–10, 138; and Americanism,
99, 140, 162; and American life,
6–8, 69, 131; anti-Catholic
sentiment, 115; and *The Christian
Examiner,* 69; doctrine of infused
grace, 92; doctrine of justification,
92; doctrine of Sacraments, 92;
and evangelism, xii, 98–100;
Hecker's catholicization, 84–98;
Hecker's conversion to, 72–83;
Hecker's lectures on, 7, 122–24;
Hecker's view of, ix, 6–7, 70, 71,
139; Hecker's vision for America,
98–117; Hecker's vision for world,
144–57; and human nature, 109;
and Methodism, 20; mysticism
and, 70, 92; nineteenth-century
apologetics of, 105–7; and
Protestantism, ix, 5–8; and
publishing in America, 133–35,
138. *See also* Church, doctrine of;
Papal infallibility, doctrine of.
Catholic Publication Society: founding
of, 135; George Hecker and, 135,
166; Paulists' relationship with,
159, 166; and St. Catherine of
Genoa, 135, 169–70.

Catholic Standard, The (of
Philadelphia), 138.
Catholic World, The: Brownson and,
134–35; Hecker and, 38, 133–35,
149, 166, 167, 170; Hewit and,
134, 160; Mrs. Craven and, 155;
Paulists and, 159.
Caussade, J.P. de: influence on
Hecker, 142–44; and Spirit, 145.
Channing, Edward, 82.
Channing, William Ellery, 30, 31, 69,
82, 105.
Chateaubriand, François René, 39.
Child's Magazine, 16.
*Christian Advocate and Journal and
Zion's Herald, The,* 16, 17, 21,
182n19.
Christian Democracy: Brownson and,
41; Hecker's interest in, 30; Loco-
Focos and, 26–27, 30, 41, 52.
Christian Examiner, The, 62, 63,
68–69.
Christian Union, The, 170.
Chrysostom, St. John, 128.
Church, doctrine of: as Body of Christ,
80, 82; Catholicism and, 81–83;
as channel of God's grace, 72–83
passim; as channel of Holy Spirit,
87; Charles Lane and, 85; Dana
and, 80; Dewey and, 32–33;
Hecker and, 72–83, 116–17, 167;
Methodism and, 35–36;
Mormonism and, 36–37; Schelling
and, 60; and social reform, 75–77.
Church and the Age, The, 149, 168.
Church Fathers, the, 58, 62.
Churchman, The, 28.
Church of the Future, 60, 63, 76, 80.
Church of the Messiah, 30, 31, 33.
Church of the Latter-Day Saints. *See*
Mormonism.
Church of St. Paul the Apostle:
Hecker's sermons in, 125–26,
139; as sign of Paulists' new era,
173, 175; Paulists and, 124–26,
159, 165; mentioned, 136, 137, 138.
Citizens' Association (of New York
City), 24.

Civĭttà Cattolica, 113, 114, 116, 192.
Civil War, 6, 122, 174.
Clapham, England, 95, 96.
Clement of Alexandria, St., 17.
Clermont, the, 10.
Coleridge, Samuel Taylor, 63, 67.
Communion: Brownson's views on, 39,
    79–80; with God, 72–73, 79, 108,
    142; Hecker's desire for, 47, 59,
    179; importance to German
    philosophy, 65; Leroux's views,
    78; of saint's (in Catholicism), 73.
Community: and Brook Farm, 47–49;
    and Fruitlands, 49; importance of
    to Hecker, xii, 17, 72,–83; and
    Methodism, 12–17, 35; and
    Mormonism, 34–36; and Paulists,
    17, 119.
Congregationalism, 102.
Congress of Malines, 137–38.
Connolly, Bishop Thomas L. of
    Halifax, 139.
Constant, Benjamin, 38, 107.
Contemplation: *vs.* action, 52–55, 94;
    Alcott and, 68; and the American
    mind, 69; Hecker and, 52–55,
    87–95; Paulists and, 120;
    Transcendentalists and, 67. *See
    also* Mysticism.
Correspondant, Le, 155.
Corrigan, Bishop Michael of New
    York, 167.
Courier, The, 23.
Cousin, Victor, 38, 39, 68.
Craven, Augustus, 155, 166.
Craven, Pauline Marie Armande Aglae
    Ferren de la Ferronays, 155.
Creation, theories of, 123.
Curtis, Burrill, 84, 86, 97.
Curtis, George: at Brook Farm, 48, 49;
    relationship with Hecker, 30, 75,
    84–85, 98; mentioned, 86, 87.

Daily Palladium, The (New Haven), 6.
Dana, Charles: at Brook Farm, 48, 49;
    his doctrine of the Church, 80;
    mentioned, 73.

Darwinism, 168.
De Caussade, J.P. *See* Caussade, J.P.
    de.
Dechamps, Cardinal Victor, 138, 153,
    155.
De Held, Rev. Frederick, 90, 102.
Deism, 31.
De Lamennais, Hughes Félicité
    Robert, 39.
DeMaistre, Joseph Marie, 157.
De Molinos, Miguel, 68.
Demonstratio catholica, 105–6.
Demonstratio christiana, 105–7.
Demonstratio religiosa, 105–7.
De Montalembert, Charles Ferbes
    René, 39.
De Richmont, Monsignor, 156.
De Sales, St. Francis, 68, 132.
De Staël, Madame, 63.
Deshon, George, 118, 172, 173.
Destiny: Hecker's belief in, 51, 54, 81,
    101–117, 131, 141–42, 175, 178,
    180; Paulists and, 122. *See also*
    America: manifest destiny of.
De Voltaire, Arouet, 148.
Dewey, Orville: his doctrine of the
    Church, 32–33; and human
    nature, 31–32; influence on
    Hecker, x, 37, 41, 45, 52, 126;
    and lectures, 31; and Loco-
    Focoism, 33; and Methodism, 33;
    and personal religious experience,
    33; and practical Christianity
    30–31, 44; and presence of God,
    31, 33, 44; his rejection of
    Calvinism, 31–32.
Dial, The, 63.
Dionysius the Areopagite (Pseudo-
    Dionysius), 69, 81.
Döllingerites, 151.
Doyle, Alexander, 173.
Dryden, John, 105.
Duffy, Rev. John, 102.
Dufresne, L'Abbe, (son of Xavier D.),
    160.
Dufresne, Xavier, 156, 160, 164, 166.
Dupanloup, Bishop Félix of Orleans,138.

INDEX

Dutch Reformed Church 10, 14, 28.
Dwight, Timothy, 5.

Eastern Spirituality. *See* Oriental
Spirituality.
Eckhart, Meister, 69, 81.
Ecumenism, ix.
Edwards, Jonathan, 5.
Elliott, Rev. Walter: his impressions of
Hecker, 123, 172–73; his *Life of
Father Hecker,* 3–4, 183.
Emerson, Ralph Waldo: and Alcott, 68;
his "The American Scholar," 66,
69, 157; his poetry and Lyceum
lectures, 85; and
Transcendentalism, 56, 62, 105.
England, John, 105.
English Romantics, 70.
Enlightenment, the, 61.
Enquirer, The, 23.
Ephraem Syrus, 17.
Episcopal Church, the. *See* Protestant
Episcopal Church.
Equal Rights Party. *See* Loco-Foco
Party.
Erigena, Johannes Scotus, 69, 81.
Eternal Spirit, the, 85.
Evangelism: Catholic, xii, 101–17;
Hecker and, xii, 98–100, 101–17;
Protestant, 6, 103, 153. *See also*
Missions.
Evening Post, The (New York), 23, 40.
Evans, George, 23.
Everett, Edward, 63.
*Exposition of The Church in View of
The Recent Difficulties and
Controversies, and Present Needs of
The Age,* 149–57, 160, 169.

Fénelon, François de Salignac de la
Mothe, 68, 69.
Ferney, France, 148, 154.
Fichte, Johann Gottlieb, 40, 57, 78.
Fichtean Ego, 106.
Fields, James Thomas, 129, 133.
Fifty-Ninth Street Church. *See*
Church of St. Paul the Apostle.

Finney, Charles G., 103, 168, 191n3.
First Vatican Council, The: and
doctrine of papal infallibility,
138–40, 150–51, 156; Hecker at,
138–40; world interest in, 139.
Five Points of the Synod of Dort, the,
19, 183n29.
"Flour riots, the," 24.
Follen, Charles, 63.
Fordham College, 88.
Forgiveness (of God), 18.
Forsyth Street Church, 14, 15, 16, 28.
Fox, George, 34.
Franchi, Cardinal Alessandro, 154.
Francis of Assisi, St., 140.
Freeman's Journal, The, 138.
Free-Soil Party (of New York), 24.
"Free Thinkers," the, 23.
Free will, 109, 121, 125.
Fribourg, Germany, 156.
Fruitlands: Alcott and, 49–50; demise
of, 50; founding of, 49; Hecker's
stay at, 49, 50, 53; Charles Lane
and, 49–50; library of, 64, 68;
mentioned, 7, 66, 69, 80, 85, 114,
143.
Fulton, Robert, 10.

Genius, the nature of, 85, 98.
Genoa, St. Catherine of. *See* Catherine
of Genoa, St.
German philosophy: and Hecker, 63;
and Transcendentalism, 63–64;
mentioned, 78, 109.
Gethsemane, Garden of, 147.
Gibbons, James , 138.
Gilded Age, the, 174.
Gioberti, Vicenzo, 134.
God: As Almighty, 142; assistance of,
99; call of, 21, 52, 86, 99, 162;
communion with, 72–73, 79, 108,
142; as Creator, 47; as creator and
sustainer, 9, 33, 127, 145;
dependence upon, 93; divine
majesty of, 142; faith in, 53; as
Father, 56, 150, 168; forgiveness

of, 18; glory of, 143, 146; grace
of, 18, 55-56, 74, 99, 159, 164;
grand scheme (plan) of, 122, 176;
as great architect, 31; as the great
Source, 67; as ground of all being,
128; hand of, 128, 152; Hecker's
experience of, 3, 8, 21, 45, 47,
72, 96, 98, 116, 129, 177, 178,
179; Hecker's vision of, 179; and
human nature, 32; hunger for,
106; as immanent, 46; inspiration
of, 51, 67, 89; as involved in
creation, 180; Kingdom of, 36, 94,
140; leading (guidance) of, 71, 74,
83, 88, 132, 145; light of, 128; as
Lord, 31, 42, 127; love for, 93,
143; love of, 18, 56, 86, 152;
man's experience of, 2, 18–19,
46, 127, 146; omnipresence of,
174; power of, 33; presence of, 9,
21, 28, 31, 33, 47, 71, 176, 178;
as Primary Director of Souls, 130;
providence of, 16, 54–55, 140,
151; purposes of, 27, 147;
revelation of, 36; search for, 116;
as Spirit, 46, 47; Spirit of, 13, 81,
127, 145; submission to, 81, 143;
as transcendent, 46, 51; union
with, 59, 91, 169, 175, 179; as
Universal Spirit, 145; waiting
upon, 99, 153; ways of, 117; will
of, 21, 55, 88, 89, 96, 97, 99,
128, 131–32, 140, 142, 144,
158–59, 160, 162–63, 164–65,
175–76; work of, 55, 73, 94, 97,
98, 99, 128, 143, 145, 150; work
through the Church, 17, 72–83,
89; wrath of, 37. *See also* Holy
Spirit; Jesus Christ.
"God and Man," 167.
Goethe, Johann Wolfgang von, 63, 64,
65–66, 105, 106.
Gower, Joseph F., 191n*14*.
Grace: Church as channel of, 76–79;
doctrine of infused _____ , 92;
growth in, 129; as life of God, 79;
need for, 71, 74, 76–79, 106,

131, 168; power of, 128; "second
experience of _____ ," 168.
Greaves, James P., 49.
Greek Fathers, the, 17–18, 128.
Gregory of Nyssa, 18, 58.
Guyon, Madame Jeanne Marie Bouvier
de la Motte, 68.

Hafkenschied, Rev. Bernard Joseph,
99, 102–103.
Hale, Edward E., 168.
Harbinger, The, 63, 64.
Harmony: Hecker's desire for, 47, 60,
179; importance to German
philosophy, 65.
Hart's flour store, 24.
Harvard, 48, 50, 63.
Hassard, John, 133.
Hawthorne, Nathaniel, 48.
Heaven (Paradise), 128–29.
Hecker, Caroline Friend: and Catholic
Church, 28; in Dutch Reformed
Church, 10; influence on home,
10–11, 12, 28; as Methodist, 10,
14, 15, 16; and religious
tolerance, 28, 29; mentioned, 44,
101.
Hecker, Elizabeth, 28, 101.
Hecker family business, 10, 21, 28,
42, 101.
Hecker, George V.: and business, 10,
21; and Brownson, 38; and
Catholicism, 28; and Catholic
Publication Society, 135, 166; and
The Catholic World, 133; as
Isaac's financial backer, 10, 111,
141; and Loco-Foco Party, 23, 24;
mentioned, 57, 101, 154, 164,
170.
Hecker, John J., Jr.: and Brownson,
38; and charity, 28; and Episcopal
church, 28; and family business,
10, 21, 24; and political activity,
23, 24, 26; and religious
publishing, 28; mentioned, 44,
101.
Hecker, John J. Sr., 10, 11.

INDEX

Hecker, Josephine, (Mrs. George V.), 11, 154, 159.
Hecker, Mrs. John, 81.
Heilig, Rev. Michael, 97–98, 99, 104.
Held, Rev. Frederick de, 90.
Helvetia, the, 101.
Herder, Benjamin, 155.
Hermes Trismegistus, 68.
Hewit, Rev. Augustine: as acting superior of Paulists, 158–60; 162, 163, 164, 172; and *The Catholic World,* 134; as consultor of Paulists, 165; as early Paulist, 118; his "Problems of the Age," 134; and Redemptorist missions, 102–3; relationship with Hecker, 108, 171–73; mentioned, 137.
Hinduism, 54.
Holden, Vincent, 3, 183n*10,* 184n35.
Holiness: general interest in, 17; Methodism and, 16, 17; Paulists and, 122; Perfectionists and, 168; "Scripture holiness," 16. *See also* Perfection; Sanctification.
Holy Land, the, 147.
Holy Spirit, the: Age of, 166, 180; awareness of, 151; *Baptism of _____* , 168–69; in believer, xi, 20, 81, 92, 130, 143, 146, 150, 155, 179; creative power of, 150; and the Church (universal), 72–83, 94, 151; devotion to, 120, 165; effusion of, 155; fidelity to, 150; as filling the whole earth, 146; gentleness of, 121; gifts of, 36, 94; Hecker and, 9, 19, 52–53, 54–59 *passim,* 74, 81, 116, 165; infusion of, 174; inspiration of, 97, 121, 148–50, 151, 153; leading (guidance) of, 54–59 *passim,* 72–83 *passim,* 86, 94, 95, 113, 116, 121, 130, 144, 146, 150, 152, 157, 161, 166; Methodism and, 13, 18–20, 58; Mormonism and, 36, 44; Office of, 154; operations (action, work) of, 19, 54, 77, 96, 99, 143, 145–46, 152, 155, 156, 168, 170, 174; in Oriental religions, 145; Paulists and, 120–21, 161; as Primary Director of Souls, 130–31; as sanctifier, 130; as Spirit of Christ, 56; as uncreated grace of God, 55; unction of, 169; union with, 81; will of, 53, 54, 57, 59. *See also* God, Jesus Christ.
Holy Trinity, the, 58.
Hopkins, Samuel, 182–83n28.
Hughes, Archbishop John of New York, 82, 90, 112, 119, 124.
Hugo of St. Victor, 69, 81.
Human nature: Brownson and, 63; Calvinism and, 20, 31, 115; Catholicism and, 109; divinization of, 56; Hecker and, 20, 46, 51, 61, 108–9, 116, 125; Lutheranism and, 115; Methodism and, 19–20; Transcendentalism and, 63, 107; Unitarianism and, 31.
Hyacinthe, Père, 138.

Idealism: Brownson and, 42, 62–63; German, 78; Hecker and, 42, 71, 86, 156; Transcendentalists and, 67–68.
Ignatian philosophy, 128, 143, 145, 157.
Ignatius Loyola, St., 94, 143, 161.
Illuminism, 156.
Immigrants, 6, 10, 88, 111.
Incarnation, the, 80.
Individualism: Hecker and, 46, 51, 60, 65, 72, 179; Paulists and, 120–22; Transcendentalists and, 62.
Infallibility, doctrine of papal. *See* Papal infallibility, doctrine of.
International Catholic, 153, 160.
International Catholic Congress in Ferney, France, 148, 154.
International Grain Elevator Company, 10.
Intuition, 61–62.

Jackson, Andrew, 23.
Jaques, Moses, 24, 26–27, 31, 41.

INDEX

Jennings, Robert, 23.

Jerusalem, 147.

Jesuits: and doctrine of papal infallibility, 156–57; and external authority, 161; mentioned, 88.

Jesus Christ: Catholicism and, 106; Democracy and, 40, 41; Gospel of, 170; Hecker and, 167; life of, 72; as living person, 58, 147; as Lord, 56; as Restorer of the Sciences, 167; as Savior (Redeemer), 18, 56, 58, 71; Spirit of, 58, 147; Transcendentalists and, 106, work of, 71. See also God, Holy Spirit.

Joan of Arc, St., 178

John the Apostle, St., 60.

John Chrysostom, St., 128.

John of the Cross, St., 94, 96, 142.

Joseph, St., 129.

Julian of Norwich, St., 68, 132, 133.

Justification: "alien righteousness," 92; Catholic doctrine of, 92; Hecker and, 109, 115, 116; Methodist belief in, 19.

Kant, Immanuel, 40, 57, 78.

Kantian philosophy, 48.

Keats, John, 85.

Keane, Bishop John of Richmond, 171.

Kehoe, Edward, 133, 166.

Kempis, Thomas à, 68, 169.

Kenrick, Francis P., 105.

King, Mrs. Jane, 129–133.

Kirby, Georgiana Bruce, 14, 28, 48.

Kirby, Monsignor Tobias, 112.

Kulturkampf, the, 148.

Lacordaire, Jean Baptiste Henri, 39.

LaFarge, John, 165.

Lallemant, Louis: doctrine of Holy Spirit, 95, 129, 145, 156–57; influence on Hecker, 94–95, 128, 132–33; his *Spiritual Doctrine*, 94–95, 128, 132; mentioned, 143.

Lamennais, Hughes Félicité Robert de, 39.

Lane, Charles: and Alcott, 49; and Catholicism, 85; and Fruitlands, 49–50; and the Spirit, 85; mentioned, 58, 70.

Lane, William, 49.

Langford, Sara, 18.

Latter-Day Saints, the. See Mormonism.

Law, William, 68.

Leo XIII, Pope, 167, 171.

Leroux, Pierre, 78–79, 108.

Liberty Hall, Chicago, 123.

Liguori, St. Alphonsus. See Alphonsus Liguori, St.

Locke, John, 61–62.

Lockeanism, 62.

Loco-Foco (Equal Rights) Party: and Christian Democracy, 26–27, 30; and "flour riots," 24; and Hecker brothers, 23, 24, 29; and social reform 23–27, 30; and Unitarianism, 31; vision for America, 26; mentioned, 34, 35, 41, 48, 52.

Longfellow, Henry Wadsworth, 105.

Lopez, Gregory, 13.

Love: for God, 93, 143; of God, 18, 56, 86; pure, 143.

Loyola, St. Ignatius, 94, 143, 161.

Luther, Martin, 92, 109, 115, 124.

Lutheranism, 73, 115, 116.

Macarius the Egyptian, 17.

McCloskey, Archbishop John of Albany, 82, 91, 112, 137.

McMahon, Ella, 143.

McMaster, James, 90.

McMillan, Thomas, 173.

Magdaline, Sister, 166.

Mahan, Asa, 168–70.

Maignen, Abbé Charles, 179.

Malines, Congress of, 137–38.

Man, The of New York, 23.

Manichees, the, 92.

Manifest destiny. See America: Manifest destiny of.

Manning, Bishop Henry of Westminster, 154–55.

Marabotto, Cattaneo, 169.

Mary Constance of Jesus, Sister, 166.

INDEX

Mauron, Rev. Nicholas, 111–12.

Mecca, 145.

Melanchthon, Philipp, 115.

Mercersburg Review, The, 168.

Mermillod, Cardinal Gaspard, 148, 154.

Merritt, Timothy, 17.

Methodism: and Calvinism, 19, 182n28; and community, 12–17, 35; and Dewey, 33; doctrine of the Church, 35–36; and doctrine of the Holy Spirit, 18–20; and family life, 14–15; and free will, 19; and Hecker family, 1, 7, 12–17, 20; and holiness, 12, 13, 16, 36, 44; and human agency, 19; and human nature, 20; influence on Hecker, 37, 45, 52, 58, 70–71, 126, 179; and Loco-Focoism, 26; Methodist Book Concern, 16, 17, 21, 133; *Methodist Quarterly Review,* 17, 133; in New York, 12–20; and Perfectionism, ix–x, 13, 17–20, 169; and personal religious experience, 18, 35; and providence, 12, 16–17, 35, 79; and religious education, 15–16; and salvation, 18; and Sunday School Union, 16; vision for America, 12, 16, 110; mentioned, 92, 103, 106, 114, 125.

Methodist book Concern, 16, 17, 21, 133.

Methodist Quarterly Review, 17, 133.

Millennialism, 26, 156.

Milner, John, 105.

Missionary Society of St. Paul the Apostle. *See* Paulists.

Missions: Hecker's desire for, 111–17; Paulists and, 119, 120, 122–24; Redemptorists and, 122. *See also* Evangelism.

Moehler, J.A., 73, 105, 116.

Molinos, Miguel de, 68.

Monde, Le, 155.

Montalembert, Charles Ferbes René de, 39.

Monopoly, 23, 26, 27, 34.

Moody, Dwight L., 153.

Mormonism: Book of Mormon, 36, 37; and community, 35–36; and continuing revelation, 36; doctrine of the Church, 36–37; doctrines of Joseph Smith, 33–34, 36–37; and Holy Spirit, 36, 44; and New Jerusalem, 36–37; and personal spirituality, 35; and providence, 36; and restoration of the people of God, 36–37; and social reform, 33–35; vision for America, 36–37, 110; and Zion, 36–37; mentioned, x, 41, 45, 52, 80.

More, Henry, 68.

Morse, Samuel F. B., 6.

Moslems, 145, 146.

Mt. Bellington, Chelsea, Mass., 44.

Mount Salève, Savoy, 160.

Mysticism: Brownson and, 81, 89; Catholic mystics and, 92; Hecker and, 81, 89, 156, 168, 178–79; Protestantism and, 108; subjectivism and, 89; Transcendentalists and, 68–69; mentioned, 108, 197. *See also* Contemplation.

Neo-Platonism, 67.

Neo-Thomism, 166–168.

Neri, St. Philip, 128, 161.

Nevins, Aloysius, 173.

Nevins, John W., 168–69.

New England Transcendentalists. *See* Transcendentalists.

Newman, John Henry, 154–55.

New York Democratic Republican Electors, 23.

New York Tablet, The, 138, 179.

Nibia, Egypt, 144.

Nile River, the, 144–147.

North American Review, The, 63.

Norton, Andrews, 62, 107.

Noteware, H. S. C., 166.

Novalis, Georg F. P. von Hardenberg, 63.

Nyssa, Gregory of, 18, 58.

O'Brien, Rev. Edward J., 5.
O'Rourke, Jeremiah, 165.
Oberlin perfectionist school, 168.
Observateur, L', 154.
Old Catholics, the, 151.
Old Dutch Church of Garden Street
(New York), 10.
Old St. Patrick's Church (Mott St.,
New York), 82.
Orange Hill, New Jersey, 170.
Oratorians, St. Philip Neri's, 161.
Order of Enoch, 34, 35, 36.
Oriel College, 107.
Oriental Spirituality, 69–70, 105,
144–46, 187n2.
Origin of the Species, theory of, 123.
Ostrander, Rev. Daniel, 15.
Othmann, Père, 94.
Owen, Robert, 23.
Oxford Tracts, the, 73–74, 107–8,
115, 117.

Palmer, Phoebe Langford, 18.
Panic of 1873, the, 166.
Papal infallibility, doctrine of: First
Vatican Council and, 138–40,
150–51; Hecker's view of,
139–40; Jesuits and, 156; world
interest in, 139.
Paradise (Heaven), 128–29.
Parker, Theodore, 48, 73, 107.
Parton, James, 124.
Paul the Apostle, St., 60, 148.
Paulists, the: as American Catholics,
162; and Catholic Publication
Society, 159; and *The Catholic
World*, 159; Chapter meeting of
1884, 172–73; and Church of St.
Paul the Apostle, 124–26, 136,
137, 138, 139, 159, 165, 173,
175; and community, 17;
community house at 59th Street,
159, 171, 176; and external
authority, 120–22, 161; founding
of, 113, 118–22, 142, 152;
Hecker's differences with,
161–62, 175; Hecker's love for,
162–63; Hecker's vision of,
118–22, 162, 174–75; and the
Holy Spirit, 121, 122, 161; and
missions, 118, 122–24, 175; as
models for world, 140, 153, 161;
and parish work, 120, 175;
problems in 1870s and 1880s,
158–61, 164–73; Programme of
the Rule and Constitution of
Missionary Priests of St. Paul the
Apostle, 119–20, 158, 171;
studentiate, 159; mentioned, ix, 3,
141, 179.
Pentecost, 147, 174.
Perfection: American interest in,
168–70; and St. Catherine of
Genoa, 129, 169–70; and
community, 17; Hecker's doctrine
of, 126–129, 130–31, 146, 179;
Mahan's doctrine of, 168;
Methodism and, ix–x, 17–20;
Paulists and, 119–20; as perfect
love, 18; "Scripture holiness," 17.
See also Holiness; Sanctification.
Perfect love, 18.
Perrone, Giovanni, 105.
Pestalozzi, Johann H., 49.
Peter the Apostle, St., 60.
Philip Neri, St., 128, 161.
Piazza di Spagna, 113.
Pictus, 70.
Pilot, The (Boston), 138.
Pius IX, Pope: Hecker and, 113, 118,
138; Hecker quoted, 96, 109;
Paulists and, 113, 118; Vatican I
and, 138; mentioned, 155.
Plato, 67, 85, 105.
Plotinus, 67–68, 105.
Poor Clares, 165–66.
Practical religion (Practical
Christianity), 30–31.
Pratt, Mrs. Minot and children, 48.
Pratt, Parley P.: Hecker and, x;
33–35, 184; and restoration of the
people of God, 36–37; his *Voice of
Warning*, 37.
Presbyterian Church, the, 115, 169.
Prince Albert, the, 90.
Princeton Review, The, 167.

INDEX

Programme of the Rule and
Constitution of Missionary Priests
of St. Paul the Apostle, 119–20,
158.
Protestant Episcopal Church, the:
Isaac Hecker and, 76, 80; John
Hecker and, 28.
Protestantism: Catholicism and, 5, 6,
92, 104; and evangelism, 6;
Hecker accused of, 156; Hecker
and, 92, 115–16, 169–70, 174;
hunger for spirituality within,
169–70; notion of alien
righteousness, 92; vision for
America, 6. *See also* Methodism;
Protestant Episcopal Church.
Providence: belief in, 17, 151;
Caussade and, 142–43; doctrine
of, 16; Hecker's belief in, 54–55,
86, 95, 96, 98–99, 112, 113, 117,
127, 135, 144, 153, 162, 167,
175, 178; Lallemant and, 94;
Methodism and, 16–17; Paulists
and, 121; toward America, 6, 177.
See also America: Manifest destiny
of.
Providential men, doctrine of, 79.
Public school question, the, 166.
Public School Society, 11.
Purchase Street Unitarian Church
(Boston), 48.
Purist Rump ticket, 24, 35.
Puritans, 110.
Pythagorus, 105.

Questions of the Soul, 104–7, 115.
Quietism, 54, 94, 143.

Ragatz, Switzerland, 141.
Rambler, The, 108.
Rationalism, 61, 69, 108.
Realism, 78.
Reason, human, 108–9, 116, 146, 174.
Redemptorists, the: in America, 90,
101–4, 111–13; appeal to Hecker,
87–90; Constitutions of, 102, 111;
in Europe, 102; Hecker at
Clapham, 95–100, 101; Hecker's

expulsion from, 112–13; Hecker
at St. Trond, 91–92, 95–100;
Hecker at Wittem, 91, 92, 95, 96,
101; mentioned, 89, 138, 142,
149, 178.
Reform: political, 1, 22–24, 76;
religious, 62–63.
——social: Brownson and, 38–42,
62–63, 76; Church's role in,
75–78, 149–50, 154–55; Dewey
and, 30–33, 41; Loco-Foco Party
and, 23–27, 41; Mormons and,
33–38, 41. *See also* Renewal,
religious.
Reformed Churches, 116.
Reformation, the, 110, 150, 156, 177.
Regeneration, 58.
Renewal, religious: Hecker's vision for
American renewal, 98–104, 110,
113–17, 118, 121, 122–24;
Hecker's vision for European
renewal, 140, 153, 161; Hecker's
vision for world renewal, 145–46,
148–57, 173–75, 178, 179.
"Renewal of The Christian Life, The,"
173.
Restorationism, 26.
Revelation, 36, 108.
Revista Universale, 156.
Richard of St. Victor, 69, 81.
Richmont, Monsignor de, 156.
Richter, Jean Paul, 63, 64–66.
Ripley, George: and Brook Farm, 48,
49, 64; his doctrine of the
Church, 77; and *The Harbinger,*
64; and Lockeanism, 62; and
*Specimens of Foreign Standard
Literature,* 64; mentioned, 73, 107.
Ripley, Sarah (Mrs. George), 48, 49,
169.
Robinson, John, 173.
Romantic Movement: in Europea, 45,
65, 131; influence on Hecker, 71;
in New England, 70, 84.
Rosecrans, Bishop Sylvester H. of
Columbus, 138.
Rosmini, Serbati Antonio, 166.
Rossi, Rev. Peter, 154.

INDEX

Ruland, Rev. George, 111–12.
Rumpler, Rev. Gabriel, 111.
Ryder, H. J. D., 168.

Sadlier, James, 135.
Saint-Gaudens, Augustus, 165.
St. Joseph's Church (Manhattan), 102.
St. Mary's Church (New Haven), 6.
Saint-Simonian school of thought, 38, 79, 138.
St. Trond, Belgium, 90–96 *passim.*
Sales, St. Francis de, 68, 132.
Salvation, 18, 127.
Sanctification: Hecker's view of, 115, 152; Methodist doctrine of, 18; Paulists and, 119. *See also* Holiness, Perfection.
Sankey, Ira T., 153.
Scaramelli, Giovanni Baptista, 96.
Schelling, Friedrich von, 60, 67.
Schiller, Johann von, 63, 65, 80, 105.
Schlegel, August Wilhelm von, 64.
Schlegel, Friedrich von, 64.
Scholastic logic, 95, 166.
"Scientific deism," 168.
Seabury, Samuel, Jr., 28
Searle, George, 173.
Second Plenary Council of Baltimore, 135.
Second Vatican Council, ix.
Sectarianism, 77.
Sedgwick, Ora, 48.
Self, the: Alcott and, 67; German philosophers and, 64–65; Hecker's concept of, 51, 74, 116, 178; self-reliance, 77, 80; Transcendentalists and, 62. *See also* Asceticism (Self-denial, self-mortification).
Self-denial. *See* Asceticism.
Self-mortifiction. *See* Asceticism.
Seventh Ward Democratic Association (New York City), 24.
Shakers, the, 50, 85.
Siena, St. Catherine of, 178.
Simpson, Richard, 107–8, 126.
Sin, 88, 115.
Sittina Miriam el Adra, 144.

Shakespeare, William, 85.
Shelley, Percy Bysshe, 85.
Smart, Robert, 15.
Smith, Joseph. *See* Mormonism.
Smith, Michael, 173.
Smith, Pascal B., 26.
Society for Christian Union and Progress, 38–39.
Society of Jesus. *See* Jesuits.
Solipsism, 56.
Spalding, Bishop John Lancaster of Peoria, 139.
Spalding, Archbishop Martin John, 105.
Spirit, the: Alcott and, 67–68, 145; Charles Lane and, 85. *See also* Holy Spirit, the.
Spiritual director: Hecker as, 129–133, 165–66; Hecker under, 87, 89, 91.
Spiritualism, 134.
Staël, Madame de, 63.
Stratton, James L., 26.
Sturm und Drang movement, 65.
Stuyvesant, Peter, family, 22.
Subjectivism: Brownson and, 78, 89; Hecker and, 42, 51, 90, 97.
Submission: in Catholic church, 82; to God, 81, 143.
Sudbrack, Josef, 2.
Sunday Schools, 11, 16, 125.
Sunday School Movement, 16.
Sunday School Union, 16.
Surin, Rev. J. J., 94, 143.
Swedenborg, Emanuel, 68, 69, 80.
Synod of Dort, 183n29.
Synthesis: Catholicism and, 82–83, 99; Hecker's desire for, x, 47, 59, 60, 69, 70, 72–83, 94, 99, 100, 126, 144, 154, 179; Protestant desire for, 167.

Tauler, John, 132.
Tammany Hall, 24.
Taylor, Nathaniel William, 5.
Taylor, Thomas, 67.
Temple School, 49.
Tennyson, Alfred, 105.

216

INDEX

Teresa of Avila, St., 96.
Thomas à Kempis, St., 68, 169.
Thomas Aquinas, St., 96, 108, 167.
Thomism, 167.
Thoreau, Henry David, 86, 98.
Ticknor, George, 63.
Ticknor and Fields Publishing Co.,
    133.
Total depravity, doctrine of: Bangs
    and, 20; Dewey and, 31–32;
    Hecker and, 115–16; mentioned,
    114, 183n29.
Transcendentalism: Alcott and, 50;
    Hecker and, ix–x, 2, 56, 58, 59,
    61–71, 72, 75, 77, 84–85, 91, 98,
    99, 106–7, 124, 128, 179; and
    Spirit, 67–68, 145; mentioned, 2,
    45, 78, 187n2, 191n14.
Tremont Temple (Boston), 123.
Trent, Council of, 73.
Tribune (New York), 41.

Unity: Alcott and, 68; among
    churches, 74; Hecker's desire for,
    60, 69, 74; of all things, 68;
    Transcendentalism and, 68.
Unitarianism, x, 61, 77, 82, 114. See
    also Dewey, Orville.
United Order, 34, 35, 36.
Universal Being, the, 56.
Universal Love Spirit, the, 145.
Upham, Thomas C., 168–70.

Vanderbilt, Cornelius, family, 22.
Varian, Isaac, 23.
Vatican, the, 112, 158.
Vatican I. See First Vatican Council,
    the.
Vatican II, ix, 179.

Vaughan, Bishop Herbert of Salford,
    England, 153.
Via ordinaria, 98.
Via perfectionis, 32, 126.
Villa Caserta (Rome), 112, 113.
Voltaire, Arouet de, 148.

Walden Pond, 86.
Walworth, Clarence, 90, 99, 102–3,
    118.
War Between the States, 6, 122, 174.
Wesley, Charles, 13, 109.
Wesley, John: and Calvinism, 19; and
    community, 12–13; and divine
    forgiveness, 18; doctrine of
    perfection, 17–20; his Doctrines
    and Disciplines, 12, 15; and free
    will, 19; his Plain Account of
    Christian Perfection, 17; and
    salvation, 18; and sanctification,
    18; and universal atonement, 19;
    mentioned, 58. See also
    Methodism.
White, Stanford, 165.
Williston, Seth, 19.
Wiseman, Cardinal Nicholas, 95.
Wittem, Holland, 91–97 passim.
Woodman, Clarence, 173.
Workingman's Party (New York), 23,
    24, 38.
Wright, Francis, 23.
Wright, H. C., 49.
Wyman, Henry, 173.

Yale University, 5, 6.
Young, Rev. Alfred, 159, 165, 173.
Young Catholic, The, 135.

Zwingli, Ulrich, 109, 115.